Revolution on the Border

Revolution on the Border
The United States and Mexico, 1910–1920

Linda B. Hall
and
Don M. Coerver

Albuquerque
University of New Mexico Press

Library of Congress Cataloging-in-Publication Data

Hall, Linda B. (Linda Biesele), 1939–
Revolution on the border: the United States and Mexico, 1910–1920
Linda B. Hall and Don M. Coerver.—1st ed.
p. cm.
Bibliography: p.
Includes index.
ISBN 0-8263-1099-0 0-8263-1234-9 (pa)
1. United States—Relations—Mexico.
2. Mexico—Relations—United States.
3. United States—Foreign economic relations—Mexico.
4. Mexico—Foreign economic relations—United States.
5. Mexico—History—Revolution, 1910–1920.
I. Coerver, Don M., 1943–
II. Title.
E183.8.M6H35 1988
303.4′8273′072—dc19 88-14222

First paperbound printing, 1990

For Donald E. Everett
Colleague
and
Friend

CONTENTS

ILLUSTRATIONS

Figures

Tables

Maps

ACKNOWLEDGMENTS

Many persons and institutions have aided us in our research for this volume, which began when we were both fledgling graduate students working with Luis Martín at Southern Methodist University. Though our paths diverged to different graduate institutions, that early experience remains crucial. Richard Greenleaf at Tulane and Herbert Klein at Columbia helped maintain our interest in U.S.-Mexican relations and the border region despite the fact that each of us during this period was focussed on internal Mexican politics as a major research interest.

As we each returned to Texas institutions for our initial teaching jobs, colleagues and friends as well as our geographical location helped maintain our interest in Mexico and the border. At Texas Christian University, Donald Worcester, and at Trinity, Allen Kownslar and Donald E. Everett, to whom this volume is dedicated, provided constant interest, expertise, and support. Individuals in innumerable archives and libraries in Mexico, Washington, D.C., and throughout the southwestern United States proved of enormous help, and we wish to thank them all.

During the course of our research we received support from many sources. In particular we wish to thank the National Endowment for the Humanities; the Joullian Fund and the Faculty Development Commission of Trinity University; and the Dean of Arts and Sciences, Michael McCracken and the Dean of Graduate Studies and Research, John Mangieri, at Texas Christian University.

Portions of this volume have appeared in other publications. For permission to reprint from these articles, we thank *Historia Mexicana*, which published "La frontera y las minas en la revolución mexicana" in Vol. XXXII, No. 3, enero-marzo 1983; *The Americas*, which printed "Oil and the Mexican Revolution: The Southwestern Connection," in Vol. XLI, No. 1, October, 1984; and *The Journal of the West*, which published "The Arizona-Sonora Border and the Mexican Revolution, 1910-1920," Vol. XXIV, No. 2, April 1985.

To David Robertson, Lester Hood, Teresa Banks, and Pat Devejian, all of whom helped in the preparation of this manuscript, our special gratitude.

Finally, special credit must be given to those members of our families whose understanding and enthusiasm were of enormous help in completing this work. To Marie Louise Coerver, Eleanor Solon, and Douglas and Leslie Hall, our enduring thanks.

Revolution on the Border

1

Introduction

Borders are volatile areas. They form a unique region in which two societies come into contact, combine, and conflict. Serving as a continuum between cultures, similar and yet different from the interiors of the two nations, events and ideas from each side of the frontier flow across, permeate, and influence events and ideas on the other side. Individuals, families, and larger groups cross, more or less freely, and populations intermingle. Thus these areas are responsive to social and political changes coming from both directions; and in times of extreme and rapid change associated with revolutions, they are likely to be profoundly affected. This, indeed, was the case on the border between Mexico and the United States during the decade of the Mexican Revolution from 1910 to 1920.

Not only was the frontier area itself affected, but it also was the carrier of change between the two nations. Border issues became national concerns during the decade. Although the driving forces were political and military between 1910 and 1920, these same events had social and economic outcomes with national—as well as local and regional—effects. In this book, we intend to examine these social and economic effects within the political and military context of the frontier region. Early chapters, therefore, will focus on political and military developments, to be followed by chapters centering on the oil industry, mining, migration, and trade. We thereby hope to present a balanced look at the border region

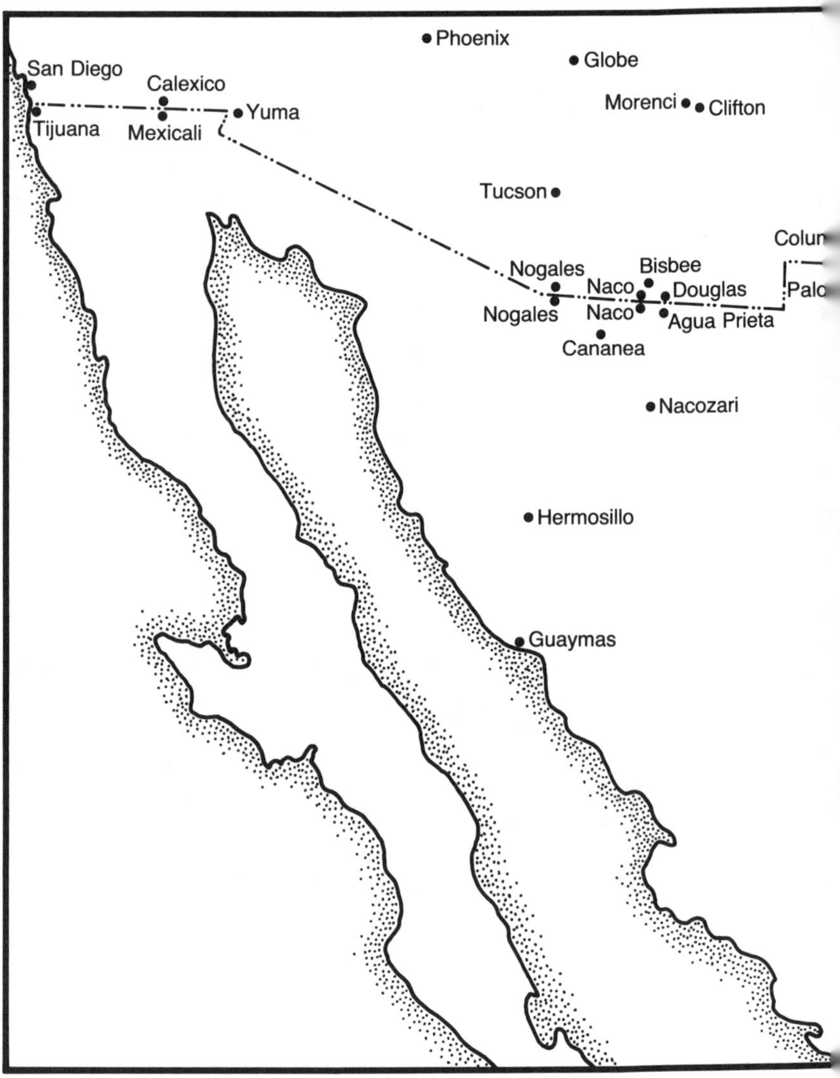
Phoenix
Globe
San Diego
Calexico
Yuma
Morenci
Clifton
Tijuana
Mexicali
Tucson
Colun
Nogales
Bisbee
Naco
Douglas
Palo
Nogales
Naco
Agua Prieta
Cananea
Nacozari
Hermosillo
Guaymas

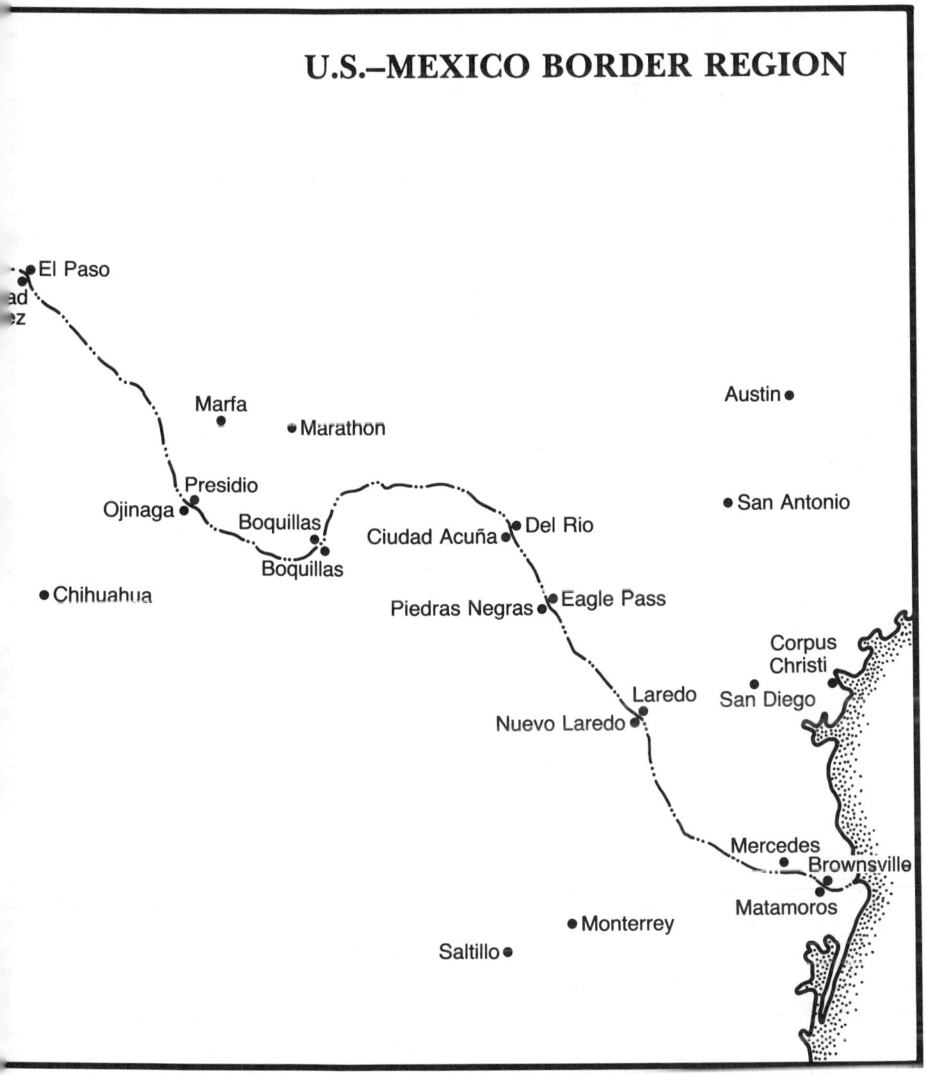
U.S.–MEXICO BORDER REGION
El Paso
Marfa
Marathon
Austin
Presidio
Ojinaga
Boquillas
Boquillas
Ciudad Acuña
Del Rio
San Antonio
Chihuahua
Piedras Negras
Eagle Pass
Corpus
Christi
San Diego
Laredo
Nuevo Laredo
Mercedes
Brownsville
Matamoros
Monterrey
Saltillo

during the Mexican Revolution. This work is intended to illuminate not only the impact of this civil war on the U.S.-Mexican border area, but also the effects that events and changes in this area had on the course of that revolutionary struggle and on the relations between these two countries.

The border itself was particularly troubled because of the key role northern Mexico played in the Revolution. Much of the fighting took place close to the border, and the northern states furnished both leaders and soldiers for the revolutionary movement. Further, the presence of the United States just to the north not only provided a contrast to the political dictatorship of Porfirio Díaz. It also offered an alternative source of employment for workers driven across the border by economic fluctuations in Mexico or attracted by greater economic opportunities. The United States was also a haven, not always equally secure, for political refugees and plotters against the government of Porfirio Díaz and for members of various revolutionary factions in the complex struggle that followed his fall.

It is important to keep in mind that the border between the United States and Mexico is one of the longest unfortified frontiers in the world. Although no major military confrontations had taken place there since the United States-Mexican war ended in 1848, the region had been far from peaceful. During the decade under consideration, the two countries came closer to direct conflict than at any other time since the Treaty of Guadalupe Hidalgo. The outbreak of the Mexican Revolution spawned an era of violence and political and economic radicalism in Mexico, which threatened the interests and lives of North Americans living in the border regions and in the interior of Mexico.

The United States between 1910 and 1920 faced many of the same problems that have been caused by conflict in Central America and the Caribbean in recent years. The proximity of Mexico and the difficulties of controlling a border almost 2,000 miles in length, however, made these problems even more acute, particularly for border residents who often were directly affected. More than once the danger of war between the two neighboring countries became acute, and possibly only the entrance of the United States into World War I prevented major hostilities. The decade saw a major military intervention by the United States in Mexican territory, the mass migration of Mexicans across the border to the relative safety of U.S. territory, important changes in economic relationships in the border area and between the United States and Mexico generally, and the beginning or acceleration of trends that would affect Mexican-U.S. relations throughout the century.

Tremendous social and economic changes took place in the border area between 1910 and 1920, and these changes were intertwined with the political and military events that were taking place at the same time.

Arizona and New Mexico achieved statehood; Texas, in asserting itself, created political tensions between state and national leaders. Simultaneously, northern Mexico was embroiled in violent struggles, first against the dictatorship of Porfirio Díaz, then against revolutionary president Francisco Madero, followed by the fight against Victoriano Huerta, and culminating in the battles between revolutionary factions led by Francisco Villa, on the one hand, and Alvaro Obregón and Venustiano Carranza, on the other. Meanwhile, mining was devastated in the region, while the oil business began to boom, led largely by southwesterners from the United States. Somewhat surprisingly, legal trade between the United States and Mexico—and almost certainly illegal trade as well—not only increased but burgeoned during these ten years. Finally, Mexican migration into the United States, particularly into the Southwest, reached enormous proportions, with probably one and a half million people fleeing the revolutionary violence, economic deprivation, and social chaos brought on by that upheaval.

Although many of the trends and changes noted above were accelerated by the Revolution, all were based in the developments in U.S.-Mexican relations and the evolving social and economic structures of the Porfiriato, that period in Mexico between 1876 and 1911 when Porfirio Díaz was the preeminent political figure of the country. While U.S.-Mexican relations had taken many dramatic turns during the nineteenth century, two major themes persisted: pressure generated by American expansionism and friction associated with a long, common border. For years after the Texas debacle, Mexican authorities were suspicious of the territorial ambitions of their northern neighbor. As late as the 1880s, considerable concern lingered over the future of the northern Mexican states. In 1881, one prominent general wrote to his superior that Sonora might very well "follow the same path as Texas" if the rate of U.S. penetration were not curtailed.[1] Mexican fears of a physical loss of territory subsided by the 1870s, only to be replaced by increasing concern over American economic penetration of their nation.

Border difficulties had been at the center of U.S.-Mexican problems since the 1820s. Even the most basic act of establishing a boundary between the two countries produced a series of acrimonious disputes lasting well into the twentieth century. The border area was a breeding ground for a variety of activities that would severely disturb international relations: Indian raids, banditry, smuggling, revolutionary activities, and even filibustering. Border problems provoked strong diplomatic pressure and often military intervention from the United States. It was under such troubled conditions that the United States and Mexico were forced to work out a relationship in the last quarter of the nineteenth century.

At the time Díaz came to power, the political situation on both sides of the border had been unsettled for some time. The United States had recently emerged from a bitter civil war, was agonizing over the problems of political and economic reconstruction, and trying to resolve the disputed presidential election of 1876. Similarly, Mexico was suffering even greater political and military dislocations. Having endured a civil war of its own, Mexico had undergone foreign invasion and occupation in the 1860s. The expulsion of the French in 1867 brought only temporary relief from the seemingly endless series of domestic rebellions. Revolutionary movements culminated in the rise of Díaz to the presidency in 1877. The Díaz government finally provided an unprecedented stability to U.S.-Mexican relations that lasted for more than thirty years.

The United States did not immediately recognize the Díaz regime, despite its usual practice of extending recognition to any government exercising de facto control over Mexico.[2] In this case, it was precisely border difficulties that led the United States to hesitate. In particular, the American government was pressing for permission to cross the international boundary in pursuit of outlaws or Indians. Recognition was delayed only a year, however, as Díaz moved additional troops to the frontier and permitted his military commanders along the border to cooperate with U.S. authorities. He also took a more flexible position on the issue of permitting U.S. troops to cross the border, provided it was on a reciprocal basis and under closely regulated conditions.[3]

The importance attached to border problems in the recognition controversy reflected the growing concern of both governments over the situation on the northern frontier. At the heart of problems along the border was the "absence of an authentic concept of a boundary between the two nations."[4] While diplomacy and military activity had gone a long way toward defining the boundary, much of the border area constituted a geographical, cultural, and economic unit. The Rio Grande was the only major geographical feature that could be used to establish international limits, and even it did not constitute a major physical barrier. In addition, periodic changes in the channel of the river produced a series of diplomatic squabbles lasting more than a century.

The border was, furthermore, not only a political frontier; it was also a population frontier. The region was sparsely inhabited, but a large percentage of the population on the U.S. side was of Mexican origin. Social and cultural ties transcended national boundaries, and little effort was made to limit the movement of people across the border. Much of the region could not support a stable economy, so many of the residents turned to smuggling and cattle rustling, which had become highly organized businesses by the 1870s. The border zone was far from the central authorities of both countries, and lawless elements encountered only limited official resistance to their activities. Both nations depended heavily upon regular army troops to maintain order in the area and concentrated a large percentage of their forces in the region. Despite this emphasis on military authority, both the Mexican and U.S. armies often proved inadequate to the task. Gen. Edward Ord, commander of the military department of Texas, complained that he had only 3,000 troops under his command, a figure representing approximately one soldier for each 120 square miles.[5]

While the international boundary did not constitute a physical barrier, it often provided legal asylum for outlaws on both sides of the border. Bandits crossed the boundary, committed crimes, and then escaped the jurisdiction of the authorities where the crimes had taken place. Since the military could not make arrests and there were few civil law enforcement officials, diplomatic response was often restricted to registering complaints about the failure of the other government to maintain law and order. The expansion of the cattle industry in south Texas caused cattle rustling to grow in importance, with transactions in stolen cattle becoming a major commercial activity. There were also frequent accusations from both Americans and Mexicans of official complicity in the banditry along the border.[6]

Indian raids across the border also created considerable friction between Mexico and the United States in the 1870s and 1880s. Under pressure from the movement of white settlers into the American Southwest, many Indians came to look upon Mexico as a refuge from the advancing whites. Mexican officials frequently criticized the U.S. policy of concentrating Indians close to the border, complaining that the reservations became, in effect, bases from which the Indians could commit "all kinds of outrages on the inhabitants of Mexico and their property."[7] Although most Indian raids were carried out from Mexican soil against settlements in the United States, the situation gave rise to an endless stream of recriminations over which party was to blame. While U.S. and Mexican authorities took turns denouncing each other, the Indians continued their raiding, "quite impartial about where they obtained their loot and equally impartial about where they disposed of it."[8]

An additional element disturbing relations along the border was the use of American soil as a base for launching revolutionary activities against the Mexican government. Díaz himself had used U.S. territory to organize his successful revolution in 1876. The defeat of anti-Díaz Gen. Mariano Escobedo in 1878, however, ushered in an era of relative calm that lasted until the final years of the Díaz regime, when revolutionary movements fomented in the United States again became a major problem.[9]

Although border problems had been a major source of friction between the United States and Mexico since the annexation of Texas in 1845, there had been only sporadic and generally unofficial efforts at cooperation in solving them. The United States had usually maintained that it had the right to pursue bandits or Indians across the international boundary. While U.S. forces normally asked Mexican authorities for permission to cross, they crossed anyway if such permission was denied.[10] This unilateral policy took its most explicit form in the so-called Ord Order of June 1, 1877, which authorized Gen. Edward Ord, commander of the Department of Texas, to dispatch troops across the border when he thought it necessary. The Mexican government replied angrily by informing Ord that any attempt to cross would be met with military force. The Ord Order continued to be a major point of dispute even after the recognition of the Díaz administration in April 1878. The revocation of the order in February 1880 opened the way for a formal agreement governing reciprocal crossing of the border by the forces of both countries.[11]

While both the United States and Mexico had discussed a border-crossing treaty for years, efforts to reach an agreement had been hampered by the reluctance of the United States to make the arrangement reciprocal. As the situation along the border deteriorated, especially with regard to Indian raids, the United States finally dropped its opposition to permitting Mexican forces to cross over into U.S. territory. In July 1882, the two parties reached an agreement providing for the reciprocal crossing of the boundary by troops "in close pursuit of a band of savage Indians." These crossings could take place only in deserted areas, and the commander of the troops making the crossing was to notify local authorities of his plan of march. The pursuing force was to return to its own territory after it had engaged the Indian band or in the event it lost the trail.[12] The reciprocal crossing agreement was renewed several times in the 1880s and 1890s and became a basic feature of border policy.

The implementation of the reciprocal crossing agreement did a great deal to eliminate the Indian problem, which had become the greatest source of border friction. The curtailment of the Indian menace was part of a broader pacification of the border zone that was developing in the 1880s and early 1890s. The growing political stability in Mexico under Díaz contributed to a calmer atmosphere along the border, as the central government extended more control over the region and was able to give it the military attention it required. The extension of the railroads into the area aided in the promotion of political peace and permitted a stronger economy to develop.[13] The amount of American investment, which started to increase significantly in the 1880s, also aided in the growing tranquility. While this helped to resolve long-standing problems along the border, it also introduced a new and equally troublesome problem in U.S.-Mexican relations: American penetration of the Mexican economy.

Before fears of earlier expansionism had completely died away, the Mexicans were confronted by a new threat to their political independence in the form of large-scale U.S. investment. Indeed, the two were often linked, with American economic penetration being viewed as the forerunner of territorial annexation.

This specter affected the early discussions involving railroad construction. There was strong opposition in Mexico to the building of railways to the northern border on the grounds that such lines would lead to U.S. commercial domination of Mexican markets and ultimately to the loss of national territory. Even when the railroad boom began in the 1880s, with the construction of two major lines running to the Texas border, the Mexican government still showed a pronounced reluctance to grant additional concessions for railways approaching the American frontier.[14]

Anti-U.S. sentiment during the early years of the Porfiriato was also evident in the lengthy negotiations over a new commercial treaty. In November 1880, the Mexican government denounced the existing commercial treaty that had been in effect since 1831. In the lengthy negotiations for a new agreement, the United States and Mexico found themselves at odds over Mexican insistence that any privileges extended to the United States be granted to other countries enjoying a "most-favored-nation" status with Mexico and that the United States agree to restriction of its ability to intervene diplomatically on behalf of North American citizens. After prolonged and often heated discussions, the senates of both countries finally approved a new treaty, but it lapsed in 1887 without ever having gone into effect, because the U.S. Congress failed to revise customs duties to conform with its provisions.[15]

Despite fears about what foreign economic penetration might mean for Mexico's future, the Díaz government never wavered in its emphasis on economic development and its conviction that foreign capital and technology were essential to the regime's development scheme. Díaz and his supporters consistently followed a policy aimed at creating an environment attractive to foreign investors. Drawn by Mexico's growing political stability and economic opportunities, foreign investors—especially North Americans—quickly responded. U.S. investment was especially heavy in such economically important and politically sensitive areas as railroads and mining.

As the United States gradually displaced Great Britain as the principal foreign investor in Mexico, there was a parallel development in Mexico's trade patterns. In the early 1880s, Britain and the United States each accounted for about 40 percent of Mexican export trade; within a decade, the United States was purchasing more than 70 percent of Mexico's exports.[16] A similar trend was evident in Mexico's import trade as the United States steadily replaced Britain as the chief supplier of foreign products. By 1890, the United States had become Mexico's principal trading partner, functioning as the chief market for Mexican exports and the main source of Mexican imports.[17] Though much of this trade was handled through maritime ports, border cities, particularly those located on the major rail lines, profited considerably.

U.S. penetration of the economy became particularly intense in the closing years of the Porfiriato, generating additional anti-American feeling and growing uneasiness over Porfirian development strategy even among the regime's supporters. In response to growing economic opportunities, American investments more that quintupled in the last decade under Díaz, reaching a total of more than 1 billion dollars by 1911.[18] American interests controlled 78 percent of the mining industry and 58 percent of the growing petroleum industry. During the first decade of the twentieth century, the United States continued its role as dominant trading partner, accounting for approximately 60 percent of Mexico's exports and imports.[19]

Porfirian land policy also encouraged foreign penetration of the economy. The Díaz administration intensified the attack on communal properties that had begun under Benito Juárez and emphasized surveying of public lands, which led to the transfer of large areas of the national domain to private individuals, often foreigners. These surveys were frequently connected with efforts to promote immigration, but the survey companies became little more than land-speculation enterprises able to obtain vast sections of public lands. Instead of opening up new lands to settlement, as was theoretically their purpose, the survey companies combined vacant lands into large tracts for speculative purposes. In the 1880s alone, these companies surveyed approximately 32 million hectares of land. Of this amount, the companies acquired as compensation for their services or through purchase more than 27.5 million hectares—a figure representing almost 14 percent of the total land area of Mexico.[20] By 1910, foreigners—mostly Americans—owned about one-seventh of the land surface of Mexico. Much of this land was located in the politically sensitive zone along the U.S.-Mexican border.[21]

By 1910, a classic pattern of economic dependency had developed. North Americans dominated transportation, communications, mining, petroleum, investments, technological transfer, and the import-export trade, all of which were particularly significant in the region near the border. The changing pattern of economic relations and the growing importance of economic issues between the two countries had their impact on diplomatic relations. Long-standing problems such as border lawlessness and Indian raids virtually disappeared in the 1890s to be replaced by new issues concerning trade and investment. A few traditional difficulties remained, particularly the mistreatment of resident aliens by both countries and the seemingly interminable dispute over the Chamizal tract. Still, what was most striking about the last two decades of the Porfirian period was the virtual absence of major issues between the two countries, a condition that continued until the outbreak of revolutionary agitation in the closing years of the Díaz regime.

At the same time, the limits of Porfirian prosperity and the problems of U.S. economic penetration were becoming increasingly obvious. While major economic advances had occurred in many sectors of the Mexican economy, particularly transportation and communication, other sectors had failed to keep pace, especially agriculture. The rural sector, which included most of the work force and population, suffered a notable decline in its standard of living as a result of the Díaz development policy.[22] The growing American presence in the economy tapped the ever-present vein of anti-U.S. sentiment and led to renewed demands for restrictions on foreign investors. The integration of Mexico into the international economy by emphasizing foreign investment and the export sector produced major economic and political problems. Beginning with a declining demand for Mexican imports in the early 1900s and culminating in the extension of the Panic of 1907 to Mexico, the hazards associated with dependent development provoked increasing opposition to Díaz and his economic policies. The economic fallout from the Panic of 1907 injured even those who had received the most benefit from Porfirian prosperity. The middle class, which had grown substantially as a result of Porfirian policies, was becoming increasingly restive in the face of political and economic restrictions. After three decades of official encouragement, American investors were deeply involved in the Mexican economy and had a vital stake in continuing the internal stability Díaz and his followers had established. When this was threatened by political developments in 1910, the United States was forced to deal not only with more traditional problems, such as revolutionary activities along the border, but also with the difficulty of protecting a greatly expanded American presence in Mexico.

As Díaz's economic problems began to mount in the first decade of the twentieth century, the aging dictator was also forced to confront growing political opposition both within Mexico and from exile groups operating in the United States. The southwestern part of the United States had frequently served as a launching point for revolutionary activities in the nineteenth century, as Díaz knew from first-hand experience in the 1870s. While these revolutionary activities had never completely died out during the Porfiriato, they had ceased to be an important diplomatic consideration in the 1880s and 1890s. Beginning in 1906, however, revolutionary plotting along the border again became a major issue between the United States and Mexico as exile activity took a more militant turn under the leadership of people such as the Flores Magón brothers, Jesús and Ricardo. Although exile attacks across the boundary were easily repulsed by Mexican forces, the Díaz administration constantly pressured the U.S. government to follow a more vigorous policy in halting such revolutionary activities. Díaz was also incensed at the growing arms trade across the border, which he thought the U.S. government was either unable or unwilling to stop. While Don Porfirio and his advisors clearly perceived the danger emanating from the north, they never completely comprehended the complications that the American system of federalism imposed on efforts by authorities to deal with the revolutionaries. Local, state, and federal officials on the U.S. side often found it difficult to sort out their various spheres of jurisdiction and coordinate their activities. Moreover, considerable disagreement existed over the gravity of the threat these revolutionary machinations posed and the emphasis that should be placed on dealing with them. The Díaz administration often mistook this confusion for lack of vigor on the part of American officials in dealing with the exile threat.[23]

U.S.-Mexican relations were further complicated by a growing anti-Americanism in Mexico. Despite the official welcome for North Americans and their investment, anti-yanqui sentiment was never far from the surface, and U.S. officials were unpleasantly surprised to discover that there was still a strong residue of resentment over such seemingly distant events as the Texas Revolution of 1836 and the Mexican War (1846–48). Mexican concern was intensified by the sudden growth in American investment in the last decade of the Porfirian period, and especially by the linking of Mexico to U.S. markets and large-scale acquisitions of property by Americans in northern Mexico. The long-standing policy of giving preferential treatment to U.S. citizens in employment and pay was also coming under increasing criticism.

This antigringo sentiment received additional impetus from two events in 1910. First, the Mexican presidential election focused attention on the system Díaz presided over and the special role given to U.S. economic and political interests in that system. There was a growing conviction—even among many of Díaz's supporters—that American influence must be curbed, especially in the economic realm. Second, the observance of the centennial of Mexican independence, which was as much a glorification of Porfirian achievements as a commemoration of the break with Spain, heightened anti-American sentiment. Critics of the regime charged that the political independence achieved in the early nineteenth century had been undermined by the Porfirian pursuit of economic development with its emphasis on American penetration of the economy. The outbreak of revolution in 1910 provided an opportunity to release anti-Americanism that had largely been repressed for three decades, with some predictable effects in the border region in the following years.

The presidential election of 1910 not only caused an increase in anti-Americanism, but also provided the background for a revolutionary movement that would lead to the overthrow of the Porfirian regime. Francisco Madero, from a wealthy family benefiting directly from the Porfirian system, challenged Díaz in the 1910 election and generated a surprising degree of popular support. As opponents of the administration began to rally to the Madero campaign, Díaz felt sufficiently threatened to order Madero arrested. Not surprisingly, the election produced a Díaz landslide. Shortly afterward, Madero fled into exile in Texas where he issued his Plan of San Luis Potosí calling for the overthrow of Díaz and the installation of a provisional president. The fact that Madero had formulated the plan in Texas and not in Mexico, as its misleading title would indicate, was a harbinger of how deeply involved the United States would become in Mexican affairs in the coming years.

2

Revolution on the Rio Grande

The violence of the Revolution greatly affected Texas. The Texas-Mexican border had been an area of dispute, lawlessness, and international confrontation from the earliest days of Texas independence. As early as 1836 disputes over territory arose when the Republic of Texas claimed the Rio Grande as its southern boundary, a claim Mexico refused to recognize just as it refused to acknolwedge the independence of Texas. A history of border raids in the 1830s and 1840s persisted after statehood in 1845; one such border incident furnished the cause for the U.S. declaration of war against Mexico in 1846. While the war ended in Mexican defeat and recognition of the Rio Grande as the international boundary, the border region continued to be a flash point in both Texas-Mexican and U.S.-Mexican relations.

The Rio Grande Valley region, even under U.S. jurisdiction, retained much of its Mexican culture and heritage. The population along the Rio Grande was overwhelmingly Mexican in origin, and movement across the international boundary was virtually unrestricted. In contrast to Arizona, Texans of Mexican origin constituted a large proportion of the population and played a significant role in the politics of southern Texas. Tejano elites joined Anglos in controlling most of the counties that bordered on Mexico, and Hispanic names regularly appeared among nineteenth-century elected officials in those counties and in Bexar County, the location of San Antonio. Illiteracy proved the major barrier to voting, but was overcome to some degree by associations with political machines, largely manipulated by Anglos. Admittedly, poor Tejanos had little political power, but it would be inaccurate to assume that they were entirely powerless. According to one authority, south Texas was "dominated by the Mexican vote," which thus became a major element in state politics. Seven south Texas counties had a Mexican population of more than 75 percent; two between 50 and 75 percent; one between 35 and 49 percent, and 12 between 20 and 34 percent. Although this vote was frequently controlled by political organizations, such as "The Ring" in El Paso or Jim Wells's group in Cameron County, these organizations nevertheless made it possible for the Mexican population to exert some influence at the local level.[1]

An uncharacteristic calm settled over the Texas border during the late nineteenth century, the result of greater cooperation between the United States and Mexico in patrolling the region as well as the growing U.S. economic penetration of Mexico. The extension of the railroads into northern Mexico and southern Texas aided in making the area more accessible. While the regime of Porfirio Díaz (1876–1911) seemed to offer the possibility of an unending period of peace and prosperity along the border, the apparent serenity was soon shattered by the growing revolutionary activity in the region that culminated in the revolution of 1910.

Texas, particularly the area from San Antonio south, had long been a favorite refuge for Mexican politicians out of power and out of favor. The last decade of the Porfiriato was no exception. In January 1904, the revolutionaries Enrique and Ricardo Flores Magón crossed the border into Laredo, where they were soon joined by other members of the Partido Liberal Mexicano (PLM). On February 5, 1904, the exiles met in that city and established themselves as the Club Liberal "Ponciano Arriaga." They laid plans to reestablish the radical newspaper *Regeneración* and plot revolution. By the end of that year, *Regeneración* was being published in San Antonio, but the would-be revolutionaries left Texas after the arrest of Enrique Flores Magón. The PLM central junta, however, returned to San Antonio from time to time between the years 1905 and 1911.[2]

Texas also harbored female radicals and revolutionaries. During the pre-Díaz period, Teresa and Andrea Villareal founded their own radical publication, *La Mujer Moderna*, in San Antonio, and in El Paso, Isidra T. De Cárdenas established the weekly *Voz de la Mujer*. Flores de Andrade of Chihuahua also worked in El Paso at this time, founding the semisecret "Daughters of Cuahtémoc," which worked with the Liberal Party. She helped the Flores Magón brothers and later Francisco Madero. Even the Saint of Caborca, Teresa Urrea, spent time leading an anti-Díaz movement in Texas, as well as Arizona, between 1890 and 1906. Her companion, Lauro Aguirre, joined the Magonista movement after her death and lived in El Paso from 1896 on, continually harassed by Díaz agents.[3]

Indeed, during much of this time Díaz had not only the help of his consuls in the United States, but also of U.S. authorities, who attempted to aid him by strict, perhaps excessive, enforcement of the neutrality laws. U.S. citizens who helped the exiles also suffered. John Murray, secretary of the Political Refugee Defense League and responsible for organizing the legal defense of the Magonistas, was harassed by Mexican-paid detectives from El Paso and San Antonio who worked in cooperation with the United States postal authorities. As a result of this cooperation, his mail was intercepted and copied, with reports made to Díaz's minister of foreign affairs. In Mexico, the U.S. consul Luther Ellsworth, in Ciudad Juárez just across the river from El Paso, kept an eye on anti-Díaz activity with the help of private detectives, postal workers, and customs authorities. In addition, he was in contact with agents in San Antonio, some of whom were paid Mexican spies and who watched over revolutionary activities in that area. With the help of the excellent telegraph, telephone, and mail services between El Paso and San Antonio, he was able to relay information and instructions to Mexican consuls and government agents throughout New Mexico and Texas. In this effort he was aided by the Texas Rangers and even Oscar B. Colquitt, governor of Texas.[4]

By 1910, the political climate was heating up considerably. In that year, elections were held in both Mexico and Texas that would have a profound influence on U.S.-Mexican relations in general and border affairs in particular. The Texas gubernatorial election of that year revolved primarily around the issue of prohibition. Oscar B. Colquitt—who had made an unsuccessful run for the governorship in 1906 and currently occupied the powerful position of state railroad commissioner—was generally identified with conservative interests. He opposed statewide prohibition and made no mention of a border policy because there were no unusual border problems. In winning the Democratic nomination and later the election, Colquitt received substantial support from Mexican American voters who strongly opposed prohibition. Influential Mexican American political leaders in south Texas, such as Francisco A. Chapa and Amador Sánchez of Laredo, played major roles in turning out the "wet" votes that produced Colquitt's narrow victory in the Democratic primary. These political debts would come back to haunt Colquitt during his governorship as he attempted to deal with growing problems along the border.[5]

The Mexican presidential elections of 1910 also promised to be uneventful. Pres. Porfirio Díaz was running for yet another term and using the centennial of Mexico's independence to showcase the peace and prosperity he had helped to bring to Mexico in the previous decades.[6] Although the incumbent was eighty, his hold on the country seemed to be secure. The elections had been briefly enlivened by the presidential candidacy of Francisco Madero. Díaz had originally welcomed Madero's opposition as proof that democratic processes had taken root in Mexico. When Madero provoked too much popular response, Díaz had him jailed and then won an easy victory in the elections.[7] Madero, however, managed to flee to San Antonio, where he established his revolutionary headquarters, following in the footsteps of the Flores Magón brothers. The Madero family had long-standing relationships with prominent Texans, and the Madero revolt would eventually cause great concern among both federal and state authorities. Much of the border population, including some officials, openly supported the revolution of Madero, whose political moderation was in marked contrast to the radical views espoused by the Magonistas. As a result, law enforcement officials at all levels had to be more diplomatic in their dealing with the Maderista rebels.[8]

As Madero plotted his revolution in San Antonio in October and November 1910, he did his best to avoid any appearance of violating American neutrality laws.[9] Federal and state authorities were uncertain as to how to proceed against his movement. While Madero had publicly acknowledged that he was the head of a revolutionary junta, he had still taken no overt action from American soil aimed at the overthrow of the Díaz regime.[10]

Federal officials in the field often did not understand the application of the neutrality laws and pursued an inconsistent course in their enforcement. The problem of enforcement was further complicated by the large number of agencies involved along the border: U.S. customs collectors, the army, attorneys from the Department of Justice, agents of the Bureau of Investigation, federal judges, and State Department officials. Despite the proliferation of agencies, federal officials found themselves shorthanded and had to call upon state officials to enforce federal neutrality laws. This was a move of doubtful legality that only served to confuse the situation further and would ultimately lead to a series of federal-state disputes over the handling of border policy.[11]

State and federal officials kept a close watch on Madero personally as the date announced for the revolution—November 20, 1910—approached. Madero, however, was able to elude this surveillance, and on the night of November 19, he crossed from Texas into Mexico without incident. In fact, Madero's entire visit was without incident. He found only a small group of rebels who were badly organized and virtually unarmed, and after two days of fitful waiting, he returned to Texas.

He soon resumed his plotting against the Díaz regime, but his initial attempt at revolution was so fruitless that federal authorities in both Mexico and the United States were still not able to produce concrete evidence that Madero had violated the neutrality laws of the United States. Pressure was mounting on the U.S. government to take action against him, particularly in view of the fact that his revolution was beginning to gain momentum along the border even if his own personal role in it had not gone well. By the time Oscar B. Colquitt was sworn in as governor of Texas in January 1911, the "border problem" was becoming much more serious, and U.S. federal officers were considering the arrest of Madero.[12]

Colquitt was in a weak position to deal with growing troubles along the Rio Grande. One of his first actions as governor was to honor his election commitment to reduce the force of Texas Rangers, although they would certainly be needed in any effort to step up surveillance and enforcement on the border.[13] Nevertheless, beginning in February 1911, state and federal officials began a cooperative effort to curb Maderista activities along the Texas border. When a rebel attack on Ciudad Juárez appeared imminent, Colquitt ordered out the Texas National Guard at El Paso to assist army troops in preventing the revolution from spilling over onto the Texas side.[14]

Not content with merely enforcing federal neutrality laws, Colquitt issued a neutrality proclamation of his own on February 11, 1911, though it differed little from federal legislation on the same issue. Still, it was a significant indication of the governor's special interest in the problem.[15]

As the Madero revolution gained momentum, particularly in northern Mexico, both state and federal authorities took action to meet the growing unrest along the border. This included President Taft's formation of the "Maneuver Division," with headquarters at Fort Sam Houston in San Antonio, Texas. Ostensibly this division would be used for field training of officers and men; by Taft's own admission, it was formed to take action should American lives and property be threatened in Mexico. At the same time, Colquitt was concentrating the Ranger force at potential trouble spots along the border and calling up units of the Texas National Guard for service at El Paso.[16]

Of particular concern was revolutionary interest in the city of Ciudad Juárez, Chihuahua. The acquisition of Juárez would give the Madero forces an important border city that would both permit the collection of customs duties and provide a point of entry for war matériel. When Maderista rebel leader Pascual Orozco attacked Juárez on May 8, 1911, hundreds of spectators gathered on the U.S. side to watch. Not surprisingly, by later afternoon the American side had suffered casualties, with four dead and nine wounded. The final figures would be six killed and fifteen wounded. Texas state officials were greatly concerned about the safety of the border population. Despite Colquitt's protests to U.S. government officials, the U.S. Army was forbidden to cross the border under any circumstances. Ciudad Juárez continued to be a major target for revolutionary attacks for some time, and the population of El Paso continued to suffer.[17]

A further problem was the overlapping and intermingling of state and federal responsibilities in meeting the threat to the tranquility of the border area. A meeting between President Taft and Governor Colquitt in September 1911 led to an arrangement in which the Texas Ranger force would be expanded, with help from federal funds, and would in turn work with federal authorities in enforcing federal neutrality laws and providing protection for the border. Thus, a state agency and state officials became involved in functions that were clearly federal, and the agency was funded largely by the national government.[18]

This confusion of jurisdictions manifested itself almost immediately in the federal and state authorities' handling of Bernardo Reyes's conspiracy against the newly established Madero government. Reyes, the former governor of Nuevo León, had long seen himself as the successor to Díaz. Díaz, however, had skillfully shipped him off on a "military mission" to Europe in 1909 when it seemed to the aging president that Reyes might challenge his authority. Reyes did not meekly accept Madero's assumption of the presidency. He began to maneuver against him, enlisting allies in Texas, particularly among Mexican American businessmen and politicians and even meeting on one occasion with Colquitt himself. When it was discovered that Reyes was planning an invasion of Mexico through Laredo, however, the governor quickly took action to break up his organization. Rangers under the command of Henry Hutchings, the adjutant general, were dispatched to Laredo, where they cooperated with U.S. Army forces in dispersing the would-be insurgents.

Although the operation was successful, no one involved quite understood what the nature of federal-state cooperation was supposed to be. In any event, Colquitt took most of the credit, despite an initial reluctance to follow the lead of the federal authorities in dealing with the conspirators. Later, the conspirators on the Texas side (Reyes having escaped back to Mexico) received ludicrously light sentences from the federal court in the border city of Brownsville, Texas.[19]

The El Paso-Juárez problems continued in 1912, despite the end of the Reyes conspiracy. In January, the Mexican garrison at Juárez mutinied when Madero tried to disband a portion of the troops. After a good deal of protest from Colquitt about the protection of Americans in this crisis, President Taft threatened Mexican authorities with a border crossing by U.S. troops to prevent firing on the U.S. side. The garrison, however, surrendered to Pascual Orozco, still loyal to Madero. Orozco then crossed over into El Paso and announced that he was glad to be there as he "always had a good time" in that city. Less than a month later, Orozco himself revolted against Madero.[20]

Another problem appeared in El Paso a month later. A U.S. Army lieutenant who had been in El Paso only three days made the mistake of taking a detail of men by streetcar for guard duty at one of the international bridges. Unfortunately, being unfamiliar with the city, he did not realize that the streetcar went through Ciudad Juárez. The Mexicans, thinking they were being invaded by means of the public transportation facilities, formed a mob led by the pistol-brandishing mayor to turn back the gringos. As the lieutenant was unable to speak Spanish, linguistic difficulties made the situation worse. Although the Americans were quickly released, the "streetcar invasion" led to panic along the border and the calling up of the Texas National Guard.[21]

President Taft's threat to send U.S. troops into Mexico to protect lives on the American side of the border was not reiterated, although troubles in the El Paso-Juárez area continued through midsummer of 1912. Revolutionaries in support of both Emilio Vásquez Gómez and Pascual Orozco threatened the area, but refused to promise that there would be no firing in the direction of the border. Colquitt was a good deal more alarmed about this possibility than were federal authorities and made plans to move artillery units of the Texas National Guard from Dallas to El Paso in preparation for trouble. He took no major action, however, until after the election of 1912, which returned Colquitt to the governorship and brought Woodrow Wilson, a fellow Democrat, to the presidency.[22]

Although the new Democratic president initially sought Colquitt's ideas about the U.S.-Mexican border situation, Colquitt ultimately got along no better with him than he had with the Republican Taft. Again, those most concerned with border security were those closest to the border. When Victoriano Huerta overthrew Madero, who was subsequently killed, new revolts broke out throughout the country, particularly in northern Mexico. This kept the border in constant turmoil almost to the end of the decade. Wilson, for his part, made the communications problem between state and federal authorities worse by adopting a personalistic style of diplomacy in which he bypassed the regular channels of the State Department and instead used personal emissaries and special agents to the various factions emerging in the revolutionary ranks.[23]

In fact, revolutionary factionalism was to be a problem in one of the major border incidents during the Revolution, the kidnapping and murder of U.S. citizen Clemente Vergara. Vergara, owner of a ranch in Palafox, Texas, was accustomed to pasturing horses on an island in the Rio Grande, although no one was certain whether it belonged to the U.S.

or Mexico. Huertista troops removed Vergara's horses on the morning of February 12, 1914, and took them to the Mexican side. Vergara was invited to cross the river and negotiate, but on arrival on Mexican territory he was arrested and subsequently hanged.[24]

Colquitt was understandably disturbed and blamed the incident on Wilson's policy of refusing to recognize any Mexican faction. Indeed, Colquitt was unable to determine with which side he should negotiate, as the Mexican state of Nuevo León, scene of the "arrest" and hanging, had two governors, a Huertista and a Constitutionalist who followed First Chief Venustiano Carranza, Madero's successor. Later, Texas Rangers seem to have crossed the river, exhumed the body, and brought it back to the U.S. side. Although Wilson was later given another, less compromising, version of the rescue of the cadaver, the incident did nothing to improve Texas's relations with Mexico or with the U.S. federal government.[25]

To the dismay of border residents, when the U.S. did intervene, it was not in response to border provocations, but to an insult to the American navy at Tampico, which led to the U.S. invasion and occupation of Veracruz on April 9, 1914. Despite Colquitt's hopes that Wilson would develop a tougher border policy, little was done beyond reinforcement of border cities to prevent reprisals for the intervention. Colquitt wrote to Wilson urging a large-scale invasion of Mexico that would include the seizure of the northern Mexican cities of Matamoros, Laredo, Ciudad Porfirio Díaz (Piedras Negras), and Juárez. He pointed out that this occupation was necessary because of the 20,000 to 30,000 refugees living along the frontier, posing a threat to Texas lives and property. He also asked for the formation of an additional quasimilitary group, the "home guards," to supplement the Texas National Guard and the Rangers in the defense of the border. The governor was unwilling to call a special session of the Texas legislature to obtain the necessary funds, however, and the national government, which had helped him during the Taft administration, was unwilling to provide financial assistance at the time. Ironically, as Colquitt prepared to leave office in January 1915, the Texas border was heating up, and Texas would have to meet the most serious period of raiding during the revolutionary period, raiding associated with the so-called Plan of San Diego.[26]

It is unclear whether the raids carried out under the Plan of San Diego between January 1915 and June 1916 were officially supported by the Carrancistas or whether they were carried out by Mexicans or Mexican Americans. It seems likely that at least some of the raids were supported by Constitutionalist First Chief Venustiano Carranza, and some were actually carried out by Mexican Americans. It also seems clear that the Carrancista commanders in the area did nothing to prevent the raiding.[27]

In any case, raiding by Mexicans and Mexican Americans in the south Texas region caused considerable hysteria. July and August of 1915 were months of particular conflict. On July 18, 1915, Ranger Caldwell of Capt. J. J. Sanders's command was killed in an encounter with Mexican rustlers at a point near the Texas coast, sixty-eight miles north of Brownsville. Two weeks later, after several other incidents, peace officers and "prominent citizens" from all over the Lower Rio Grande Valley met in "secret" session in San Benito, Texas, to make plans to suppress the raiders' activities and to inflict "summary punishment . . . upon any suspected bandits who may fall into their hands." On the same day, a raid on Sebastian, Texas, stirred feelings up even further. A. L. Austin and his son, prominent local farmers, were kidnapped from their corn-shelling facilities and taken to a nearby field where they were shot. A witness, who apparently survived because he had formerly lent one of the attackers ten dollars, recognized some of the bandits as local residents. Most of the Anglo community at Sebastian, however, believed that these individuals were joined by others from across the river. The bandits also robbed T. Alexander's store in Sebastian, and, though pursued by a detachment of the 12th Cavalry, eluded apprehension. The hysteria in south Texas reached its August peak when, on the seventeenth of that month, two hundred and seventy Mexicans were reported to have crossed the river near Progreso and be moving toward Mercedes in Hidalgo County. In fact, what apparently had happened was that a patrol of twenty-one U.S. soldiers had been fired upon from the other side of the river. One was killed and two others injured. The explanation given for the mistake was that a sharp bend in the river made it appear to a witness that the fighting was on the U.S. side. Meanwhile, eight hundred U.S. soldiers were put on guard near Progreso.[28]

Despite the concerns of the Texans, however, in the twelve-month period between July 1915 and July 1916, thirty raids into Texas produced only twenty-one American deaths, including civilians and military personnel. Nevertheless, the reprisals against Mexican and Mexican American residents of Texas were significant. The Plan of San Diego led to a number of executions by various groups ranging from Texas Rangers to groups of armed citizens operating as vigilantes. The resulting racial tension created a sizeable exodus of Mexicans and Mexican Americans from the Lower Rio Grande Valley. One estimate indicates that as many as three hundred Mexicans had been executed without trial on the Texas side of the river. Although overshadowed by the Pershing Expedition, which had followed Pancho Villa into Mexico after his raid on Columbus, New Mexico, in March, 1916, the Plan of San Diego caused significant violence in south Texas and led to fears of a race war in the area as well as the real threat of a war with Mexico. Though U.S. authorities ultimately backed away from a major confrontation, given the shadow of the conflict in Europe, the possibility of war between the United States and Mexico was significant for a period of time.[29]

Meanwhile, Texas continued to be a favorite spot for those Mexican exiles plotting to return to the fray in their native country. Prominent among these were former persident Victoriano Huerta and erstwhile Madero supporter and opponent, Pascual Orozco. Huerta may have chosen Texas as a likely site because of the large number of former Díaz supporters who had settled there and might be expected to support him against the Constitutionalists of Venustiano Carranza and Alvaro Obregón.[30] Orozco had become the nominal leader of a number of prominent Mexican exiles in the United States loosely referred to as the "El Paso Group," while Huerta had been negotiating with Germany for aid in mounting an armed movement to recapture power in Mexico. In March 1915, Huerta came to New York to prepare such a movement, and Orozco met with him there.

Huerta's plotting was by no means well hidden, with even the newspapers reporting on his movements. The San Antonio *Express*, for example, accurately reported on June 14, 1915, that Huerta and many of his adherents, "former military commanders and legislators," were on their way to El Paso to mount a new military effort to regain control of Mexico. Orozco was also reported to be in El Paso, and Gen. José Ynés Salazar was close at hand in western Chihuahua.[31] Huerta and Orozco—hoping to throw off unwanted observers, particularly federal authorities—scheduled their meeting for Newman, New Mexico. No one was deceived, however, and both were arrested and taken to El Paso, where they were charged with violations of the federal neutrality laws. Within a few days, other Huertistas and former Porfiristas in various parts of the state were also arrested.[32]

Initially, both Huerta and Orozco were released on bond, although they were kept under constant surveillance by federal and state authorities. Nevertheless, Orozco was able to escape about three weeks later, climbing out a back window of the house in which he was staying, sneaking through the bushes, and departing into the alley. Huerta was immediately taken back into custody. The Villistas in charge of Ciudad Juárez and Tom Lea, mayor of El Paso, both requested military reinforcements to deal with the possibility of a renewed Orozquista attack on the Mexican border city.[33]

Reports of Orozco's whereabouts filled the Texas newspapers for the next two months, but in fact the situation was resolved by the deaths of both Orozco and Huerta. Orozco was the first to die. Surrounded by a posse of federal and state authorities including marshals, Rangers, and members of the 13th Cavalry, he was shot to death in the Green River Canyon. Huerta, abandoned by the German authorities, began to drink heavily again and rapidly fell ill. He died on January 13, 1916, and was buried in the El Paso cemetery next to his co-conspirator, Orozco.[34]

Huerta's death, however, did not end the German threat in Mexico. Pancho Villa now became the target of German attention, and throughout much of 1915, German agents helped to finance arms purchases for the Villistas. Although it is difficult to prove conclusively that German agents encouraged Villa in his attack on Columbus, New Mexico in March 1916, Villa continued to receive their help in the wake of the raid. Additionally, Germany attempted to establish a closer relationship with Carranza himself. Carranza's antipathy for the United States made this rapprochement more likely. In January 1917, the German Foreign Minister, Arthur Zimmermann, offered Carranza an alliance in the event that the United States declared war against Germany. Germany would provide Carranza's government with substantial financial assistance in a war to reconquer the territory that had been lost by Mexico in 1848. The Zimmermann Telegram, as this communication came to be known, was intercepted by the British and subsequently pubished on March 1, causing a sensation in the border area and in the nation generally. The demobilization of U.S. troops on the border following the withdrawal of the Pershing Expedition from Mexico was reversed, and the Texas National Guard was mobilized on March 31. On April 6, the United States declared war on Germany.[35]

Throughout the war, American officials and border residents continued to be concerned about German activities, potential or actual, on the border. The Texas Ranger force was expanded, and the State Adjutant General organized a force of volunteers known as the Loyalty Rangers to aid them in border enforcement activities. In addition, a special investigation bureau was also established under the Adjutant General for the purpose of gathering information about possible subversive activities in the border region. The new bureau was directed by W. M. Hanson, an individual who had had considerable law enforcement experience along the border starting in the 1880s and who had also been a resident of northern Mexico from 1906 to 1914.[36]

Despite the fears of border residents, however, violent activity in the area diminished greatly toward the end of the decade. When another threat did emerge in 1919, the response of U.S. officials indicated that they had lost their earlier patience. Pancho Villa, though no longer in control of Ciudad Juárez, had remained a power in the state of Chihuahua, and in June of that year he decided to move against that border city. The United States quickly reinforced El Paso and was ready to act at the time of Villa's attack on June 15. Having received prior authorization to move across the border in the event of firing into El Paso, Army troops crossed almost as soon as shots started to fall on the U.S. side. The Villistas were dispersed within twenty-four hours, having suffered one hundred killed; army casualties were two killed, ten wounded. This action reflected a much tougher U.S. policy toward Carranza's government. Fortifications had been increased in the area, and there were twenty-four Army posts in Texas alone. Brownsville and El Paso housed the two largest Army ordnance depots in the United States, and Newton Baker, the secretary of war, was quite open in threatening intervention should Villa or Carranza continue to cause border violence.[37]

By the end of 1920, major border problems caused by the Mexican Revolution had come to an end. The presidential inauguration in December 1920 of Alvaro Obregón—a Sonoran highly familiar with the border area—led to considerable optimism on the part of William P. Hobby, the governor of Texas, who enthusiastically remarked at an El Paso dinner honoring Obregón, that Texas and Mexico could be "pals."[38] The major border violence had come to an end, although Texas would continue to furnish a haven during the following decade for Mexican dissidents.

3

The Arizona-Sonora Border and the Mexican Revolution

The Arizona-Sonora border was also significantly affected by the events of the Mexican Revolution. Though Arizona was less troubled by raids across the frontier than was south Texas, it nevertheless suffered from dangers to its citizens and their property along the border and experienced considerable disruptions of the cross-border economy. The decade of the Revolution also saw Arizona emerge from territorial status to statehood, while Sonora moved from its position on the periphery of national power to place one of its sons, Alvaro Obregón, in the Mexican presidency. These two states—coping with similar problems of geography, environment, resources, and isolation from the political centers of their respective nations—developed along quite different lines. Their symbiotic relationship, despite occasional clashes, was of major importance in determining the course of historical events.

In both states, the major industries were mining, cattle, and irrigated agriculture. Both were influenced by the considerable development of the copper mining industry, especially in response to World War I; by the growth and development of large land companies, which frequently also served as construction companies that created irrigation facilities; and by the continual problem of insufficient water, which led to disputes over water rights and to the eventual development of a policy of public works designed to deal with this shortage.

Further, the border between Arizona and Sonora was just as permeable as other parts of the frontier. North Americans had been present in Sonora in considerable numbers at least from the 1880s, when the closing of the U.S. frontier led the adventurous to seek new opportunities to the south. By the same token, Mexican laborers had been migrating, temporarily or permanently, from Sonora into the territory of the United States from the time of the Treaty of Guadalupe Hidalgo in 1848. Many of these migrants had been prospectors, drawn by the California gold rush, and many continued to prospect in Arizona. As the copper mining grew to be a major industry in Arizona, more workers were needed. A large number of Sonorans, attracted by the economic opportunities afforded by this industry, moved across the line, returning to Mexico should the desire or the necessity arise. Thus, economic, social, and even family ties bound the two areas. Further, coping with similar problems and the similarity of economic development led in turn to similarities of technology and business practice in the two areas; engineers and businessmen, such as the prominent mining engineer Louis D. Ricketts, worked in both Arizona and Sonora.

The development of the border area until 1910 had not been entirely peaceful. As in Texas, the presence of the border itself had created major problems of law enforcement, with rustlers running cattle back and forth across the line, Indian raids a constant menace, smuggling an everyday occurrence (as it still is), and ordinary barroom shootouts far from unusual. Order was enforced on the Sonora side of the line in the Díaz period by the Federal police force known as the Rurales, led by Emilio Kosterlitzky, and in 1901 Arizona established its own force, the Arizona Rangers. In existence only nine years at the beginning of the Revolution, the Rangers performed their duties of patrolling the border, enforcing the law, and keeping the labor force, particularly Mexican, in line. This latter function they pursued on both sides of the border. The Rangers' first captain was Burt Mossman, formerly superintendent of the Aztec Land and Cattle Company. He recruited men noted more for their toughness and willingness to take action than for their judgment. In fact, some sources report that some Rangers had formerly served on the wrong side of the law. In any case, they were violent and effective in what they saw as their duty. Mossman soon resigned, following some irregularities, to take a position with William C. Greene, cattle baron and mine owner in the Arizona-Sonora area.[1]

The Rangers came into constant conflict with Mexican migrants, with the most flagrant outbreaks occurring during mine strikes. In 1903, a strike of the Mexican, Italian, and Slavonian workers at the mines of the Arizona, Detroit, and Shannon copper companies operating at Clifton, Morenci, and Metcalf, Arizona, was broken by fifteen Rangers, the sheriff, and fifty deputized civilians, later joined by national guardsmen and several troops of regular cavalry. A number of Mexicans were ultimately arrested for inciting a riot, although in fact no riot had occurred. Three years later the Rangers, under Capt. Thomas Rynning, along with a number of Arizonan volunteers, went into Sonora to put down a strike at the Cananea Copper Company, owned by Greene and heavily staffed by U.S. citizens. After the U.S. group had scattered the strikers, Kosterlitzky and the Rurales arrived to take over, but the Rangers were apparently loathe to leave the scene. Eventually persuaded that the situation was under control, they went back to Arizona. This incursion was followed by considerable outrage on the Mexican side of the line, despite the fact that the Rangers had been invited by Gov. Rafael Yzabal. Theodore Roosevelt, who had served as Rynning's commanding officer in the Spanish-American War, was more pleased than the Mexicans and commented with delight, "Tom's all right, isn't he?" The last captain of the Rangers was Harry Wheeler, who was later sheriff of Gila County and responsible for the deportation of more than one thousand striking workers from Bisbee, Arizona in 1917.[2]

The year 1910 saw the beginning of Arizona's final and successful drive for statehood. While Arizona's delegates were meeting to draw up a constitution, the rumblings of revolution were beginning to the south. The young, Mexican presidential candidate, Francisco Madero, who was running against Díaz, had made a campaign visit to Sonora in December 1909. After repeated harassment by Sonoran authorities, he left the state through Arizona. He was arrested in June 1910; and in October of that year he fled to San Antonio, Texas, at almost exactly the same time that the Arizona constitutional convention began meeting (see Chapter 2).

Simultaneously, Sonoran landowner José Mariá Maytorena, who later supported the Maderista revolution, made his way to Tucson, where he helped direct revolutionary forces crossing back into Mexico. Chihuahua, however, not Sonora became the major scene of the battles against Federal forces during this stage of the Revolution, and intense problems between the two states did not arise at this time. Nevertheless, the situation was watched with interest in Arizona, which achieved statehood on February 14, 1912.[3]

The state of Arizona was politically controlled by Anglos from the outset. Indeed, one historian has concluded that a major problem in the long drive for statehood was that Arizona needed to acknowledge its Spanish-speaking population in order to make the territory eligible, but did not want Hispanics to vote. When, in 1902, a committee headed by Sen. Albert Beveridge had visited the territory, Marcus A. Smith—Arizona territorial representative in Congress—angrily accused committee members of trying to prove that so many of its people were non-English-speaking that it did not merit statehood. The Mexican-born population was indeed significant—29,542 in 1910 according to the census count, as compared with a total of 294,353 residents in that year. Other estimates place the number of Mexican-born at double or triple that figure.

In any case, the problem was resolved to some degree by a bill introduced in the territorial legislature in 1909 by the future governor of the state, George W. P. Hunt. This bill provided that only those who could read and write English would be eligible to vote. Even before that time, though, Anglos had been preeminent in politics, with only eight individuals with Spanish surnames appearing on the rosters of the territorial Council and House of Representatives between 1864 and 1909.[4]

From statehood on, however, Arizona was increasingly affected by the revolution developing on its southern borders. Though Sonoran fighting in the initial stage of the Revolution had been minimal, the assassination of Francisco Madero in February 1913 and the refusal of the Sonorans to accept his successor, Victoriano Huerta, made Sonora a major focus of revolutionary violence. Further, Sonorans and other Mexicans of all factions moved back and forth across the border, and Arizona "hardware" and "sporting goods" stores began to do a land-office business in the arms trade, both legal and illegal (See Chapter 9).[5] Another complicating circumstance was the large number of Mexican laborers who came into Arizona during the decade, pushed by the danger of Mexico's revolutionary violence and unstable economy and pulled by jobs in the rapidly developing Arizona copper industry. Thus, the histories of Arizona and Sonora between 1910 and 1920 were deeply intertwined.

The most spectacular encroachments of the Revolution on the populace of Arizona were the border battles. Immediately upon receipt of the news of Madero's death in February 1913, plans were made by Sonoran leaders to gain control of a border town, which would permit supplies to come freely into the state. Contingents of the Federal Army, controlled by Huerta, occupied the border towns of Naco and Nogales and also had troops in the mining town of Cananea. The Federal Army also controlled the southern part of the state, and most important, the port of Guaymas, the only major port on the Sonoran coast. The Sonoran revolutionaries were effectively isolated, and rather than attack through the Federal forces in the south and face the Federal gunboats in Guaymas, they decided to move against Nogales, which was guarded by four hundred well-armed and well-trained men under Colonels Reyes and Kosterlitzky.[6]

The battle began on March 13, 1913, and was observed from the Arizona side by the citizens of Nogales, Arizona, and the sightseers who had come from all over the state. In fact, Nogales, Arizona, and Nogales,

Sonora, are physically one town, separated only by a street, and stray bullets from the Mexican side continually fell onto the U.S. side. The commanders for the Constitutionalists, as the Mexicans who had refused to recognize Huerta were calling themselves, were Juan Cabral and Alvaro Obregón, the latter a farmer from the area of Huatabampo who became the most successful general of the Revolution and eventually president of Mexico.

The battle began at 5:15 A.M. and continued all day, many bullets striking the Arizona side. The fighting accelerated toward nightfall as the Constitutionalists pushed the attack. At about the same time, a company of U.S. soldiers set up a machine gun at the top of the hill on the Arizona side and ordered the Federal troops to stop firing, which they did immediately after seeing the machine gun. Soon, Mexican Federal troops began crossing over to the U.S. side of the line, leaving their uniform coats and caps in a heap at the Mexican customs house and stacking their guns. Many of these men were Rurales, who were confined with their commander, Kosterlitzky, for several months in the army camp on Cavalry Hill before being returned to Mexico. Crossing in the other direction at the same time were two hundred Chinese residents of Sonora who had come over to the U.S. side earlier and had been held under guard at the Masonic Hall all day for their own protection. Shortly after their departure, trains began coming into Nogales, Sonora, from the south for the first time in two weeks. Some 1,200 to 1,500 Constitutionalist troops had arrived by evening on four trains, including a construction train that was rebuilding bridges damaged by the Federals.[7]

The loss was costly for the Federals, not so much in casualties, as in men crossing the line and being taken prisoner by U.S. troops. Obregón reported that his opposition had lost 250 men in that way and also claimed that the damage and injuries on the Arizona side had not been caused by his troops. At 7:00 P.M. he had received word from the North American commander in Nogales that U.S. troops were pulling back from the line because order had been restored. The U.S. commanding officer, according to Obregón, exonerated the Constitutionalists from any responsibility for the shots that fell on the Arizona side, though it is difficult to imagine who else might have fired them.[8]

Within two weeks, the Constitutionalists controlled the northern part of Sonora, and with it the border.[9] The fighting, however, was far from over. By August 1914, Constitutionalist troops had taken Mexico City, but within Sonora, factional fighting among Constitutionalists had already broken out. Maderista Gov. José María Maytorena, who had fled to Tucson in February 1913, returned several months later when the danger was past. He had, however, became jealous of Obregón, who had won victories with his Army of the Northwest all the way to Mexico City and stood high in Carranza's favor. Pancho Villa, fighting in Chihuahua, had likewise become jealous of Obregón and for various reasons was on the verge of a rupture with Carranza, whom he neither liked nor trusted. As early as July 1914, Maytorena had broken with Plutarco Elías Calles, then military commander in the state, over control of the town of Cananea, where the copper mines were still operating and continuing to provide a major source of revenue for the Constitutionalists. Thus Maytorena looked to Villa, who had not yet broken openly with Carranza, for support against Calles, who supported Carranza and Obregón. Calles then controlled the north, and Maytorena remained dominant in Hermosillo. Meanwhile, the main body of Constitutionalist forces had moved far into the interior of the country, and in August 1914, Constitutionalists under Obregón took over Mexico City. Huerta had already fled the country. Even this victory, however, could not prevent the Sonorans from fighting each other.

In October 1914, while representatives of the various revolutionary factions were meeting in Aguascalientes to try to preserve peace among themselves after the defeat of Huerta, open warfare again broke out in Sonora. Villa and Obregón had met with Maytorena earlier to try to resolve the difficulties, but they had been unsuccessful. By late September, Maytorena was besieging the forces of Calles and Obregón's close friend and associate, Benjamin Hill, at the border town of Naco, just north of the copper mining town of Cananea. The siege lasted for more than two months, and the number of casualties from stray bullets falling on the U.S. side led the U.S. border population to clamor for military action. The siege was replete with bizarre incidents, including the desertion of a black trooper, who, apparently disgusted with the U.S., joined Hill's forces and occasionally used his machine gun to strafe the North American side of the town.[10] Another incident was the Villistas' arrest of several gringos. Charged with high treason, they were accused of having attempted to dynamite one of Maytorena's troop trains en route from Del Río to Nogales and of having tried to steal Maytorena's private airplane. One of the men was actually arrested on the U.S. side of the line. Some of these men were released after a month's confinement, but the fate of the others remains unknown.[11]

In any case, by December 1, forty-one residents of Naco, Arizona, had been injured by the fighting on the other side, and on December 4, two more were killed by snipers. At this point, Pres. Woodrow Wilson at last responded to the outraged demands of the citizens of Arizona, and authorized the secretary of war, Lindley M. Garrison, to send Hugh L. Scott, the Army chief of staff who was experienced in border negotiations, to try to resolve the situation. Though Garrison told Scott that "the President wants you to go down and drive those armies away," it was clear that Scott's duties were to be diplomatic rather than military.[12]

His recommendation to both factions was that they pull out of Naco, with Calles and Hill taking control of a port of entry to the U.S. at Agua Prieta to the east and Maytorena at Nogales to the west. Calles and Hill agreed immediately, since they were losing, a fact that Scott noted, but Maytorena proved more intransigent. He eventually agreed, however, after Scott went directly to Villa, who had at last broken openly with Carranza and Obregón. Villa agreed to put pressure on his subordinate, and Maytorena finally evacuated Naco in January 1915.[13]

Estimates made in a report by the United States Army in April 1915 of troops belonging to the two factions had rated them somewhat higher for the Villistas: 5,230 as opposed to the Carrancistas' 3,500. However, the Carrancistas had 2,000 more troops in Mazatlán, just down the Pacific Coast, making the totals in or near the state approximately even. The Villistas under Maytorena, however, had a considerable advantage in armament and ammunition received during the preceding months: 15,568 rifles and 8,542,470 rounds of ammunition, as opposed to 5,282 rifles and 5,195,160 rounds of ammunition for Calles and Hill. Much of this, of course, had been expended in the battle. Nevertheless, it is fair to assume that the Carrancista forces were at a disadvantage.

The same report assessed the commanders as well. Calles was reported as "a man of some executive ability," but "not very friendly to Americans." Further, it was claimed that he was using his position for personal economic gain, sending $1,000 to $2,000 every week or so to his brother-in-law, Fernando Chacón, in Nogales, Arizona, for deposit to his personal account. Maytorena was described as from a "very old and aristocratic Mexican family." The report went on to say that "he is well educated and possesses some little executive ability, though his lack of knowledge of the military art is pitiable." His greatest weakness, it was pointed out, was in "the poor quality of material selected for his officers. They are ignorant, of exceeding intemperant[sic] and low moral habits; due to jealousies among them, coordinated action in any direction is impossible."[14]

In July, Calles began driving westward along the border, taking Naco and attacking Nogales, as Obregón moved northward from Mexico City against the main Villista force in the center of the country. Apparently Maytorena's problems with his officers had virtually undercut his ability to deal with Calles.

Villa was poised to come into Sonora. Embittered by his losses to Obregón at Celaya in April and León in June and by the U.S. de facto recognition of the Carranza government in October 1915, his depredations throughout the state were particularly brutal. During the months that Villa had been fighting Obregón in the center of the country, Calles had fortified himself at Agua Prieta, opposite Douglas, Arizona, where he was threatened by Maytorena to the west and Villa from his Chihuahuan base to the east. When it was reported that Villa would move against Calles at Agua Prieta, President Wilson, to aid the de facto government he had recognized, permitted the reinforcement of the town through the United States. Calles had surrounded Agua Prieta on three sides with deep trenches behind barbed wire and had placed machine guns in positions to sweep the entire front. Since the Villistas frequently attacked at night, Calles had prepared for this by installing a huge searchlight to illuminate potential areas of attack.

The number of border raids had accelerated in the months just before the battle at Agua Prieta, and U.S. officials, hoping that a quick defeat of Villa might end them, cooperated as much as possible with the Carrancistas, who were even allowed to move troops along the railroad on the U.S. side from El Paso to Arizona. The Carrancista troop train was joined in El Paso, on October 29, 1915, by several United States infantry companies assigned to guard the train along its route from El Paso to Douglas, Arizona. A number of U.S. troops remained at Douglas during the fighting at Agua Prieta, the trenches being manned for three days by units of the Seventh, Eighth, Eleventh, Twentieth, and Twenty-second Infantry Regiments, Ninth Cavalry, and Sixth Field Artillery.[15]

The Villistas did not wait long, mounting a massive attack at 1:30 A.M. on November 1, 1915. The searchlight did its job, and the Villista ranks, running into the barbed wire, were cut down by the machine-gun cross fire. Hundreds of bullets fell on the North American side, but the U.S. commander, Frederick Funston, reported that, though authorized, he had not fired across the border, since both Mexican commanders were already trying to "prevent injury to Americans," and that the only effective way to control firing into Arizona was to cross the line and drive the Mexicans southward. The fighting was soon over, however, and to everyone's surprise Villa took his troops and turned south, to make an unsuccessful attack on Hermosillo, the Sonoran capital. It was some weeks before he reappeared, defeated and frustrated, on the border.[16]

When Villa returned, he was full of anger, as were his troops. In late November, shortly before Obregón's arrival on the border, Villa took the town of Nogales from the Constitutionalists, but then decided to abandon it before he could be challenged. As the Villistas pulled out of Nogales, looting of the town began. With trouble expected, five companies of the Twelfth Infantry were placed on the street dividing Nogales, Sonora, from Nogales, Arizona. About noon on November 26, the last Villista train pulled out of Nogales, but broke in two because of the heavy load of loot. As a result of the accident, part of those troops returned to join the three hundred Villistas who were still in town, drinking, smashing, and burning. One drunken soldier deliberately fired at least two shots at the U.S. troops, who immediately returned the fire. The Villista fell dead with some dozen bullets in his body. Villa's troops then opened up on the Twelfth Infantry, most of whom were in the street without cover. With the Villistas in houses, on roofs, or in automobiles, a fierce but brief battle took place. No American casualties resulted, but some fifty Villistas were killed and many wounded.[17]

Shortly thereafter, the Carrancistas began to fire on Company "L" of the Twelfth Infantry, believing them to be Villistas. One U.S. trooper was killed in the firefight that followed and two wounded. Estimates were that the Carrancistas suffered more than one hundred casualties before the error was discovered by a Carrancista officer, who then quickly notified the North Americans.[18] General Obregón himself arrived in Nogales a few days later to take over the northern army. He was successful in quickly running the Villistas from Sonora, and border problems of this nature subsequently shifted eastward, culminating in Villa's raid on Columbus, New Mexico, on March 9, 1916. The Arizona-Sonora border entered a new, if not more relaxed, phase.

The Villista attacks at Santa Ysabel, Chihuahua, and Columbus (see Chapter 5) terrified U.S. citizens returning to Sonora's mining zones after Obregón had promised on November 23, 1915 that the de facto government would guarantee the safety of employees and their properties.[19] The Columbus raid and subsequent threats by Villa led to a general evacuation of North American employees from Nacozari, where Phelps-Dodge had extensive mining operations, and North American soldiers were sent in to guard the copper smelters on the Arizona side.[20]

The Carranza government was completely opposed to the Punitive Expedition under Gen. John J. Pershing sent into Mexico in pursuit of Villa's band. Talks between Obregón and Gen. Hugh L. Scott, the Army chief of staff, in April and May failed to bring about U.S. withdrawal (See Chapter 5). It began to seem possible and even likely that war would break out between Mexico and the U.S., and, as troop movements began on both sides of the Arizona-Sonora border, more North Americans began to leave. Concern was especially high that Cananea, which had a large number of Villa sympathizers among the workers, might be endangered.[21]

In an attempt to avoid problems, General Calles, well aware of the economic importance of the Cananea mines to the Sonoran economy, telegraphed the presidente municipal of Cananea to "maintain a prudent attitude" and protect Americans residing in Cananea.[22] Despite the telegram, there was an immediate demonstration against the U.S. citizens at

Cananea, but major violence was averted by careful patrolling of the streets and guarding of the houses by "responsible citizens."[23] Evacuation of the women began the following morning. Reports from the border led Chief of Staff Scott to write to his friend, Col. H. J. Slocum, in Columbus, New Mexico, that:

> It seems to me we are verging rapidly toward war. I told the President to look out for an attack upon Pershing by the national forces of the Mexican government; that there will be no way to stave off war, and that we should at once seize all the border towns—Cananea, El Tigre, Nacozari, etc.—and shove the Mexicans into the desert beyond.[24]

It is interesting that Scott mentioned areas that were not, in fact, "border towns," but mining camps in which there were major U.S. copper concerns. On the same day, L. D. Ricketts, the American mining engineer mentioned earlier who had now become the manager of the Cananea mine and an important official in the Amalgamated Copper Company, wrote Scott that all but thirty or forty Americans had been evacuated and that Calles had promised to send a troop train to bring them to the border. One American had come hurriedly down from Arizona at 2:00 A.M. in Ricketts's car to bring out the mine records. Nacozari, site of the Phelps Dodge mines, was reported completely evacuated, with the mines running under Mexican direction.[25] Calles meanwhile had promised to send in troops to protect the towns, but as of June 21 they had not arrived.[26]

Scott replied that the situation did indeed seem very threatening, but that he had instructed Frederick Funston, commanding general of the Southern Department, to watch over the mines and "try to save the large amounts of money invested there before the properties are destroyed by Mexicans." He went on to say that troops were very thinly distributed, but that National Guard units were being moved in along the border "just as fast as we can get hold of them," freeing the regular Army to enter Mexico across the length of the border in the event that Pershing were attacked.[27]

By June 27, virtually all U.S. mining employees had left the state, though food was being shipped in to the Mexican employees still on duty, and mining properties, including railroads, were being operated by Sonoran authorities. Calles was reported to have brought a force of between 6,000 and 7,000 troops south of Agua Prieta, presumably to attack Douglas should hostilities ensue.[28]

In the midst of the excitement, Ricketts, a friend of Scott, sent him a handwritten note about the Sonoran leaders. He described Calles as "a pretty good man—a good organizer and disciplinarian and a *poor fighter*. On the whole he is among the best of the Mexicans." Ricketts dismissed Gen. Benjamin Hill as "not personally brave and not personally honest."

As for Obregón, he was "not particularly able—very stubborn and narrow-minded."[29] Scott replied that Ricketts's views coincided exactly with his own.[30] Perhaps he was still exasperated by talks he had conducted earlier with Obregón that had failed to legitimize the North American military presence in Mexico. In any case, both were at least partially wrong. Obregón was particularly able, both militarily and politically, and emerged later as the consensus candidate for president of Mexico in 1920.

Although war was never declared, Calles kept the mines safe while the Americans took refuge across the border and rose a great deal in the good opinion of Walter Douglas, the general manager of Phelps Dodge, and Ricketts. Douglas already thought well of him, indicating to the U.S. Army commander at Douglas, Arizona, that he believed that Calles would do everything possible to protect U.S. lives and property, as long as "the integrity of the state is not seriously menaced." By July 3, the municipal president at Nacozari had ordered the Moctezuma Copper Company mines back into operation, though the Phelps Dodge management did not choose to send any of the North American personnel back at that time.[31]

By December 1916, the fear of war had receded, and Ricketts was again in communication with Scott about Calles. Ricketts commented that Calles, "while he may be severe to foreign interests," was an excellent administrator with a "pretty good head on him." Ricketts went on to praise Calles for adopting payment in silver for employees, since government-issue paper money was worthless, and for prohibiting the sale of alcohol, putting the mining camps on an "effective prohibition basis," an action pleasing to Ricketts both as an employer and as a witness to the violence of the area.[32]

Calles was elected civilian governor of the state in May 1917, but his term of office was more eventful than had been hoped. In fact, in the pre-Constitutional period, Calles had given indications that he might make life difficult for the companies, both because of his attitude toward labor and his taxation policies. Calles had served in 1915 as the Carranza-appointed governor of the state, and at that time he had ordered that all exports of metals be taxed and that payment be made in gold and silver. His stated rationale was that since metals were a resource of the state and usually exported, the state itself should realize some financial benefit.[33] In June 1916, he and Adolfo de la Huerta, whom Ricketts had referred to as "a young and inexperienced radical who has no judgment," had made attempts to cancel the concessions of the Cananea Copper Company and the Moctezuma Copper Company, presumably with an eye to renegotiation. The matter languished, however, and Calles was at least temporarily appeased by the Cananea Company's offer of $7,000 to improve the schools in that mining town.[34]

Further, he and De la Huerta were making considerable strides in improving the legal and actual status of labor in the state. De la Huerta had established a Cámara de Obreros, with one representative for each one thousand workers. The Cámara was to function as an official government body to study organizations and systems for improving workers' well-being, pass judgments on industrial accidents and award indemnities, act as arbiter in worker-employer conflicts, and arrange for the inspection of plants to avoid health hazards to workers.[35] At the time of the Mexican Constitutional Congress of 1916–17, Sonora already had an advanced labor code, providing for a minimum wage, the eight-hour working day, special protection for women and children, and a six-day work week.[36] Further, both Calles and De la Huerta had encouraged labor to organize, and a number of unions were emerging throughout the state, especially in the mining regions.[37]

When Calles assumed the constitutional governorship of Sonora in 1917, he immediately began to demand increased taxes from the copper companies, which were potentially the major source of income for the many social programs he hoped to put into operation, especially in the field of education. His tax demands, when combined with labor problems, forced shutdowns almost immediately in Cananea, Nacozari, and El Tigre, the three principal U.S. companies.[38]

Calles's initial reaction to the shutdowns was fury, and he rapidly took measures to resettle the miners on properties in Sonora and Sinaloa that the revolutionary government had taken over. His thought was that in this way, the workers would have work, the land would be cultivated, and the agrarian problem resolved. Given the critical nature of the situation, he announced that he was bypassing the usual red tape and taking immediate possession of these lands in order to colonize them. On the same day, he ordered a train to Cananea to transport the workers from the mines. By quick action, he hoped to prevent the migration of these workers to the U.S., "where they encounter a difficult situation shameful to our race."[39] Two days later, he specified several properties that were to be divided, indicating that the resettled miners would be given the means to work the land, and announced that in this way, residents of Sonora would cease to be subject to the "whims of foreign capital." At the same time he sent a report of his actions to President Carranza, who had several months before forbidden such distributions of land without his prior approval.[40]

This sort of drastic action, however, failed to solve the economic problems of the state, and the commanding officer of the U.S.S. *Yorktown*, visiting Sonora in August, observed that the state was in economic chaos. No money but fractional Mexican silver and U.S. currency was circulating, no banks were open, food was scarce and prices high, and neither industries nor mining camps were operating. He estimated that Calles's taxation policies had thrown ten thousand Mexicans out of work.[41]

Calles therefore moved to appease the copper companies and return them to operation. The U.S. consul in Nogales, E. M. Lawton, reported that Calles had abolished by executive decree the Cámara de Obreros "which has caused so much trouble in the mining camps of El Tigre, Cananea, and Nacozari." Lawton emphasized Calles's unfriendly attitude toward North Americans, however, and indicated that only the bankruptcy of the Sonoran treasury had caused Calles to back down.[42] At about the same time, Cananea representatives indicated that negotiations with Calles were promising.[43] By December 1917, the mines began to reopen and thereafter suffered no interruption of their operations. In 1918, production stood at 52,694,731 pounds, up from 16,333,081 in 1915.[44]

Calles's anger toward the copper companies had no doubt been exacerbated by the harsh crackdowns on striking laborers in Arizona during July 1917. In the most bizarre and flagrant of these incidents, Henry C. Wheeler, sheriff of Cochise County, had deputized two thousand men, including Phelps Dodge employees from Douglas, Arizona, to break the strike at the Copper Queen mines in Bisbee. Twelve hundred miners were rounded up, loaded in cattle cars, and shipped to the army post at Columbus, New Mexico. When the army refused to accept the "prisoners," the train carried them back to Hermanas, New Mexico, where the engine was unhitched and the cars containing the men were left standing in the rain with the doors unlocked. The strikers were first warned never to return to Bisbee, where many of them had families, and then abandoned. Eventually a detention camp was set up to provide for these men, and many of the Mexican citizens involved filtered back across the border. Nevertheless, as late as September, attempts were being made by a Sonoran committee to go to the aid of the Mexicans still at the camp to help arrange for their return and provide food and other provisions for them. In early October, ninety-one deported Mexicans entered Sonora at Agua Prieta, many still without word of their families in Bisbee.[45] This incident, and the many less glaring abuses to which Mexican citizens were subjected, strengthened Calles's resolve to reconstruct the economy of Sonora and to provide jobs for Mexicans in their own country.

The problems of the copper companies thus influenced the problem of agrarian reform, which Calles considered a key to economic recovery, particularly since Sonora was suffering widespread hunger in 1916 and

1917. The richest agricultural area of the state was the Yaqui Valley, which had been the site of extensive development by a U.S. corporation, the Richardson Construction Company, since 1904. Irrigation works underwent a great deal of damage during the Revolution, particularly from the Yaqui Indians, who had earlier been pushed out of their native homeland along the river and up into the mountains. As revolutionary factions fought one another, a group of Yaqui "broncos" took advantage of the opportunity and began to attack the new settlements sponsored by Richardson. By 1916, much company property had been abandoned, and the Sonoran government ordered Alfonso Echeverría to take over and administer the irrigation works so that the harvest would not be lost and new crops might be planted.

This action led to continual problems between Calles and the company, since Calles attempted to cancel the Richardson concession. Calles blamed the company for all delays in repairing the works, as well as any shortage of water, and the controversy became increasingly bitter. The Richardson Company's holdings were gradually eroded by state action, and several years later, the national government acquired rights to what remained. Although the company had made major advances in agricultural techniques and irrigation works during its short tenure in Sonora, the problems involved in the monopolistic development of a vast agricultural area by one company, particularly a U.S. firm, were made vividly clear to Calles and his associate, Alvaro Obregón, and were important in influencing their decision to invest heavily in nationally financed public irrigation projects after their rise to national power.[46]

The Yaqui problem had ramifications for the U.S. citizens living in the Yaqui Valley and on the border as well. The Richardson Construction Company had confined its sales of irrigated land almost exclusively to North Americans, and the raiding by the Yaqui "broncos" put these U.S. citizens in considerable peril. As early as June 1915, the United States was considering landing an expeditionary force at Guaymas, should it become necessary to evacuate Americans. The flagship *Colorado*, carrying three companies of the Fourth Regiment U.S. Marine Corps, along with the cruisers *Chattanooga* and *Raleigh*, sailed for the Sonoran coast, but the situation calmed down, and they were not required to take action. In the next two years, as the Yaqui raids continued, many U.S. citizens left the area, being replaced in some cases by German sailors whose ships had been interned in the area at the outbreak of the First World War.[47]

The Yaquis' principal source of weapons was the U.S., and though they did not raid on the U.S. side, they made frequent trips into Arizona to acquire arms and ammunition. Some worked for a time in the cotton and citrus ranches and in the Arizona mines to acquire the money to purchase needed supplies. After Villa had been driven from Sonora, Calles was able to turn his attention to the Yaquis, declaring a war of extermination against them in 1917. The Yaquis' efforts increased proportionally. They had a certain advantage in that they had regular routes for smuggling, whereas arms shipments to Calles's forces were held up by the U.S. export laws. Nevertheless, Calles's appeal for help across the border was heeded, at least to some degree, by the North American authorities, which led to the last Indian battle fought by the U.S. Cavalry.[48]

In the late fall of 1917, ranchers south of Arivaca in Arizona began to discover the remains of partially butchered cattle, evidence that the Yaquis were using the area for regular crossings of the Arizona-Sonora border. The U.S. Army, therefore, increased its patrolling of that particular region. On January 10, 1918, Capt. Blondy Ryder and Troop E of the black Tenth Cavalry spotted a column of Yaquis along a skyline ridge. The majority of the Yaquis escaped safely, leaving behind a group of ten to hold off the cavalry. Both sides used the natural cover of the boulders and bushes, the Yaquis falling back gradually for protection. After about thirty minutes the Yaqui rear guard was pinned down and quickly surrendered. Only one Yaqui, the eldest and apparently the chief of the group, had been seriously injured when a shot had hit and exploded one of the cartridges in his belt, laying his stomach open. Although he was given medical attention, he subsequently died on the way to the hospital in Nogales. One of the nine remaining Yaquis was an eleven-year-old boy, the grandson of the chief, who had fought along with the others using a rifle reported to be almost as long as he was tall.

The Yaquis were held for some time by Colonel Ryder's command, and such a cordial relationship developed between the prisoners and the captors that the Yaquis asked to enlist in the U.S. Army. They were turned down, however, and subsequently brought to trial for exporting arms without a license. Calles was eager for them to be returned to Mexico, where they undoubtedly would have been executed. This eventuality was avoided by the judge, who, by sentencing all but the boy to thirty days in the Pima County jail, managed to avoid the possibility of deportation.[49]

Sporadic incidents on the Arizona-Sonora border continued, such as the "little battle of Nogales," in which a confrontation at the customs house led to an exchange of fire between the U.S. and the Mexican armies, the latter taking up a position in Gen. Alvaro Obregón's home on the Mexican side and firing out the doors and windows. Evidently the General was not in residence at that time, and in any case the fighting quickly stopped when the superiority of U.S. firepower became clear. On the U.S. side 2 officers, 3 soldiers, and 2 civilians died; reports indicated that the Mexicans buried 129, possibly including 2 Germans.[50] In general, however, the border calmed down considerably.

By 1920, Arizonans supported General Obregón for president of Mexico, evidently holding no hard feelings over the use of his home in the 1918 Nogales fighting. For the most part, they had been impressed with his business talent in organizing the garbanzo growers of Sonora and Sinaloa into a productive and efficient cooperative, and his work as an import-export agent had led to many contacts with Arizona businessmen. Gov. Thomas Campbell of Arizona met with him several times after his election as president. A large Arizona delegation attended his inauguration in December 1920.[51]

Former Governor Hunt had become a strong admirer of Obregón, and Sen. Henry Ashurst recommended to the president of the United States that Obregón's government be officially recognized. The Arizonans had faith in his ability to control the country and to end the sporadic and sometimes continuous violence that had been going on since 1910. Further, they felt that he understood the role that foreign and particularly U.S. capital could play in the development of Mexico. In short, they found Obregón acceptable as president because they knew him, thought him to be a practical man, and believed they could deal with him. Thus, the view of the Arizona-Sonora border at the end of the decade was colored by considerable good feeling and optimism about the future relationship of the two nations.

4

The Military Response: From Nonintervention to Veracruz

The possibility of American military intervention along the border had been considered even before the actual beginning of the Mexican Revolution in November 1910. The secretary of war, Jacob Dickinson, had authorized American military commanders along the boundary to aid civil authorities in enforcement of the neutrality laws, warn Mexican military commanders about actions threatening North American life and property in Mexico, and give notice to Mexican military commanders that United States forces would be used to prevent actions by Mexican troops that endangered life and property on the American side.[1] At the same time, orders were issued specifically prohibiting the crossing of United States troops into Mexico without prior approval from Washington.[2] It was a policy from which the administration of William Howard Taft would not deviate despite rebel provocations and domestic criticism.

As the situation along the border deteriorated and Taft began to entertain doubts about the viability of the Díaz administration, the Republican president took actions that seemed to indicate an early departure from his policy of nonintervention. In March 1911, he ordered the creation of the so-called "Maneuver Division" with headquarters at San Antonio, Texas. While the formation of the division was supposedly designed only to provide "field training for officers and men," its organization quickly gave rise to reports that it would be used to intervene in Mexico. Authorities later expanded its official role to include the enforcement of the neutrality laws. Secretary Dickinson reiterated the administration position that American troops would not cross the boundary and that the United States had no intention of intervening in Mexico. At the same time, public skepticism about the administration's intentions increased with the announcement that U.S. warships would make "friendly visits" to Mexican ports and a report that the U.S. Army had ordered 4,500 maps of Mexico from a San Antonio firm.[3]

Taft's private views on the mobilization shed more light on United States policy than his public pronouncements, but were still basically consistent with his policy of nonintervention. Taft viewed the Maneuver Division as a prepositioning of troops in the event that a substantial deterioration in the Díaz regime might require intervention to protect American lives and property. Even if such a situation developed, Taft said he doubted that he had the authority to order troops across the border. In any case, he would not intervene without "express congressional approval." The president hoped that formation of the Maneuver Division would have a deterrent effect on his domestic critics as well as anti-Díaz revolutionaries operating in northern Mexico.[4]

Both Díaz and his opponents were influenced in the conduct of their political and military operations by the possibility of American intervention. The rebel chieftain, Pascual Orozco, warned the U.S. consul of his intention to attack Juárez in February 1911, so that North Americans could seek safety. Although the February attack on Juárez never occurred, much the same thinking prevailed when the rebels once again prepared to mount an attack on Juárez in May 1911. When lengthy negotiations failed to produce the surrender of the city, Madero was prepared to break off the siege and move south rather than attack and risk stray shells falling in El Paso and the possibility of intervention by the United States. Although Orozco eventually led a successful attack, it was in defiance of Madero's direct orders to end the siege. The rebels conquered the city in two days, producing several casualties in El Paso but no North American intervention.[5] After hearing of Díaz's offer to resign, Madero ordered his revolutionary forces to withdraw from the frontier in order to avoid any possible complications with the United States.[6] Even the losers in the confrontation were concerned about the possibility of U.S. intervention. In his letter of resignation, Ramón Corral, vice-president under Díaz, warned of the "danger from the North and the designs of the Department of State."[7]

Although the American casualties resulting from the Maderista capture of Juárez produced some national criticism and greatly angered state and local officials in Texas, it did not lead to any change in Taft's policy of nonintervention.[8] Díaz's resignation on May 25, 1911, led shortly to Madero's election to the presidency, but there was no indication that Taft believed that the former president's fall would lead to a destabilized political situation requiring intervention. The U.S. ambassador, Henry Lane Wilson, however, took an unrelentingly pessimistic view of the prospects for the Madero administration and long-term peace in Mexico. Even before Díaz's resignation became effective, Wilson was warning of Madero's incompetence and the possibility of a "long period of turbulence and political unrest."[9] Despite the gloomy prognostications, however, Taft moved even further from intervention. In July, the dismantling of the Maneuver Division began; in early August, all units of the division that had not returned to their regular posts were permanently transferred to the Department of Texas. Taft's display of force—the largest peacetime maneuver to that date—had cost more than 2 million dollars.[10]

Growing revolutionary activity by anti-Madero forces on both sides of the border soon revived the possibility of intervention. The most serious development was the revolt by Pascual Orozco in March 1912. Orozco was one of Madero's most respected generals and was especially influential in the key border state of Chihuahua. Orozco's original revolutionary pronouncements were strongly anti-U.S., although he later retreated from this position and even apologized to President Taft.[11]

With another battle for Juárez looming, the Taft administration considered, but quickly rejected, intervention as a possible course of action. The general feeling among administration officials was that intervention along the border would almost certainly lead to large-scale fighting and would endanger American lives and property throughout Mexico. Taft's response was to impose an arms embargo on March 14, 1912, from which he soon exempted the Madero government. This selective embargo had the effect of converting Juárez, now under Orozco, into a strategic liability. Trade between Juárez and El Paso in nonmilitary goods was permitted until May 1912, when the United States terminated all commerce. Madero's troops recaptured the city in August 1912, and the following month Orozco was forced to retire to the United States.[12] Taft had succeeded in substituting the arms embargo for intervention. While the selective nature of the embargo helped to strengthen the Madero government, Taft's ability to promote political stability in Mexico was greatly limited.

The failure of the Orozco rebellion brought little relief to the beleaguered Madero administration. Madero's opponents in Mexico and in the United States continued their revolutionary plotting amidst increasingly hysterical reports from Mexico City by Ambassador Wilson. Wilson characterized the Madero regime as "incompetent to meet the situation" and as rapidly losing "what little prestige it gained from victories in the North." The ambassador also had a warning about the border: "I urge the most rigid precautions relative to the state of Sonora where the

Chihuahua barbarities will doubtless be repeated in worse forms and on a larger scale."[13]

Wilson's effort to move administration policy toward a tougher stance achieved partial success on September 4, 1912 when President Taft personally warned the Mexican ambassador that, if the situation continued to deteriorate, it might be necessary to seek congressional guidance. Since Taft had often spoken of intervening only with congressional approval, the implication of intervention was certainly made. Shortly afterward, Wilson presented an even stronger indictment of the Madero regime to the Mexican minister of foreign affairs. Dismissing Madero's efforts to pacify Mexico as "apathetic, incompetent, or both," the ambassador bluntly warned that "the situation as it exists now cannot be allowed to go on indefinitely. Continuation of the current conditions may force the United States to abandon its current policy."[14] Since the most prominent feature of the "current policy" was nonintervention, the indication seemed to be that the Taft administration was moving toward a more interventionist stance.

The harsh words directed toward the Mexican ambassador and the minister of foreign affairs proved deceiving. Taft had no intention of departing from his long-standing policy of nonintervention. Administration policy was still based on the contention that intervention would endanger more American lives and property than it would protect. It would be more productive to rely upon diplomatic measures aimed at encouraging the Madero government to provide greater protection for all U.S. citizens, rather than to have the United States intervene to improve the protection offered only to a limited number. The State Department solicitor, J. R. Clark, summarized the administration position when he said that "the time to intervene will be when we can save more American lives by going into Mexico than by staying out of Mexico."[15] Clearly, Taft believed that the time had not yet come.

In his message to Congress in December 1912, Taft described his Mexican policy as one of "patient nonintervention." He nevertheless cautioned that "we must not wait for events to overtake us."[16] Only two months later, it appeared as though patient nonintervention was indeed about to be overtaken by events. Ambassador Henry Lane Wilson's oft-repeated prophecies of doom for the Madero administration were about to become reality. Yet another gloomy report from the ambassador served as a preface to the events that would place new strains on the policy of nonintervention. On February 4, 1913, Wilson warned the secretary of state in a lengthy report that the Madero government "seemed to be utterly unable to cope with the situation." The military forces of the administration were in a "hopeless state, united only in contempt and dislike for the present Government." The economic situation was "hourly assuming more threatening proportions." As for President Madero, he seemed unable "to remedy or offer any solution for the rapidly accumulating dangers." Wilson prophetically warned that there were an "infinite number of intrigues and political deals" taking place in Mexico City.[17]

One of these intrigues came to light on February 9, when a major coup was launched against Madero by forces under two long-time opponents of the regime, Gen. Bernardo Reyes and Gen. Félix Díaz. Although Reyes was killed on the first day of the revolt in an unsuccessful attack on the National Palace, the coup produced a ten-day battle in the heart of the capital that resulted in many civilian casualties and new demands by Ambassador Wilson for American intervention. Early in the fighting, Wilson suggested to the secretary of state that he be permitted to make statements of a "menacing character" to both the Madero government and the rebels in hope of ending the fighting. Permission was refused on the grounds that such an action might "precipitate intervention."[18]

Although the ambassador's request had been denied, Wilson proceeded to act as if it had been approved. Taft had dispatched warships to both coasts, a fact Wilson seized upon to threaten the Madero administration with marine landings if the situation did not improve. In reality, the administration had no intention of sending in the marines and had not authorized Wilson even to hint that such an action might be taken. Taft did take the precaution of positioning additional troops and transports at Guantánamo Naval Base in Cuba and at Galveston, Texas. Despite widespread rumors of intervention, there was no increased military activity along the border. With less than a month to serve as president, Taft was not about to abandon his consistent policy of nonintervention.[19]

The coup came to a successful conclusion on February 18, when Gen. Victoriano Huerta, commander of Madero's forces, went over to the rebels and arrested Madero and his vice-president, José María Pino Suárez. There was renewed speculation about U.S. intervention when Madero and Pino Suárez were killed while being transferred to prison on the night of February 21. Huerta's version of the incident—confirmed by Ambassador Wilson—was that Madero and Pino Suárez were accidentally killed when a group of Madero's supporters attempted to free them. It was widely believed, however, that Huerta had ordered their executions. President Taft quickly indicated that the killings would not change his policy of nonintervention and that no special military preparations were under way.[20] Taft did not extend recognition to the Huerta regime because he had only a few days remaining in office and he hoped that recognition could be used to obtain concessions from Huerta on a number of outstanding issues, especially border problems and damage claims.[21]

Madera's overthrow and assassination occurred at a time when it was particularly difficult for the United States to frame a coherent response. Woodrow Wilson took office in early March with U.S. policy toward the Huerta regime still undetermined. Ambassador Wilson strongly advocated recognition of Huerta, whom he viewed as the man capable of pacifying Mexico and protecting North American lives and property. President Wilson, however, early on developed a strong personal dislike for Huerta. The situation was further confused by the rapid development of revolutionary opposition, located primarily in the northern border states, to the Huerta regime. The rise of the so-called "Men of the North"—Venustiano Carranza, Pancho Villa, and Alvaro Obregón—focused attention on the border and once again created a situation where revolutionary action could become an international incident prompting U.S. intervention.

It became obvious very quickly that President Wilson intended to interfere in Mexican affairs, if not actually to intervene in Mexico. He repeatedly put off Ambassador Wilson's suggestions to recognize the Huerta regime and recalled the ambassador to Washington in July 1913. The following month, Henry Lane Wilson submitted his resignation.[22] Through a series of personal representatives sent to Mexico, President Wilson worked to get a commitment from Huerta that he would not be a candidate for the presidency in the elections that were to be held. Unsuccessful in that goal, Wilson then instituted a policy of eliminating Huerta from the presidency.[23]

Wilson's policy of "watchful waiting" did not preclude frequent consideration of the possibility of military intervention, though the president and his closest advisors had doubts about the advisability or even feasibility of U.S. intervention.[24] The secretary of the navy, Josephus Daniels, indicated that "the principal cause of this whole situation in Mexico was a contest between English and American oil companies."[25] Col. Edward House, Wilson's closest advisor, expressed doubts about the readiness of the army and navy to intervene in Mexico.[26] State Department counselor John Bassett Moore offered a different perspective on the subject of intervention. He advocated recognition of Huerta, warning that "inaction might drift into intervention."[27] Wilson's first personal representative in Mexico, William Bayard Hale, maintained that intervention was unnecessary since "firm representations, politely made, as by a perfectly friendly, yet fully determined and powerful neighbor, would save Mexico."[28]

While politicians discussed the advisability of intervention, military officials were examining the more practical problems associated with it. This scrutiny placed considerable emphasis on the problems that intervention might pose along the border. The U.S. Army's plan for intervention in Mexico was known as the "Alternative Plan." Gen. Tasker Bliss, commander of the Southern Department, pointed out the dangers of the plan for the border region in a letter to the president of the War College. Bliss warned that American intervention would almost certainly unite rebel and federal troops in Mexico and that there were approximately 50,000 such troops within a short distance of the border. The existing plan assumed a "general American military superiority" that did not exist along the border, where combined Mexican forces greatly outnumbered existing U.S. troops. Bliss said the United States forces were "trivial" in comparison to potential Mexican forces and that distribution of American troops was based on political rather than military considerations. The general believed that the success of a local invasion of U.S. territory by Mexican forces was a "foregone conclusion." He flatly stated that the "present regular force cannot guarantee the integrity of the border" and that "a soldier like Huerta" would quickly exploit U.S. weakness in the region. As the military commander most directly affected by the situation, Bliss recommended that the "political branch" give ample advance warning to the military of intervention so that forces could be concentrated on the international boundary.[29]

The secretary of war, Lindley Garrison, expressed similar sentiments in a letter to the secretary of state, William Jennings Bryan. Garrison warned that it was possible and even probable that intervention would lead to a Mexican invasion of U.S. territory. Mexican troops near the border greatly outnumbered U.S. forces, which numbered no more than 4,000 along the border. Huertistas in the vicinity of Juárez alone numbered 5,000, while the combined national guards of Texas, New Mexico, and Arizona could boast a strength of only 3,700. Mexican forces had been concentrating recently at points where railways crossed the border; El Paso, Laredo, Eagle Pass, and Brownsville were identified as likely targets for attack.[30] In spite of his views, Garrison subsequently told the secretary of state that there were no major troop movements planned.[31]

Wilson's policy toward Mexico continued to be influenced by a desire to avoid intervention and by doubts about American military preparedness. On August 27, the State Department "earnestly urged" that all U.S. citizens leave Mexico at once.[32] While many in Mexico interpreted this action as a prelude to intervention, the actual motivation was a desire to avoid further American casualties in the escalating conflict between Huerta and his opponents. The president also prohibited all arms shipments to Mexico in hope of restricting the fighting.

Military authorities continued to warn that intervention would mean war and that the United States was not prepared for such a struggle. Garrison wryly pointed out that the New York City Police Department was about three times the size of the American force on the border, while W.

W. Wotherspoon, assistant chief-of-staff for the army, stated that the United States was "wholly unprepared for war" and the U.S. Army "woefully small."[33]

Wilson's latest personal representative to Mexico, John Lind, also counseled nonintervention. Despite a pessimistic evaluation of the Mexican situation, Lind advised against intervention on the grounds that the "utter helplessness of the Mexicans to deal with the situation has not been sufficiently demonstrated to the world." Lind matter-of-factly observed that, if Huerta initiated a "reign of terror," then immediate intervention would be necessary; if "matters continued to drift with only occasional murders," then intervention would not be required. Lind did identify one cause for optimism: "It is good to be a Democrat these days even down here in Veracruz."[34]

Actions by Huerta in October 1913 quickly raised the possibility of intervention once again. On October 10, Huerta dissolved the Mexican congress—a relic of the Madero regime—and arrested 110 congressmen. The action completed the transformation of the Huerta regime into a military dictatorship and prompted new thoughts in the Wilson administration about more aggressive action. Wilson was contemplating the possibility of extending belligerent status to the Constitutionalist forces under Carranza and blockading Mexican ports to cut off Huerta's principal sources of revenue. The president was even considering plans to send U.S. troops into northern Mexico in the unlikely event that the Mexican border states would consent to their movement.[35] Wilson, however, had so strongly argued against involvement that there were fears that public opinion would not support military action against Mexico. Sen. Augustus O. Bacon, chairman of the Senate Foreign Relations Committee, warned the president that "we have so industriously preached nonintervention in the past few months that the idea has taken very deep root and it may be difficult to effect a change of views in this regard."[36] Later, the administration indicated that it would continue its policy of trying to isolate Huerta, but threatened to "use less peaceful means to put him out" if he did not resign.[37]

As the president moved toward a more belligerent stance, it became more difficult to keep foreign policy synchronized with military policy. Gen. Leonard Wood, the U.S. Army chief of staff, complained to Sir Cecil Spring Rice, the British ambassador, that the army and the navy were being kept in the dark on Mexican policy by the White House. Wood thought that intervention was inevitable and would not be as difficult as generally conceived, estimating that the loss of American lives would be no more than 2,000 or 3,000. He further expressed his belief to the ambassador that the Wilson administration did not now have, and had never had, "a deliberate plan in Mexico."[38] General Wood's undiplomatic observations seemed at least partially justified. Although the White House was following a path that would lead to confrontation with Huerta, there were neither major changes in the disposition of U.S. forces on the border nor in the standing orders under which those forces operated.

Wilson's effort to isolate Huerta was based on the assumption and hope that the Constitutionalist forces would be able to overthrow Huerta without direct military intervention by the United States. To hasten that end, Wilson partially lifted the arms embargo on February 3, 1914, permitting the Constitutionalists, but not the Huerta administration, to import arms. Wilson had come to consider the embargo counterproductive since Huerta could still import arms from Europe, while the Constitutionalists depended almost exclusively on the arms trade across the U.S.-Mexico border. As had Taft in 1912, Wilson hoped that a selective embargo would be an adequate substitute for American intervention. Wilson's action brought an effusive response from Pancho Villa, one of the leading Constitutionalist generals: "I think President Wilson is the most just man in the world. All Mexicans will love him now, and we will look upon the United States as our greatest friend, because it has done us justice."[39]

While the partial lifting of the embargo led to increased military activity by the Constitutionalists, ironically this new military activity created a situation ultimately leading to U.S. intervention. When it came, it was over an incident far removed from the earlier border incidents that had threatened intervention, and at a location far distant from previous border trouble spots such as El Paso, Texas, or Nogales, Arizona.

By late February 1914, John Lind—still serving as Wilson's personal representative in Mexico—was actively lobbying for United States intervention. Lind did not believe that increased Constitutionalist military activity would succeed in overthrowing Huerta. While in Veracruz, he dispatched a Marine officer to Mexico City to gather intelligence data about Huerta's military installations. He then proposed a plan to Secretary of State Bryan in which U.S. Marines would be secretly taken by railway to Mexico City to capture key installations and arrest Huerta. An interim military government would be established until the Constitutionalists could assume control, and Huerta would then be granted political asylum in the United States. Bryan notified Lind that the matter had been referred to the president, but no action was ever taken.[40] His plan rebuffed, Lind continued to agitate for intervention, warning that if the Constitutionalists "fail to take active and efficient action by the middle of March, it will be incumbent on the United States to put an end to Huerta's saturnalia of crime and oppression."[41]

The incident that prompted the intervention so strongly advocated by Lind was an otherwise minor incident at Tampico on April 9. Constitutionalist advances in the North had led to a siege of the oil center at Tampico, which was still under Huertista control. The threat to oil supplies and the large number of American citizens in the area had resulted in substantial activity in the region by the U.S. Navy. On April 9, Huertista soldiers detained a small party of United States sailors sent ashore to acquire gasoline. Higher-ranking Mexican officers quickly ordered the release of the North Americans, but Rear Adm. Henry T. Mayo, commander of the American squadron at Tampico, demanded a twenty-one-gun salute in addition to the apology that officials had already offered. President Wilson and Secretary of State Bryan both supported Mayo's demand. When subsequent negotiations over the incident proved unsuccessful, Wilson requested congressional authorization to use military force to obtain redress. Before Congress could act, Wilson received news that a large order of arms and ammunition destined for the Huerta government was about to be landed at Veracruz. The president then ordered the seizure of Veracruz to prevent the arrival of the arms. On April 21 U.S. forces seized the customs house and dock facilities at Veracruz; the following day, as a result of unexpectedly heavy opposition, they moved in to occupy the remainder of the city.[42]

The militant response to this relatively minor incident must be contrasted to the apparent lack of concern the U.S. government exhibited toward seemingly more serious events on the border. On April 7, for example, just two days before the incident at Tampico, the town of Madero, Texas, was attacked by armed men from across the border. As reported in the San Antonio *Express*, this incident marked the "first 'invasion' of American soil in the lower Rio Grande Valley." Sixty heavily armed Mexicans, either bandits or revolutionaries, entered the town, "imbibed freely of various intoxicants," and shot up the town. Though no one was injured, residents of the town were reported to have been "thoroughly frightened." The only response, however, did not come from Washington, but from the deputy sheriff of nearby Mission, Texas, who rushed to the scene with reinforcements in a number of automobiles. The invaders, however, had already fled across the river.[43]

At the same time, the border was flooded with refugees fleeing from the Villistas, who had recently dominated the cotton-rich Laguna district with their victory at Torreón. On April 8, eight hundred Spaniards arrived at Ciudad Juárez, ejected from their homes by Villa, who soon arrived on the border to sell the cotton confiscated from their estates. Residents of El Paso mobilized a group of vehicles to help the displaced Spaniards and their belongings, "bedding and clothes, parrots, and kitchen utensils," across the border.[44]

Wilson's more belligerent attitude was met with approval on the border. Gov. Oscar B. Colquitt of Texas greeted the news that Wilson was holding out for the twenty-one-gun salute, indicating that should war with Mexico result, by stating that the "entire Texas National Guard, if necessary, will be called out." He went on to add that he was "gratified to learn that the Washington Government is awakening to the situation in Mexico, and that President Wilson has his ear to the ground and hears the rumblings." He further indicated that if intervention was contemplated, he wished to be notified in time to protect the people of South Texas. He was particularly concerned with the possible effect of intervention on the "swarming" Mexican refugees in the area, who he predicted would cause much trouble in the event of war, and he even foresaw widespread "assassinations unless proper protection has been arranged for before the declaration of war."[45] Indeed, on April 20, detachments of the U.S. cavalry were ordered from Mercedes to Brownsville, and another squadron was stationed at Sanderson to protect Texas citizens. The Texas National Guard was alerted to protect the armory at San Antonio, which was located in the Hispanic section of town. Meanwhile, the mayor, sheriff, district judge, and local military commander met in El Paso to provide their own force. The mayor had organized a posse of five hundred special deputies to be summoned by fire whistles. Each deputy was reported to have a secret, assigned task, including the immediate arrest of "certain Mexicans known to be agitators" and searching specific localities for arms and munitions. Meanwhile, Colquitt put the El Paso militia at the service of the sheriff, should he need it to preserve order. Moreover, he called on the president to seize the Mexican border towns of Nuevo Laredo, Matamoros, Ciudad Porfirio Díaz, and Juárez as the only measure that would protect the United States from the "menace" of the twenty to thirty thousand Mexican refugees he estimated to be in the border area.[46]

When the president requested congressional authorization to move against the Mexicans, virtually the entire Texas delegation supported him, with only one legislator abstaining while a second was absent. They were joined by the representatives of New Mexico and Arizona, who also voted with the president. Texans supported Wilson editorially as well. The San Antonio *Express* commented on April 21 that "when the flag is trampled upon and redress is sought of the ruling power, there can be no tolerating of quibbling pleas of extenuation."[47]

Still, there was resentment that, while there had been the threat of U.S. intervention for three years, the eventual location and occasion for intervention were on the Mexican Gulf Coast. After years of problems along the border involving loss of life and property, the United States had chosen to intervene over a minor misunderstanding at a place that had not been involved in the original incident. As one congressman pungently observed during the debate over the resolution to use military force: "If we are to use force, it should be on the northern border, where our flag has been insulted, our citizens plundered."[48]

The discrepancy lay in the changing status of U.S.-Mexican relations and in particular Wilson's new attitude toward the Huerta administration. Both Taft and Wilson had sincerely hoped to avoid intervention for fear that it could not be contained and would rapidly escalate into a full-scale war. While there were occasions when intervention might have been justified, such as El Paso in 1911 or Nogales in 1913, there was no occasion when intervention was required in the broader strategic view. By the spring of 1914, however, Wilson had decided to remove Huerta from office. While Constitutionalist military activity had increased, there was no indication that a Constitutionalist victory was either certain or imminent. The decision to intervene, therefore, was not based on a desire to protect American lives or property, which certainly were not in danger at Veracruz. It was instead a product of Wilson's determination to put an end to the Huerta regime.

Nevertheless, the intervention at Veracruz had a substantial impact on the border. The secretary of war authorized the dispatch of additional troops to the international line and sent warnings to all military commanders to be prepared for possible reprisals by Mexican forces. Since the Mexican military presence along the frontier was still considerably larger than that of the United States, there were fears that the possible invasions spoken of earlier by General Bliss might come to pass.[49]

Some officials misinterpreted the occupation of Veracruz as the first phase of a broader program that would include the border area. Governor Colquitt of Texas was "gratified to learn that the officials in Washington are finally awakening to the situation in Mexico" and hoped that the Wilson administration would "listen to the voice of the people who have been so long demanding protection against atrocities committed by marauding bands of Mexicans along the Texas border."[50] Senator Borah of the Foreign Relations Committee spoke in terms reminiscent of Manifest Destiny in the 1840s. Borah believed that, once the American flag was raised in Mexico, "it will never come down. Once U.S. forces enter Mexico as an armed body, we are starting on the march to the Panama Canal."[51]

Those who hoped for a broadening of the intervention were to be severely disappointed. There was no change in the orders governing border military operations. Army commanders were still prohibited from crossing the international boundary without prior consultation with Washington, and the Wilson administration still would not grant such permission. Even the occupation of Veracruz was restricted to the city and its immediate environs.[52] In the absence of any U.S. intention to broaden the intervention, the only action that might have produced a greater military response would have been military opposition by the Huertista or Constitutionalist forces. Huerta was unable and unwilling to seek such a confrontation. With the exception of Pancho Villa, who tried to avoid offending the United States, Constitutionalist leaders denounced the occupation but offered no military response. Villa publicly said he would not make war on the United States and privately told President Wilson that he approved of the occupation of Veracruz. The Constitutionalists finally agreed that they would oppose U.S. forces only if they invaded Constitutionalist territory.[53] Since the Constitutionalists were strongest in the northern border states, such a decision potentially had great significance for the border region. The determination of the Wilson administration to contain the intervention, however, rendered the decision irrelevant.

The Wilson administration harbored two underlying concerns about the intervention at Veracruz: that intervention might provoke a united military response by the Mexicans or that it might lead to reprisal attacks along the U.S.-Mexican border. If either of these had been realized, major U.S. military action in the area would have almost certainly resulted. Reprisal attacks would have meant the opening of a "second front" along the northern frontier by both Mexican and U.S. forces. Fortunately, neither united military opposition nor reprisal attacks developed. Wilson, with help from his Mexican antagonists, had prevented the intervention from escalating into war. The occupation may have even hastened the downfall of Huerta. It did not, however, bring peace either to Mexico or to the border.

5

The Military Response: the Punitive Expeditions

The United States had severely miscalculated when it thought that the overthrow of Victorano Huerta would pacify the border area. Instead of bringing peace, Huerta's departure from the presidency led to the most violent phase of both the Mexican Revolution and of border troubles. The Constitutionalists were an uncertain coalition of anti-Huerta forces under the nominal leadership of the "First Chief," Venustiano Carranza. The lack of unity in the Constitutionalist ranks surfaced very quickly once the "usurper" Huerta had been eliminated. This revolutionary factionalism had particular significance for the border region since the three principal leaders were the so-called "Men of the North": Carranza, Pancho Villa, and Alvaro Obregón. Each of these leaders had his power base in a northern border state: Carranza in Coahuila, Villa in Chihuahua, and Obregón in Sonora. Civil war soon broke out, with Carranza being supported by a reluctant Obregón while Villa was nominally allied with the southern leader, Emiliano Zapata. Since Wilson's policy in Mexico extended beyond the mere ouster of Huerta to influencing the direction of the Mexican Revolution, the president's factional preference would have a major effect on revolutionary politics as well as on border developments.[1]

The Wilson administration pursued an uncertain policy. With the growing split within the revolutionary factions, it was hard-pressed to choose among the contenders, particularly on ideological grounds. However, the divergent attitudes of Villa and Carranza on the Veracruz occupation initially encouraged support for Villa. Carranza's uncomprising nationalism contrasted markedly with Villa's pro-American response and influenced the president to look for a promising Mexican pupil to tutor in the ways of democracy and capitalism. Villa, however, proved a controversial and less than pliable student from the start. While opponents described him as a bandit and murderer, his supporters characterized him as an authentic social revolutionary sincerely concerned with improving the lot of the masses from which he had risen. A War Department profile of Villa described him as illiterate and immoral, but "susceptible of advice and improvement when this advice is received from those he respects."[2] It was this characteristic that most commended Villa to Wilson.

Military events ultimately determined which faction the United States recognized. Villa's forces were no match for Carrancista troops under the able leadership of Alvaro Obregón. The Villistas suffered a series of defeats during 1915, culminating in military disaster at the Battle of Celaya, where Villa's unsuccessful efforts to overrun the Carrancista defenses produced massive Villista casualties.[3]

Military activities along the border also helped to influence the decision about which faction would ultimately be recognized. Carranza went so far as to launch raids into Texas under the Plan of San Diego in an effort to hasten U.S. recognition of his government.[4] The continuing crisis at Naco, Sonora, as Carrancistas and Villistas maneuvered for military advantage along the Arizona-Sonora border, also encouraged a settlement of the recognition question in an effort to avoid intervention.

On October 19, 1915, Wilson extended de facto recognition to the Carranza regime, the first Mexican government recognized by the United States since February 1913. Shortly thereafter, Gen. Frederick Funston, the head of the Southern Department of the Army in charge of the area, suggested a new approach to border problems: the use of bloodhounds and Apaches. In a telegram on October 22, 1915, he asked the adjutant general of the U.S. Army to ship twenty bloodhounds express to his area of operations, adding that "the prejudice against blood hounds [sic] arises from ignorance on the subject, and is based upon fiction. They are simply a breed of dogs with a sense of smell greatly developed and could not be made to attack a man, being no more dangerous than a pointer." As for the Apaches, "they would be used simply as trackers for troops and would never operate alone." Whether or not the bloodhounds actually arrived is unknown, but Apache scouts were later used in Mexico by the Punitive Expedition. Funston went on to explain that the "jungle-like character of the country and the many bends in the river" made it exceedingly difficult to prevent crossings by "bandits," or, presumably, revolutionaries. He closed by saying that the best that could be done was constant day and night patrolling. Bandits would be dealt with after they had crossed to the U.S. side. Funston, never one to mince words, suggested to James Ferguson, the governor of Texas, that conditions in the Big Bend area of the Texas-Mexican border were so out of control as to call for the imposition of martial law.[5]

Future problems concerning Pancho Villa and intervention on the border were foreshadowed by events in two Sonoran border towns, Agua Prieta and Nogales, in November 1915. Agua Prieta was under Carrancista control and had been reinforced when the Wilson administration permitted Carrancista troops to travel through American territory. During the unsuccessful Villista attack, hundreds of bullets fell on the U.S. side. Although authorized to return fire, the U.S. commander on the scene, Gen. Frederick Funston, had declined to do so on the grounds that the combatants had tried to avoid firing onto the American side. Funston believed that the only effective response would have been to cross over and drive the Mexican forces south, which he was prevented from doing by existing orders. Later in November, as the Villistas were retreating from Nogales, Carrancista forces accidentally fired on U.S. forces, resulting in three United States casualties and approximately one hundred Carrancista casualties.[6] This violent, confused situation on the Arizona-Sonora border served as the immediate background for the most daring Mexican raid into the United States and the most significant military action in Mexico undertaken by the United States during the Revolution.

Despite his lack of military success against the Carrancistas, Villa was still a powerful military force and a leader of regional importance. Since the area where Villa operated was on the U.S. border, he was still to be reckoned with in U.S.-Mexican relations as well. Much dismayed when first informed that the United States had extended de facto recognition to Carranza, Villa was becoming more anti-American in his pronouncements and actions. As his military fortunes waned further with defeats in Sonora at the hands of his old rival Obregón, his men broke into small groups of marauders, one of whom galloped across the border at Nogales shouting obscenities and insults. Though no casualties seem to have resulted, Funston reinforced the garrison and ordered that in the future armed Mexicans crossing the border without authorization be shot. Villista resentment showed itself again in early January 1916, at Santa Ysabel, Chihuahua, where a group of U.S. and Mexican employees of the Cusi Mining Company were taken off a train and shot by a group of Villistas[7] (See Chapter 7). This was Villa's attempt to promote trouble between the United States and the Carranza government, but the U.S. took no action at this time.

Again, in early March 1916, there were indications that Villa was nearing the border. Col. Herbert W. Slocum, commander of the 13th Cavalry stationed at Columbus, was informed on March 7 by a Mexican employee of the American-owned Palomas Land and Cattle Company that a group of five hundred men were camped in the area. Two Americans, including a man named McKinney who was a foreman for the company, had been captured by the band. Moreover, unidentified Mexicans, thought possibly to be Villistas, had been seen prowling around Columbus since January. By March 8, several reports on the large, armed camp were received. Nevertheless, the predawn attack on Columbus on March 9 caught both civilian and military authorities unprepared, as reports from both special agent George Carothers and from the U.S. Army had indicated that the border was quiet. In fact, Carothers thought that Villa was headed toward Sonora. Thus, the residents of Columbus were shocked when the Villistas came across the border at night, and, after creeping along ditches that edged the U.S. cavalry camp, rushed into the town firing at will. The Villistas torched buildings in the town, shooting civilians who emerged fleeing. According to the Dallas *Morning News*, some of the "bandits enticed a number of civilians into the open with English spoken invitations." The *News* did not speculate on what might motivate civilians "into the open" in the midst of a pitched battle. Despite a raid on the post office, only one "small registered package" was taken. Other stores, however, were looted and then burned. Although the army unit of 350 men stationed at Columbus immediately went into action, seventeen Americans were killed.[8] Villa's casualties were estimated to have been as high as 100.[9]

Villa had now succeeded in causing major difficulties between the United States and the recently recognized Carranza government. The raid led to immediate, if unauthorized, intervention. United States military commanders along the border were still operating under orders prohibiting them from sending troops across the international boundary without prior approval from Washington. Despite the standing order, Col. Herbert Slocum, commander at Columbus, immediately ordered a detachment of cavalry led by Maj. Frank Tompkins to pursue the raiders into Mexico. The forces, only twenty minutes behind the Villistas, soon encountered five stranded Americans, including two women, two officers, and an enlisted man. One of the officers joined Tompkins's small detachment, bringing the total number of men to thirty-two pursuing a force of several hundred Villistas. They soon spotted the Mexicans retreating southward toward the border and parelleled them, cutting through the wire fence on the international boundary.[10]

About three hundred yards south of the fence, the Villistas had deployed a covering detachment for their retreating forces. Tompkins and his men attacked without delay. As Tompkins described it, "our fellows socked in the spurs, let out their charging yell and swept forward." The Mexicans then retreated in disorder, and Tompkins hurriedly wrote a note to Slocum asking permission to pursue with his troop of twenty-nine men and officers as well as another troop of twenty-seven who had joined him. Slocum gave his permission.[11]

They proceeded under almost constant fire, fighting a total of four separate actions without losing a single man. Tompkins returned to Columbus seven and a half hours after beginning his pursuit. His small detachment had killed between seventy-five and one hundred Mexicans, "on Mexican *soil*," and recovered much abandoned war matériel, including two machine guns. In Tompkins's words, however, the major importance of the action was psychological and presaged the American attitude that quickly developed as word of the Columbus raid became known around the country: "most of all, we took the fight to the Mexicans."[12] Tompkins's action had been misleadingly easy, however. It was to stand as the most successful U.S. attack against the Villistas and certainly the most satisfying. The Punitive Expedition that followed was marked throughout by frustration.

In the face of Tompkins's success, Southern Department commander Gen. Frederick Funston heartily endorsed the unauthorized crossing, describing it as "entirely justified" and indicating that it would have continued longer "had our force not been so small."[13] The Wilson administration also quickly approved of the operation.[14] The Mexican reaction to the raid, of course, was considerably more complex. The Mexican ambassador to the United States reported immediately to his government that Villa himself was reported to have led the attack with the intention of causing conflict between the United States and Mexico by provoking his own pursuit. Although it seems that Villa was not actually present, the Mexican assessment of his motives was almost certainly correct. Unfortunately, American anger and impatience quickly forced the issue of the border crossing. One the same day as the raid, Gen. John J. Pershing inquired of the Mexican consul in El Paso if Carranza would accept his help in the pursuit of Villa. The consul nervously referred him to Carranza.[15]

Meanwhile, plans were immediately set in motion for a larger expedition to enter northern Mexico in pursuit of the raiders. Pershing assumed command of the force being organized at Columbus, even though General Funston himself had indicated an interest in leading any movement into Mexico.[16] Orders from the War Department directed Pershing to capture Villa and disperse his raiders so that they would no longer be a threat to the border. Pershing was instructed to cooperate with Carrancista authorities and to withdraw if there were sufficient Mexican forces to continue the pursuit. The expedition was to be kept small to avoid creating any suspicion of a "larger object" for the border crossing.[17]

Before launching the operation, the Wilson administration hoped to obtain the agreement and the cooperation of the Carranza government in eliminating Villa, who had long been its major military antagonist. In reality, Carranza was more concerned about a potential U.S. military presence in Mexico, and he considered any U.S. troop movement across the border to be an "invasion of national territory."[18] Still, the United States hoped to obtain Carranza's consent to a reciprocal crossing agreement, similar to the one in effect during the Porfirian period. Carranza had earlier suggested such an agreement in an effort to forestall the entrance of the Punitive Expedition into Mexico. Both sides agreed to a protocol providing for reciprocal crossing in pursuit of bandits on March 13. The Wilson Administration conveniently interpreted this as authorization for entry of the Expedition into Mexico, and the first elements crossed the border on March 15.[19]

The precipitate U.S. action ignored several important considerations. First, the protocol had been approved by the Mexican ambassador in Washington, but it had not been approved formally by the government at Mexico City. The agreement was thus not technically in effect when U.S. troops crossed the international boundary. Second, the agreement applied to future raids, not to future crossings. Carranza did not intend for the agreement to apply to the Columbus raid and the Punitive Expedition, and his proposal stated clearly that crossing would be permitted *only* if another raid took place.[20] Third, the concept of "hot pursuit" was central to the Mexican position. Even if the agreement were retroactive, it would not have applied to a force sent across the border six days after the incident provoking the crossing. Indeed, one of the biggest problems faced by Pershing was the lengthy headstart that the Villistas had on the expeditionary force. Also, the Carranza administration clearly envisioned the crossing of relatively small forces, not the sizeable body under Pershing's command. The Punitive Expedition was quite large; organized as a provisional division, it originally consisted of more than five thousand troops and reached a peak strength of more than eleven thousand. Finally, there was never any intention that the forces crossing would venture deep into the territory of the other nation or remain for any extended period of time. Certainly Carranza could not have condoned a penetration exceeding three hundred miles and lasting for almost a year.

Despite these obvious inconsistencies, the Wilson administration remained optimistic about avoiding a clash with the Carrancistas while pursuing Villa.[21] Meanwhile, Mexican consuls in the United States reported

THE PERSHING PUNITIVE EXPEDITION

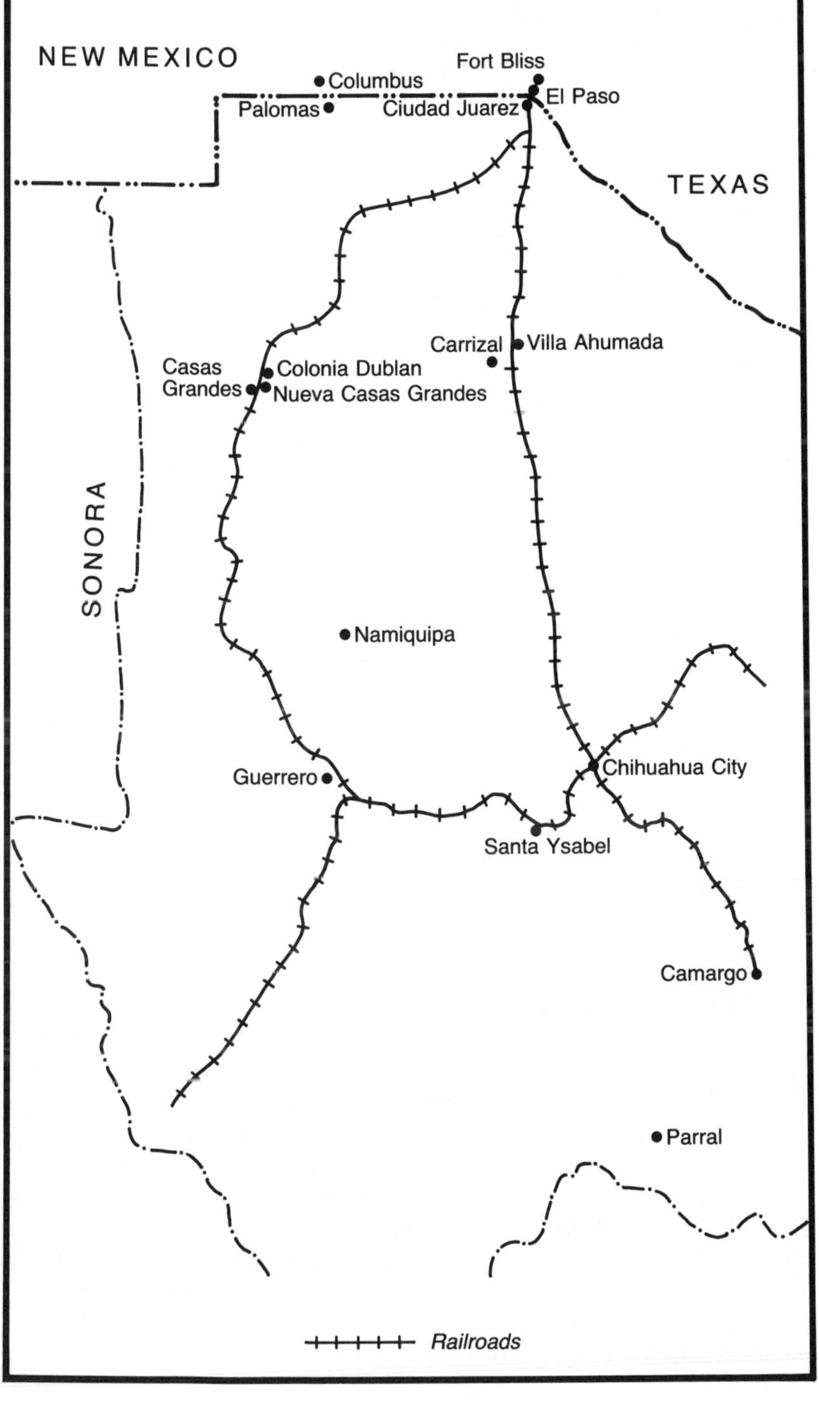

that Mexicans of many political views were expressing their desire to return to their homeland and take arms against what they and Carranza saw as an imminent United States invasion of Mexican territory.[22]

The Carranza government immediately challenged the entrance of the expedition and indicated that it did not consider that any reciprocal crossing agreement was in effect. The United States responded by saying that it "sincerely regretted" the misunderstanding, but wanted to continue negotiations for such an arrangement. While the Carrancistas offered no military challenge to the expedition, they also refused it any cooperation, despite the Wilson administration's hopes. A major problem was the refusal by Mexican authorities to let the North Americans use the railroads, which had figured prominently in the logistical plans for the expedition. U.S. forces were also warned to stay away from population centers, which further complicated supply.[23]

Early military reports about the expedition were also discouraging. Pershing informed the Army chief of staff, Hugh Scott, that he should not be "optimistic over the capture of this brigand, Villa" and that Scott would know from his own experience the difficulties of such an operation. He did express some minor optimism that the U.S. forces were "somewhere near his trail," but by no means was the confidence and enthusiasm being communicated to the American public ever present in the dispatches of the commanding officer of the Punitive Expedition. He went on to complain about the delay in launching the expedition and the refusal of the Carranza administration to permit use of the railroads, which Pershing found particularly infuriating in view of the fact that Carranza had used United States railroads to move his own troops earlier in the revolutionary period. He added, ominously for the Mexicans, that should he be able to use the railroad line between Juárez and Casas Grandes, where he had established his base of operations, "it would enable our troops to reach perhaps two hundred miles further into the interior, which may become necessary in the near future."[24]

Pershing's lack of optimism was shared by General Funston, his immediate superior. Funston wrote to Scott on April 5, 1916, just a few weeks after the Columbus raid, suggesting that the lines of communication from Columbus be given up as "the whole scene of operations is shifting farther and farther into the interior," and that a new base that could be supplied from El Paso be set up somewhere in Chihuahua. Thus, "we would be in a position to continue our advance, may be [sic] as far as Parral or Torreón if necessary, or at least until Villa stopped running and turned to fight, which is just what we want." He went on to add that "it is really an infernal shame that we have to haul our supplies over that stretch of sand and mountains for three hundred miles while the Mexican Central Railway almost parallels our route."

Of course, penetration deep into Mexico was exactly what Carranza's government was trying to avoid. Three weeks earlier, Luis Cabrera, a prominent member of Carranza's government, had described the lack of understanding between the two sides to an American friend: "The spirit on the American side is mere 'jingoism.'" According to him, both Texans and Mexicans believed that intervention was coming, and that the purpose of the Pershing Expedition would be considerably more serious than the simple pursuit of Villa. He went on to say, "How can we convince Mexicans that the purposes of the expedition are not hostile, when in Texas they are beginning to disarm all of the Mexicans and to arm all of the American inhabitants?"[25]

Other Mexicans saw the potential for disastrous misunderstandings with North American troops in Mexico. As one reminded a friend, during the wars with the Apaches, U.S. troops had crossed the line disguised as Indians. Mexican forces, thinking that these troops were indeed hostile savages, had killed their leader, and the Mexican government had had to pay an indemnity of $40,000. Indeed, from the beginning, Mexican officials had assumed that Villa's attack had been directed toward provoking conflict between the United States and Mexico by forcing the U.S. to retaliate against him.[26]

United States officials, including Funston, were aware that serious problems with the Mexicans could come at any time. Nevertheless, Funston urged that pressure be put on Carranza for concessions in the matter of the railways, reminding an associate that in dealing with the Mexican First Chief during the Veracruz invasion such pressure had been effective. Funston suggested that should Carranza not yield, his supply of arms from the U.S. be cut off. Recalling the measures taken in Veracruz, he mentioned that when Carranza had closed the port after the invasion, Funston himself had suspended railway shipments of coal and oil between Veracruz and Mexico City, making it difficult for Carranza to operate the railroads in other parts of the country. Thus, Funston "saw at once that I had Carranza where his hair, or rather his beard, was long." Carranza had yielded at once. "It was like taking candy from a sick baby; Carranza came off of his high horse at once, and lifted the embargo."[27]

Still, Funston recognized the dangers of continuing the expedition farther into Mexico, although earlier fears that the people of Chihuahua would mount a general uprising in support of the Villistas had not been realized. Funston had been informed that a number of Carrancista generals were becoming increasingly distressed about the presence of U.S. troops in northern Mexico, particularly General Ricaut, whom Funston had regarded as friendly. Though Funston had underestimated Carranza's intransigence, he was concerned about the increasing impatience of the Mexican military. The situation was exceedingly dangerous, and "we are not going to gain anything by hiding our heads under the bedclothes like children afraid of the dark. It is my opinion that unless we should get Villa quickly, a not likely outcome, and consequently be able to withdraw gracefully and victoriously, we are going to have to fight, and fight hard." Meanwhile, he noted rail movements of Mexican troops in northern Mexico that he correctly assessed as having more to do with the U.S. presence than with the pursuit of Villa.[28] As Funston accurately surmised, Carranza had from the beginning been preparing for war with the United States, positioning his forces for such an eventuality.[29]

As the Pershing Expedition had moved father south and increased in size, the likelihood of a major incident grew. By early April, the Expedition had penetrated more than three hundred miles into Mexico and now comprised almost seven thousand troops. With little cooperation from local inhabitants, these forces were having minimal success in tracking the elusive Villa, much less capturing him or dispersing his men. Carrancista officials confused the situation, perhaps deliberately, by circulating rumors that Villa was dead in hope that this would lead to a U.S. withdrawal; and indeed it seems that Villa had been wounded, either by Mexican forces, possibly in late March near Namiquipa, or later at Guerrero by American troops. Americans later questioned a doctor claiming to have treated him who reported that one of Villa's legs had been badly broken by a gunshot. His followers seemed to have carried him to a cave in the mountains nearby, where he recuperated for the next two months. In any case, he dropped out of sight for most of April and May.[30]

Although Villa was now out of the action, the long-anticipated incident between U.S. troops and Mexican citizens finally occurred on April 12. A cavalry unit under the command of Maj. Frank Tompkins, the original pursuer of Villa at Columbus, entered the town of Parral, Chihuahua, to purchase supplies. Tompkins believed that he had the permission of local Carrancista officials to enter, but the U.S. force soon attracted an angry mob. Local citizens began shooting at the gringos; when the cavalry unit attempted to withdraw, Carrancista troops also attacked the column. The incident resulted in two U.S. dead and several wounded; Mexican casualties were estimated at forty.[31]

The Parral incident gave a new direction to U.S.-Mexican relations as well as to the intervention itself. On the day after the Parral incident, the Mexican government announced that it was going to suspend discussion of any reciprocal crossing agreement. The Carranza administration said that it was "now time to treat upon the subject of the withdrawal" of U.S. forces.[32] Changes in the composition of the Punitive Expedition also hinted at new motives behind the intervention. While artillery and infantry units had accompanied the original force into Mexico, the emphasis had been on the highly mobile cavalry forces needed to pursue Villa. Later reinforcements for the Expedition, however, were mainly artillery and infantry units better suited for garrison duty than chasing bandits in the deserts and the mountains. The Parral incident not only definitively shattered the idea that the Carrancistas would cooperate with the North Americans; it also showed that Mexican troops might actively oppose the U.S. advance. Funston, therefore, ordered Pershing to assume a defensive posture until new negotiations could be conducted concerning the movements of the Expedition.[33]

These new negotiations involved the leading military figure in each country: Gen. Hugh Scott, U.S. Army chief of staff, and Carranza's secretary of war, Gen. Alvaro Obregón. The site selected was an appropriate one for a U.S.-Mexican confrontation: El Paso-Ciudad Juárez. Before the Scott-Obregón Conference, Scott went to San Antonio to confer with General Funston, who was to accompany him to El Paso. The result of this preliminary meeting was a gloomy report to the secretary of war. Scott reported that Villa's location was unknown and that he was no longer being trailed by the Expedition. Lack of supplies continued to restrict operations, and Carrancista troops were being concentrated to oppose any southward advance. Three possible courses were now open. The first was to resupply and reinforce the Expedition, seize a railroad for supply, and continue to drive south. Scott rejected this because he believed it would not lead to the capture of Villa, "who can go clear to Yucatán." A second option was to withdraw the Expedition, which would cause considerable embarrassment for the Wilson administration. A third choice was to concentrate the Expedition around Colonia Dublán, Chihuahua, where it could be readily supplied and "maintained indefinitely as an incentive to Carranza forces to kill or capture Villa."[34] Scott recommended that the final option be implemented, a recommendation Wilson quickly approved.[35]

The instructions given Scott and Obregón virtually ensured that the conference would fail to produce an agreement. While Carranza wanted an American commitment to withdraw, Scott was instructed to discuss "the future military operations of our forces in Mexico." Scott was to warn Obregón that "the danger exists of American public opinion being irritated to the point of requiring general intervention." The central theme of the instructions was to obtain Carranza's cooperation in dealing with the threat posed by Villa. The United States was amenable to a plan in which U.S. forces remained in northern Chihuahua while the Carrancistas drove "Villa and his associates toward the north." The United States was not concerned with which side made the capture as long as it was done "expeditiously."

One of the most important parts of Scott's instructions dealt with the question of the withdrawal of the Punitive Expedition. If Obregón made a demand for the immediate withdrawal of U.S. forces, then Scott was to say that the matter was a "diplomatic question," which would have to be worked out through diplomatic channels. Scott was given full power to deal with all matters "which relate purely to the military situation."[36]

Obregón, for his part, arrived in Ciudad Juárez to discover, as he wired to Carranza, that "all the alarmist American press on the border is predicting a rupture between you and me and reporting that I have made statements on this subject." Indeed, rumors about a coming break were rife. Meanwhile, one of Carranza's closest advisors wired Obregón with concern about his own potential relationship with Scott. By telegram, he urged the general to make it clear that the Carranza government bore no grudge against Scott as a result of his former friendship with Villa.[37] Thus, personalities and press reports were beginning to add to the difficulties of conflicting instructions to prevent agreements between the two countries.

After the first negotiating session with Obregón on April 29, General Scott was already warning that a "deadlock was imminent." Obregón had called for the immediate withdrawal of the Pershing Expedition and had refused to discuss any form of cooperation with the North American forces, especially use of the railroads that figured so prominently in U.S. Army thinking. The Carrancista position was that the goals sought by the Expedition had already been achieved, with Villa's band dispersed and Villa himself possibly killed.[38] The conference then adjourned until Scott could receive further instructions from Washington.

The new instructions held out the hope for a compromise, but also recognized the possibility of a broader military confrontation. The United States offered to relocate its forces "in a convenient number of days to a place nearer the border." Immediate withdrawal was not possible as long as there was "any danger to our people on the border." Scott was once again to suggest cooperative action with Carrancista forces to pacify the region. The United States would withdraw the Expedition completely once the area was safe from further attacks. If the conference broke down over the question of immediate withdrawal, Scott was to concentrate his forces for a possible Carrancista attack and should it occur, to "take all necessary steps to make [our] answer decisive and speedy."[39]

Scott's reply to the new instructions was pessimistic. He believed that the Mexican generals were "certain of our entire lack of [military] preparedness" and would continue to demand immediate withdrawal of the Punitive Expedition. Scott opposed such withdrawal since it would be considered a "complete victory by the already arrogant Mexican people" and would "encourage further aggressions." Instead, he advocated a strengthening of forces on the border to deal with "expected eventualities" in northern Mexico and to repel any attempted invasion of U.S. soil.[40] The Wilson administration responded by calling into federal service the national guards of Texas, New Mexico, and Arizona. The mobilization was deemed necessary in view of "possible further aggression upon the territory of the United States from Mexico and to properly protect the frontier."[41]

Meanwhile, Carranza's attitude was becoming more belligerent. Obregón wired the First Chief for permission to deny a false Washington press report that had quoted Obregón as claiming to have forty thousand men near the border preparing to push U.S. troops out of Mexican territory. Carranza replied that such a statement might be misconstrued as an act of weakness or irresolution. He added that "although we do not want war, we will accept it if thrust upon us."[42]

Nevertheless, though military preparations increased along the border, there was an apparent breakthrough on the diplomatic front at El Paso. Despite harassment by a mob of reporters, Scott and Obregón were able to hold a marathon meeting on May 2, during which they reached a compromise agreement calling for the gradual withdrawal of the Punitive Expedition, with the process to begin immediately. In return, the Mexican government promised to distribute its forces along the international line to prevent any future invasion of U.S. territory from Mexico. The agreement said that the withdrawal process could be halted if the Mexican government was unable to prevent further invasions of the United States.[43]

The agreement was a partial victory for Scott because it avoided the setting of a specific date for withdrawal; it was acceptable to Obregón because it at least started the withdrawal process immediately. The text of the memorandum of accord, translated from the Spanish, ran as follows:

> Since the punitive expedition of American forces has destroyed and dispersed many bands of revolutionaries and since the Mexican government is effectively pursuing those elements that remain at large and will continue to do so, the United States government has decided on the gradual withdrawal of the expedition, beginning immediately. In fact, some troops have already been pulled back one hundred miles from the farthest penetration south. The Constitutionalist government will distribute forces to prevent another invasion of U.S. territory. Withdrawal will only be impeded by evidence that the Constitutionalists cannot control the situation.

Obregón hoped to persuade Carranza to agree to the new document by indicating that he had discussed it with several of his most prominent generals, who had indicated that they were "highly pleased." Carranza, however, immediately objected to United States claims of success and called the last sentence completely unacceptable, "the poison that can kill us," as any problem along the border could be used as an excuse for U.S. troops to remain.[44]

Indeed, a new invasion of American territory by Mexican bandits soon threatened the tentative agreement, and made it clear that the Constitutionalists were not yet able to control the border. On May 5, a group of approximately eighty bandits crossed the Rio Grande and raided the towns of Glenn Springs and Boquillas, Texas. A cavalry detachment of nine men serving as a border patrol at Glenn Springs was present when the attack occurred, and three U.S. soldiers and one civilian were killed at Glenn Springs. At Boquillas, bandits took two Americans captive: Jesse Deemer, the owner of the general store there, and his clerk, Monroe Payne. When the raiders returned across the Rio Grande, they took Deemer and Payne with them. The bandits also attacked the company store of the American-owned mine at Boquillas, Mexico, located just across the river from the Texas town of the same name. Several more prisoners, including the mine physician and superintendent, joined Deemer and Payne as captives.[45]

This raid came at a particularly unfortunate time. In spite of the conferences still under way at El Paso, there was growing fear of a clash between elements of the Punitive Expedition and Carrancista forces. Unlike the American reaction to earlier raids across the river, the response this time was more bellicose. The Wilson administration ordered forces to pursue the raiders across the Rio Grande and rescue the captured North Americans. A "second punitive expedition" crossed into northern Mexico on May 11 under the command of Maj. George Langhorne, while another force under Col. Frederick W. Sibley crossed into Mexico in pursuit of the Glenn Springs raiders on May 26.[47] Despite a three-day headstart by the raiders, Deemer and Payne were quickly rescued, but Langhorne did not return to American soil until the bandits were dispersed.[48]

The Mexican response to this latest incursion also indicated a hardening posture. Carranza maintained that the raid had been organized on the U.S. side of the river and that the raiders were deliberately trying to provoke U.S. intervention. He directed Obregón to reject "emphatically" the tentative agreement of May 2 and warn General Scott that any American force crossing the border prior to the signing of a reciprocal crossing agreement would be "considered as an invading force and will be fought." Carranza instructed his commanders along the border to be prepared for a break in diplomatic relations with the United States and to avoid any "surprise" by American forces in the event of a break.[49]

Although the latest incursion into northern Mexico by American forces had not produced any further confrontations with Carrancista troops, both U.S. and Mexican authorities were making preparations for a broader conflict. In addition to approximately four thousand national guard troops from New Mexico, Arizona, and Texas, reinforcements from the army were also en route to the border. The Wilson administration even transferred forces from the coast artillery on the Atlantic and Gulf coasts to serve as infantry on the border.[50] On the Mexican side, Carranza instructed military and civilian officials to attack immediately any U.S. forces crossing the frontier.[51]

U.S. commanders were even more belligerent than the Mexican president. General Funston warned Pershing of "suspiciously large" Mexican troop movements in northern Mexico and instructed him, in the event of a Carrancista attack, "to destroy all of their forces within reach, taking care not to become too deeply involved," although he made no suggestion as to how to avoid such involvement.[52] In a provocative letter to the adjutant general, Funston bemoaned his shortage of troops while advocating an advance into northern Mexico by those same troops. Funston proposed a crossing in force of the international boundary to capture strategic points forty or fifty miles below the border. Such a movement would provide better protection for the frontier area and would take the initiative away from Mexican troops and bandits who would have to worry about "protecting themselves, their families, their own soil, and their interests."[53] The Wilson administration, trying to devise a formula to extricate the forces it already had in Mexico, declined to act on Funston's suggestion.

The Mexican government summarized its attitude toward the worsening situation in a lengthy and argumentative note to Secretary of State Lansing on May 22. In the note, the Carranza regime reviewed U.S.-Mexican relations since the crossing of the Pershing Expedition in March. The message pursued familiar themes: the entrance of the Expedition without Mexican permission, the need for immediate withdrawal of the Expedition, and the continuing failure to reach an agreement on reciprocal crossing. The Mexican government denounced the "new invasion of our territory" by the Langhorne-Sibley expedition and said that it could not be held responsible for bandit raids such as the one that had provoked the latest incursion. While the U.S. government had made repeated demands for the protection of the frontier, anti-Carranza rebels were operating "on the American side under the tolerance of the authorities of the State of Texas." Unless there were a complete withdrawal of American troops, the Mexican government would "have no other recourse than to defend its territory by appeal to arms."[54]

The U.S. response came in an equally lengthy and contentious note from Secretary of State Lansing. Claiming "it would be tedious to recount atrocity after atrocity," Lansing maintained that the frontier along the lower Rio Grande was in a "state of constant apprehension and turmoil" because of frequent "bandit raids from Mexico." These raids involved not only Carrancista supporters but even Carrancista soldiers. The Carranza government, instead of stopping such incursions, had protected and promoted bandit activity. Reviewing the Santa Ysabel massacre, the Columbus attack, and the Glenn Springs raid, Lansing accused Carranza of being more concerned with the form of a reciprocal crossing agreement than in actually pursuing bandits. The secretary of state summarized the thrust of the note and the basic American position when he observed that the "United States government can not and will not allow bands of lawless men to establish themselves upon its borders with liberty to invade and plunder American territory with impunity."[55]

While the battle of words continued between the diplomats, military authorities on both sides were preparing for a real struggle along the border. The U.S. Army continued to follow a policy of "hot pursuit" of bandits across the international boundary despite the possibility of a major conflict with Carrancista forces, which had in turn been ordered to resist any penetration. Despite the deteriorating situation, there were still limited efforts at cooperation. General Obregón sent additional troops to the area south of the Big Bend region and dispatched forces to pursue the remnants of the Glenn Springs raiders. Obregón's basic goal was to convince the Americans that the border was secure so that the Punitive Expedition would be withdrawn. While these initial efforts impressed General Scott, the chief of staff still warned: "If they [the Carrancistas] start any funny business, we intended to meet it."[56]

By the end of May, however, General Funston, from his headquarters in San Antonio, was hoping to avoid further hostilities. In a letter to Scott, he indicated that he wished Pershing would "act more conservatively," and in fact had suggested that Pershing fall back to a position closer to the border. Funston feared that a fight might break out at any time between the Punitive Expedition and Carranza's forces and that such an event would put "the fat . . . in the fire for good." As he told Scott:

> There will be no more hope of localizing the difficulty than of localizing a typhoon. Regardless of the result of such a conflict, it would be heralded all over Mexico as a victory, and the whole country will be aflame with the tabasco sauce brand of patriotism prevalent there.

He went on to lament the scarcity of officers such as Obregón, Treviño, and Ricaut, "all of whom are intelligent enough to know what war with the

United States means. So many of them are ignorant and pompous hotheads." Should a war between the United States and Mexico begin, he announced that the U.S. was "preparing a little surprise for our charming friends in case they kick the bean pot over." This surprise would be a cross-country operation with a small force from Del Rio, Texas, which would hasten to save and seize the railroad bridge at Sabinas, ninety miles south of Piedras Negras. Troops would at the same time attempt to take some of the nearby coal mines, which were not currently in operation. In a foreshadowing of modern warfare, Funston indicated that it would be infantry in trucks that would take the lead, not the cavalry. He noted that though this procedure would be "getting the cart before the horse," the horses of the cavalry simply could not keep up with the "automobile procession." At the same time, U.S. forces would seize the two international bridges at Eagle Pass and the town of Piedras Negras, and the large railroad bridge three miles south of that town. The Piedras Negras groups would then rush to join up with the Del Rio expedition at Sabinas, striking the Mexicans "a fierce blow below the belt."[57]

The danger was real, as a series of raids in June led to still more "little punitive expeditions." Major attacks took place in the Lower Rio Grande Valley near Brownsville, San Ignacio, and San Benito, leading to major incursions by U.S. forces. Hot pursuit in this region was especially dangerous since there were large numbers of Carrancista forces in the area. During the penetration near Brownsville, they fired upon American troops withdrawing across the river. The U.S. forces returned fire, killing two of the Carrancistas and forcing the rest to retreat. Fearing an invasion, the Carrancista commander at Matamoros distributed weapons to civilians and ordered the destruction of the railroad tracks on the Mexican end of the international bridge to prevent use by invading U.S. forces.[58]

By mid-June, there was a growing possibility that the continuing border clashes and the presence of the Pershing Expedition might lead to a full-scale war between the United States and Mexico. On June 16, General Scott directed the War College to draw up a new plan for the invasion of Mexico "on the lines of the various railways from the north," as he feared Carranza might "be compelled to commit some overt act against the United States in order to quiet his people." The old plan calling for a landing at Veracruz followed by a march to Mexico City was out-of-date, since most of the Mexican army was now concentrated in the northern states where it threatened the U.S. border. A new plan should provide for both an invasion and protection of the border and include protection of American property near the frontier.[59]

The clearest indication of the worsening situation was the federalization of the national guard units of the remaining forty-five states on June 18. The Wilson administration ordered all of these units to the border to join the earlier-federalized units of Texas, New Mexico, and Arizona. Ultimately some 110,000 national guard troops served on the border.[60]

The Carrancistas also began mobilizing in anticipation of a major military conflict. The commander of the garrison at Juárez, which presumably would be one of the first points attacked, distributed weapons to more than one thousand civilians. Gov. Adolfo de la Huerta of Sonora ordered local officials to organize armed groups of civilians in anticipation of a U.S. invasion. Gen. Alfredo Ricaut, Carrancista commander at Matamoros, informed U.S. military officials that he would attack any American force encountered on the Mexican side of the river. There was a general call to arms in Chihuahua as well as a prohibition on border crossings by Mexicans into the United States.[61] The most ominous threat came from Gen. Jacinto Treviño, commander of Carrancista forces in Chihuahua. Treviño warned Pershing that he had orders to resist any new crossings by American forces and to attack forces of the Punitive Expedition unless they were withdrawing to the north. Pershing replied that he was under no restrictions on movement from the U.S. government and would therefore use his own judgment as to which direction he would move his troops. Pershing also had a warning for Treviño: if the Mexican army should attack the Expedition, "the responsibility for the consequences will lie with the Mexican government."[62]

In an environment where any engagement might lead to a general war, a clash between Carrancista forces and U.S. troops occurred at Carrizal, Chihuahua, on June 21. Worried about reports of Carrancista troop movements, General Pershing had dispatched two reconnaissance patrols to determine the location and number of Carranza's forces. Pershing's orders specifically stated that the patrols were to avoid a fight if at all possible and were not to enter any town garrisoned by Mexican forces. Since the reconnaissance involved troop movements Treviño had warned against, Pershing was especially explicit in his instructions. Later, the two patrols joined under the command of Capt. Charles T. Boyd, one of Pershing's most trusted field commanders. Strangely, however, Boyd indicated to his noncommissioned officers that they would move south to test Treviño's threat. In any case, the reconnaissance brought the American force to the town of Carrizal where there was a Carrancista garrison under the command of Gen. Félix Gómez. Boyd asked Gómez for permission to march through the town, a violation of his orders. When Gómez refused, Boyd angrily replied that he would go through anyway. As Boyd's troops started to enter Carrizal, a fierce firefight broke out, leading to heavy casualties on both sides. American casualties were twelve dead, including Boyd, and ten wounded; twenty-four survivors of the fight were prisoners of the Carrancistas. Mexican casualties were at least seventy-four.[63]

Because of the isolated location of the incident, U.S. military and civilian authorities found it difficult to obtain details of the encounter. Funston angrily telegraphed Pershing on June 22 inquiring, "Why in the name of God do I hear nothing from you? The whole country has known for ten hours through Mexican sources that a considerable force from your command was apparently defeated yesterday with heavy loss at Carrizal."[64]

While Pershing attempted to sort out the details, high-ranking U.S. Army officers in the United States continued their preparations for a wider conflict. The adjutant general wrote to General Funston reviewing the procedures for implementing martial law along the border if it became necessary. General Scott notified Funston that he was rushing the federalized units of the national guard to the border as quickly as possible: "We are going to throw the whole militia of the country in there at the first possible moment."[65]

As the national guard moved toward the border and Pershing formulated plans for an all-out attack on Carrancista forces, the details of the Carrizal incident gradually became known. President Wilson began to prepare a message to Congress asking for permission to use American armed forces in northern Mexico. At the same time, Wilson pressured the Carranza government to release the prisoners taken at Carrizal. What followed was a rapid retreat from what seemed only days earlier an inevitable conflict. A detailed report of the Carrizal incident clearly indicated that Boyd had violated his orders, causing even Pershing to lament "the error of judgment on poor Boyd's part." On June 28, the Carranza administration announced that it would release the troops taken prisoner at Carrizal. In early July, Mexico and the United States agreed to submit their disagreements to a joint commission.[66]

While war had been avoided, the status of the Pershing Expedition was still unsettled. The only immediate military result of the agreement to negotiate on border problems was a slowing down of the transfer of national guard troops to the border. Despite the peaceful turn of events, General Scott was pessimistic about the upcoming meeting of the joint commission and the long-term prospects for intervention in Mexico. As he commented to George Carothers, formerly President Wilson's personal envoy to Villa, "I understand that there is going to be a commission to do practically what Obregón and I did at El Paso." He added, ironically, that Carranza had delayed the departure of U.S. troops from his country through his own intransigence.[67] Scott predicted that the Mexicans would continue to insist upon the immediate withdrawal of the Pershing Expedition as they had done at El Paso. The U.S. forces would pull out, however, only if the Carranza administration would reinforce the border and clean out the bandits along the international boundary. As for the prospects of that occurring, Scott stated, "they haven't done it and don't propose to do it, and, what is more, they can't do it." He added that he saw very little that a commission could actually accomplish and that he was in "great hopes" that he would not be on it. As for the future policy of the United States, there "seems to be no light on the situation in any direction short of intervention."[68]

Scott's predictions about the Mexican position quickly came to pass when the joint commission finally met in September. While the Americans wished to discuss a broad range of topics, the Mexican representatives were interested in discussing only specific border problems and particularly the withdrawal of U.S. forces. The U.S. position was indicative of the changing purposes to which the Punitive Expedition was being put. Having been sent in to disperse Villa and his raiders, the Expedition was increasingly viewed as a way to interfere with the internal development of the Mexican Revolution. As early as August 17, Funston had stated that the Expedition had accomplished its mission and recommended its withdrawal. In September, Pershing informed Scott that there was no military reason to keep the Expedition in Mexico.[69] Scott acknowledged the changing role of the Expedition, saying it was "the only way in which we can have influence on the actions of the Mexican government."[70]

The negotiations of the joint commission continued through the fall of 1916 without producing a final agreement. The commission had drafted a preliminary agreement that Carranza ultimately rejected because it called for a phased withdrawal of the Punitive Expedition and would have permitted the return of American forces if the border situation required it. Carranza was still insisting upon immediate withdrawal of U.S. forces as a prerequisite for further negotiations.[71]

While Carranza was unsuccessful in pressuring the U.S. forces to withdraw, the Wilson administration was moving toward a unilateral decision to recall the Expedition. Military authorities continued to stress that there was no military reason for retaining the Expedition in Mexico. Pershing acknowledged the diplomatic value of the Expedition as "a club that the administration can use over the Mexican government," but maintained that, "from a military standpoint alone, there has been no particular reason for its retention here."[72] A further consideration was the fact that the War Department estimated that the cost of the Expedition and the mobilization of the national guard was running at approximately $15 million per month.[73] By late 1916, the demobilization of the national guard on the border was moving swiftly; more than six thousand troops per week were leaving the frontier in November and December. In January 1917, the Wilson administration decided to withdraw the Punitive

Expedition as quickly as possible, and by January 27, a phased withdrawal had begun. On February 5, the last of Pershing's troops returned to U.S. soil after spending almost eleven months in northern Mexico.[74]

The return of the Pershing Expedition brought to an end the most interventionist phase of U.S.-Mexican border relations during the 1910–20 period. Concern over military involvement in Mexico was rapidly giving way to concern over military involvement in Europe. The Pershing Expedition and the "little punitive expeditions" together had served as a prelude to the larger military undertaking of the American Expeditionary Force in World War I that Pershing would also lead. Although the attention of the United States was increasingly focused on Europe, peace had still not returned to the border, and continuing disagreements with the Carranza administration brought new possibilities for intervention until the end of the decade.

Revolutionaries pose on the steps of the customs house in Ciudad Juárez, May 10, 1911. (Courtesy El Paso Public Library)

In 1914, this house in Naco, Sonora, Mexico shows the effect of the struggle between revolutionary factions. (Courtesy of the Arizona Historical Society Library)

The library in Ciudad Juárez, badly damaged by the fighting in 1911. (Courtesy of El Paso Public Library)

The border was in the 1915 war, in many cases, an imaginary line down the main street of town, as shown here at Nogales. (Courtesy of Northern Arizona University)

Bodies began appearing on the International Line between the United States and Mexico from the earliest years of the decade, as shown here in Naco. (Courtesy of the Arizona Historical Society Library)

Rebel Headquarters in Cananea, Mexico in the early part of the decade. (Courtesy of the Arizona Historical Society Library)

The interior of the reduction works at the Cananea Consolidated Copper Company, owned by U.S. entrepreneur William C. Greene. (Courtesy of the Arizona Historical Society Library)

Tenth cavalrymen captured by Mexican forces at the Battle of Carrizal. (Courtesy of the Arizona Historical Society Library)

Refugees from the fighting in Mexico, shown at Ft. Bliss, Texas at the time of the Punitive Expedition in 1916. (Courtesy of the Arizona Historical Society Library)

The U.S. cavalry drilling near the border at Warren, Arizona. (Courtesy of the Arizona Historical Society Library)

The burn-out ruins of the Commercial Hotel in Columbus, New Mexico after the Villista attack in March, 1916. Six charred bodies were found in the rubble. (Courtesy of the El Paso Public Library)

Squadron of Military Airplanes being use in the campaign against Pancho Villa on the Mexican Border, 1916. (Courtesy of the Arizona Historical Society Library)

Caterpillar tractor and motor trucks struggle up a hill in Northern Mexico during the Pershing Punitive Expedition, 1916. (Courtesy of the Arizona Historical Society Library)

Seventh Cavalry detachment on the trail of Pancho Villa, 1916. (Courtesy of the Arizona Historical Society Library)

Tractor pulling hay for the cavalry horses during the campaign against Villa, 1916. (Courtesy of the Arizona Historical Society Library)

U.S. armored tanks stationed on the border, 1916. (Courtesy of the Arizona Historical Society Library)

Mexican refugees from the violence making their way to the border. (Courtesy of the El Paso Public Library)

Refugees coming into Nogales set up shantytowns on the U.S. side. The automobile forms a marked contrast with the poverty of the area. (Courtesy of the Arizona Historical Society Library)

Mexican refugees at Fort Bliss, Texas. (Courtesy of the El Paso Public Library)

Watching the Revolution from the relative safety of the U.S. side of the river was a major spectator sport for Americans, shown here at El Paso. (Courtesy of the El Paso Public Library)

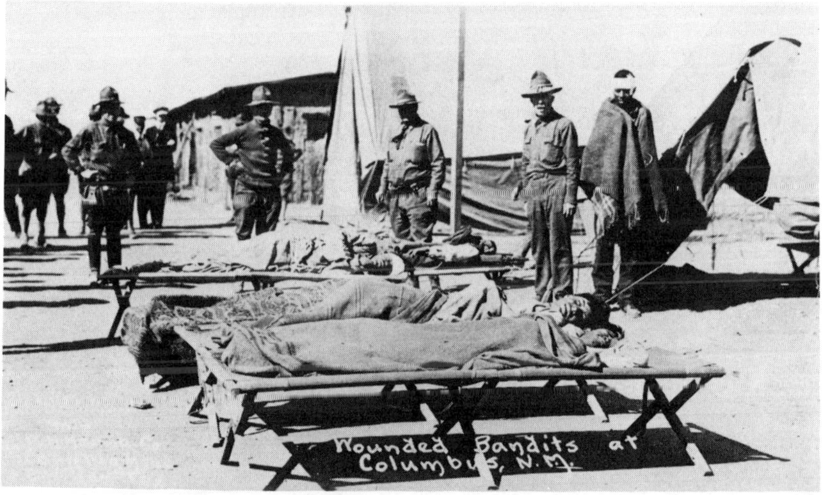

Wounded Mexican bandits apprehended after the Columbus raid. (Courtesy El Paso Public Library)

Pancho Villa, shown with associates Toribio Ortega and Colonel Medina. (Courtesy of the El Paso Public Library)

Francisco Madero chats with federal general Juan Velasco after Madero's forces took Ciudad Juárez in May, 1911. (Courtesy of the El Paso Public Library)

Mexican rebels in the hotly contested border town of Agua Prieta, Mexico. (Courtesy of the Arizona Historical Society Library)

6

Oil and the Mexican Revolution: the Southwestern Connection

The United States was not only concerned with Mexico because of security problems along its southern border. Another important consideration was the extensive economic involvement of U.S. citizens in Mexico as well as the expanding economic ties between the two countries. During the first decades of this century, and particularly during the Mexican Revolution, oil was the critical industry in this emerging relationship. The oil industry in Mexico was from the beginning closely tied to developments in the American Southwest, where the oil business began to boom as early as 1901.

The oil business developed in waves. As new fields were discovered, individuals and companies rushed to that area to seek their fortunes. Just after the turn of the century in the United States, the wave headed for Texas and Oklahoma, and shortly thereafter turned farther south toward the Mexican Gulf Coast. Although Mexico was going through a revolution between 1910 and 1920, entrepreneurs, engineers, geologists, and skilled workers from the American Southwest poured into the area and participated in bringing Mexican oil production up to 25.2 percent of total world production in 1921. At the same time, United States participation in the Mexican oil industry rose from 38.5 percent of a total investment of $51,900,000 in 1911 to 61 percent of $819,600,000 ten years later.[1] This effort was both dangerous and romantic for the participants, and for many of them the profits were substantial. The relationship between the United States and Mexico was considerably affected by this influx of capital and personnel and became particularly significant with the advent of the First World War in Europe. By the end of the decade, it had become clear that oil had paid most of the cost of the Mexican Revolution and that future institutionalization by the Mexican government would depend greatly on oil revenues. Further, North American companies had gained preeminence in the industry. Although the capital involved frequently originated in the eastern United States, many of the men who went to Mexico to take part in the boom went there via the American Southwest.

The decade between 1900 and 1910 had seen tremendous development in the oil business in the southwestern United States, particularly in the states of Oklahoma and Texas. Major oil strikes took place there, the most notable being at Spindletop, near Beaumont, Texas, in 1901. This gusher, brought in initially with a flow of 75,000 to 100,000 barrels a day, produced 18 million barrels in its first year, amounting to 20 percent of the production of the United States in that year and initiating one of the most spectacular booms in the North American experience. That discovery was followed in late 1905 by another highly productive well brought in at Glenn Pool, Oklahoma, leading to intense activity in that region, and particularly attracting the Texas Gulf Coast producers. By 1907, the Oklahoma-Kansas region was the largest producer in the United States, followed by California and then Texas, down slightly from the peak between 1901 and 1904.[2] This tremendous activity in the oil industry in the southwestern United States led, quite naturally, to North American interest in possible extensions of the Gulf Coast fields into Mexico, although Mexico was already on the eve of the extensive period of civil war connected with the Mexican Revolution.

Unlike most other economic activities, the oil business in Mexico advanced substantially during the revolutionary years between 1910 and 1920. It was not that the difficulties of operation were less significant for oil than for mining, agriculture, or trade; nor were the personal dangers less pervasive. Moreover, foreigners, principally British and North American, dominated the industry; and because of the newness of the technology involved and the large amounts of capital necessary to keep going, most companies generally found it prudent to keep at least some foreign employees on hand most of the time. The oil business, however, was immensely profitable. Oil money was a significant factor in financing the Mexican Revolution, in the form of taxes, forced loans, and outright theft. The oil fields were located close to the Gulf Coast, and thus foreign employees were in a position to be supported morally and practically from outside the country or to be evacuated in an emergency. The development of the Mexican oil industry was in the strategic interests of Allied governments during World War I, when the major shift from coal to oil propulsion was undertaken by the United States and British navies. Thus, the oil business had considerable incentive to continue despite the terrible difficulties of operation in a revolutionary setting. The industry's success can be measured by the fact that U.S. imports of Mexican oil increased from .8 percent of U.S. domestic production in 1911 to 14 percent in 1919.[3]

Particularly because of the importance of potential oil revenues to the various Mexican factions, however, the oil fields were dangerous places to be. During the phase of the Revolution when Villistas fought Carrancistas, the fighting near or even in the fields was frequently heavy, giving rise to fears that fires would be set off causing economic and environmental catastrophe. Both sides made demands on the oil camps for all kinds of help and supplies. Small groups of bandits, as well as private armies led by local caudillos, principally Manuel Peláez, also extorted money and services from the oil camps. Still, yearly Mexican domestic production of oil rose from 3,634,080 barrels in 1910 to 157,068,678 barrels in 1920.[4]

It was largely the entrepreneurs that had been active in Texas, California, and Oklahoma booms, along with young men being trained in the new profession at southwestern universities, who headed south to develop the Mexican resources. As one observer noted, every summer the Mexican Gulf coast was inundated with new graduates from the University of Texas who had come to Mexico to make their fortunes.[5] North American companies also began to be interested. In 1911, Texaco made its first investments in Mexican oil, Gulf made its first foreign investments of any kind, and Magnolia purchased more than four hundred acres in Tampico. Texas newspapers began to describe the potential of the Mexican oil fields, reporting, for example, that "prominent" operators estimated a 250 percent increase in production between 1911 and 1912. On June 23, 1912, the San Antonio *Light* ran a half-page advertisement in which the Continental Investment Company emphasized the glories of the Gulf port of Tampico, soon to become the lifeline of the oil region. This early ripple of interest led to a tremendous wave later in the decade.[6]

Even British firms used the talents of southwesterners. Everette DeGolyer, an undergraduate student at the University of Oklahoma at the time, took several years off from his studies to work as a geologist for the Mexican Eagle Oil Company, an enterprise of Sir Weetman Pearson, Lord Cowdray, the engineering genius who had constructed the Hudson River Tunnel. DeGolyer, twenty-four years old at the time of his great strike, located the famous Potrero del Llano #4, at a site on the banks of the Buena Vista River, forty miles northwest of Tuxpam in the state of Veracruz. The well came in just after Christmas in 1910, surprising the crew at 2:00 A.M. on the morning of December 28. Unfortunately, a drilling valve had not been placed on the wellhead, and when the oil came in it rose to a height of 250 feet, with spray and gas going even higher. The countryside around for a radius of a mile was rapidly covered with oil, an environmental disaster of the sort that would later lead Mexican revolutionary president Venustiano Carranza to call for controls on drilling. The river itself was covered with oil, and the Tuxpam River, into which the Buena Vista fed, had oil six inches deep on its surface all the way to the Gulf. It took two months and all of Pearson's engineering genius to cap the well. Later in 1911, DeGolyer returned to Oklahoma, where he was known as the richest student on campus, to complete his degree in geology. Subsequently, he went to Mexico again and stayed until 1914, when he and his family were evacuated during the anti-American demonstrations that took place in Tampico during the U.S. invasion of Veracruz. The story is told that while he was watching the fighting from the fifth-floor deck of the hotel where the North Americans had been taken for refuge, a bullet creased his porkpie hat right through the crown. DeGolyer then gave up the violence of the Revolution to focus his energies on the development of oil in his home state, but he left a legacy of interest on the part of North American firms, which, spurred by the enormous Potrero del Llano strike, began to accelerate their entrance into the Mexican petroleum industry.[7]

Another southwesterner who sought his fortune in Mexican oil was William F. Buckley, Sr. Buckley was born in Washington, Texas, where his father was a rancher and a sheriff, and later lived on the border at Eagle Pass. At some point he became fluent in Spanish and taught this subject at the University of Texas while attending school there. He graduated with a B.S. in 1904 and obtained his law degree in 1905. After working as the Spanish translator for the General Land Office in Austin, Texas, he went to Mexico City, where he set up a law practice. In 1911, following the oil boom, he went to Tampico to open a law office with his brothers, Claude, another recent University of Texas graduate, and Edmund. Since no particular model for oil contracts had been developed in Mexico, the forms commonly used in the United States were adapted to the Mexican situation. The Buckleys, trained in the law and fluent in Spanish, were the ones who became the adaptors and translators. Their business flourished, and English-speaking companies that came to Tampico "employed the Buckley brothers to make all their contracts and advise them as to all the legislation and different methods of operation in the oil business." William Buckley remained in Mexico until 1922, and, according to the testimony of one witness, cut a dashing figure as a bachelor until his marriage in 1917.[8]

Buckley also participated in the oil business in a more direct way, becoming president of the Mexican Investment Company in 1913. In 1915, he sold that interest and founded the Pantepec Oil Company with Edmund. He became one of the leaders of the U.S. community in Tampico and in the oil industry, working energetically in the American Association of Mexico to protect U.S. interests. In fact, he even established a network of agents and informants to keep an eye on Mexican revolutionary activities and then on the new Mexican revolutionary government itself. Naturally, these activities were resented, and an order for Buckley's arrest was issued in November 1921. Ultimately, however, he was given a safe-conduct to the border, and expelled from the country. Buckley became a bitter opponent of Pres. Alvaro Obregón, aiding the antagonistic investigation of Mexican affairs conducted by Buckley's long-time friend, U.S. Sen. Albert Fall.[9]

Yet another Texan who went south was Sam L. Kone, a native of San Marcos, Texas. Kone arrived in Mexico after his graduation from the University of Texas engineering school in 1912. He first went to work with the Mexican National Railways, which was building a line from Mexico City to Tampico to Matamoros, but his interest was in the oil business from the start. In fact, he had learned of the possibility of a job with the railroad when looking at one of the oil journals in the library. Kone soon left the railroad business, however, as the revolutionaries took over the trains and all construction work ceased. He took a job with Gulf Oil, which had opened an office in Tampico in 1911. The many duties he performed for Gulf included serving for a time as the agent who made the payments for the lease rentals on the oil fields. This task was more complicated than it seemed, because very few of the owners were easily accessible. Most had fled the violent zone around the oil fields and were hiding in the mountains. In the search for the owners, according to Kone, he "never travelled the same trail twice."

Even more serious was the fact that the payments had to be made in gold, according to the contract, making delivery very hazardous. This provision was reasonable, of course, because several revolutionary factions were issuing paper money, all of it equally valueless. Kone traveled in the mountains with large amounts of money, taking along a notary public, whose presence was necessary to make all transactions legal. Not surprisingly, government notaries were not eager to go into areas under control of the revolutionaries, where most of the landowners were.

The job was complicated still further by the fact that different Indian groups in the oil areas spoke different languages. Violence, bureaucratic restrictions, language barriers, and the difficulties of locating people who were, in effect, refugees from the Revolution, contributed greatly to the problems of doing business. Payments to the landowners were nonetheless urgent, for if the leases were not paid, they would lapse. As Kone stated, "It was a very precarious and unusual situation." Eventually, Kone left Gulf to form his own drilling contracting company, staying in Mexico for a total of twenty years.[10]

Perhaps the most important southwesterner to make a fortune in the Mexican oil industry was Edward L. Doheny. Doheny had arrived in Mexico before the turn of the century, fresh from his successes in oil prospecting in California. Before that, he had been a surveyor in Kansas, a law student, a schoolteacher, a soldier in the Indian campaigns, and a horse trader in Oklahoma. In his extensive travels, he had met A.A. Robinson, who had built the Santa Fe Railroad from Kansas to the Pacific Ocean and in 1889 had migrated to Mexico to become president of the Mexican Central Railway. As Mexican coal was of a poor grade, he became interested in the possibility of using fuel oil and invited Doheny to come and look for it. The railroad engineers also built jetties to clear the sand bars away at Tampico, in order to open up this port.

Doheny and his associates bought 450,000 acres of land west of Tampico, later adding 170,000 acres to the south toward Tuxpam. His first major well came in at El Ebano, thirty miles west of Tampico, in 1901. Although he ultimately lost the railroad contract when the Mexican Central hired a new president, Doheny set up a paving company in Mexico City, used his oil for asphalt, and paved first the capital and then Guadalajara, Morelia, Tampico, Chihuahua, and Puebla. Doheny, like others, did not really strike it rich in Mexican oil until the decade of the Revolution. Eventually, through his holdings inside and outside of Mexico, he became the biggest U.S. oil magnate after John D. Rockefeller.[11]

Meanwhile, educational institutions in the southwest, particularly the Universities of Texas and Oklahoma, were developing curricula that would contribute to the oil boom. Oklahoma, spurred by the discoveries at Glenn Pool, was already developing a fine school of petroleum geology before 1910. Prof. Charles N. Gould and E. G. Woodruff were reported to be able to teach their students "to find oil under any rock in Oklahoma." Their first geology assistant, Everette DeGolyer, certainly found a great deal in Mexico. During the decade from 1910 to 1920, the University of Texas added courses to its rather limited offerings. In 1910–11, the economic geology course was described as "especially designed for mining engineers who wish to practice in Texas, and for those who wish to engage in business with a view to developing the natural resources of the state." Field trips were scheduled to lignite mines, cement factories, and brick yards. By 1913–14, the same course discussed "coal, oil, natural gas, asphalt, building stone, cement, lime, gypsum, salt, etc." In 1916–17, a new course was introduced, "The Geology of Petroleum," which was "a discussion of the geological and geographical occurrence of petroleum and of the problem of oil field development." By 1919–20, the law school was offering "Oil and Gas Law."[12]

It was not only the remarkable southwestern entrepreneurs, geologists, and engineers who were moving to Mexico. According to one participant, "All the skilled workers in the oil well drilling were foreigners. . . . All of the drillers, tool dressers, were experienced workers and had worked in the oil fields before they came to Mexico." Most of the drillers were most recently from Texas, California, and Oklahoma, and some of them had actually started out in Pennsylvania, the first major petroleum-producing area in the United States. Many of them went to Mexico because they were in contact with other friends who were drillers, or because they knew the bosses. Many heavy equipment operators went as well, particularly after World War I, when such equipment as four-wheel drive trucks, track-laying tractors, and other heavy machinery was purchased from the U.S. armed services. Kone and his partner, Jack Willis, employed a number of men from San Marcos, Texas, who had served together in World War I in an army transportation company. Kone put out the word in San Marcos that as soon as they were demobilized, he would give any of them who would come to Mexico a job in Tampico. According to him, "practically every one of them did come." Many of these men became drillers or supervisors.[13]

All these individuals, both the entrepreneurs and the skilled workers, were operating in Mexico under extremely hazardous conditions. Many people were killed by revolutionaries or by bandits, and almost everyone who was in the oil fields during this period was harassed at one time or another. Particularly dangerous was the situation of the men who had to carry large amounts of money, either for payroll purposes or to pay off leases. The Chijol Canal, which was used to carry men, money, and supplies by launch from Tampico to the nearby oil fields, was a popular spot for ambushes. Eight attacks on launches in this area were reported in the month of February 1918 alone, with a number of oil company employees being wounded and at least one killed. A typical incident involved the Texas Company, whose launch, the *Alex I*, was stopped by bandits on February 21, 1918, on the assumption that it was carrying the paymaster and payroll. Other arrangements had been made, and neither the man nor the money was on board. The bandits nevertheless threatened to kill one of the passengers, were finally dissuaded, and then took all the personal belongings of the individuals on board. As this episode was drawing to a close, two other launches passed by, and both were fired upon. One got through, but the other was stopped when the man at the wheel was hit. The second launch was carrying both the paymasters of the Island Oil Company and the Texas Company. When the latter refused to surrender his shotgun, a gun battle resulted. The Texas Company paymaster was killed, and the Island Oil man was wounded along with two other U.S. citizens. About 14,000 pesos was stolen in this particular encounter. Typically, the report ends with the note that none of the bandits was caught or punished.[14]

By all accounts, bringing money in for payrolls and other purposes was the most dangerous and difficult job of all. One participant recalls that the money was hidden in various ways, sometimes in the flue of a boiler that would be put on a barge, sometimes in a keg of nails, sometimes inside one of the tires on an automobile or a pickup, and might take a week to arrive. The latter ruse, however, was quickly discovered by the bandits, who began to check all the tires.[15]

Other problems occurred within the oil camps themselves. During a large part of the revolutionary period, there were frequently two or three military groups operating in the area in addition to the bandits. First the revolutionary Constitutionalists fought Victoriano Huerta's Federalists. Later, Constitutionalists under the banner of Venustiano Carranza fought Villistas. An independent group under local caudillo Manuel Peláez operated in the area and actually controlled a large part of it during the later years of the period. Thus, oil camps were called upon to support first one and then another group as they came through and were subject to reprisals for their support. Generally, the oil companies did the politic thing and cooperated with the group that was there at the moment. This cooperation could take the form of serving meals to soldiers, burying their dead, repairing their weapons, shoeing their horses, and even cutting down the bodies of the men they lynched. In addition, payoffs for "protection" were regularly made to caudillos in their area, but this practice did not prevent the "requisitioning" of important supplies by the troops of these same men. From 1914 to 1917, for example, the Penn-Mex Fuel Oil Company suffered both peaceful and violent visits to their Alamo camp by Villistas, Carrancistas, and Pelaecistas. One of the camp's most important functions for the various factions was to provide food, and as the troops moved back and forth through the region, the camp cooks might find themselves serving meals for two or three groups in succession. In January 1916, the camp reported providing corn for the Pelaecista troops, 26 meals for Carranza forces, and 351 meals for Villistas. Pelaecista troops helped themselves to mules, horses, saddles, chain and leather traces, reins, harness oil, blankets, sheets, towels, quilts, and medical supplies. They also took personal property such as wool shirts, wool trousers, one blue serge suit and a safety razor and shaving brush (perhaps for one of the nattier dressers), underwear, and one dozen pairs of socks from the unfortunate and unwilling Pantalión Chino. The camp also provided corn for Villista horses on February 2, the *same day* they were forging horseshoes and shoeing the mounts belonging to the Pelaecistas. By April, it was the Carranza and Paláez forces that were taking turns going through the camps. Not surprisingly, by June 1916 the North American employees were being evacuated from the camp. Mexican employees stayed on, however, and the various warring groups were supplied with thousands of kilos of ice in the hot Gulf Coast summer.

By mid-1917, harassment of the camp had declined. Total losses, according to the company's account, were $84,252.39 in gold and 594,544.99 in pesos, furnishing the major portion of a total loss during the decade of $110,367.98 and 646,064.53 pesos. The violence did not stop although by 1919 most attacks were carried out by bandits rather than real or self-styled revolutionaries.[16] Although one might wonder why the companies would wish to continue to operate under these conditions, it is interesting to note that even during the terrible months of March and April 1916, production from one or two wells at the Alamo Camp averaged between 8,000 and 9,000 barrels a day.[17]

Even more serious was the danger to the oil fields themselves, from either sabotage or accident. The battle of El Ebano, between the Villistas and Carrancistas, actually took place on the property of the Mexican Petroleum Company. The fighting lasted from March 21 through May 31, 1915. The Carrancista forces took over the company's headquarters two kilometers from the El Ebano railway station, placing artillery pieces on the top and side of the hill on which it was located. The Villistas, also supported by artillery, stationed themselves at the foot of the hill on all sides except the east. Naturally, enormous damage was done to company buildings, which were directly in the line of fire. Carrancista fire also destroyed some of the oil tanks and other company property located within the Villista lines. Surprisingly, only one North American, Isaac Ely, was killed, when the Villistas took possession of a pumping station. Fortunately, the oil fields themselves were not gravely damaged in the battle, but the loss of oil tanks and reservoirs—combined with fire damage to facilities—was substantial.

After the battle, the victorious Carrancistas did not leave, "re-visiting and re-occupying the camp" for another year or so. Company employees and machine shops were used during this time to repair railway rolling stock, automobiles, firearms, and other equipment. The usual "requisitioning" of provisions and materials continued, and the troops were fed in the employees' dining rooms. Adding insult perhaps to injury, the soldiers required the company to make coffins for their dead and forced employees to bury the corpses. The Mexican Petroleum Company set its losses in the period from March 1914 to February 1916 at 1,624,064 pesos, with 770,000 pesos of this amount from the loss of oil either through fire or from damage to storage facilities.[18]

Eventually the oil companies developed a modus vivendi with the caudillo and landowner Manuel Peláez. In return for money and supplies, Peláez "protected" the oil fields from other bands of revolutionaries or bandits. As one North American described the arrangement, "the land owners had a small army composed of their ranch workmen, and the oil companies subsidized payment to these soldiers . . . known as Pelaecistas."[19] This group came to control most of the oil area away from the ports, while the government controlled Tampico, Tuxpam, and Veracruz. Thus, the oil companies had to deal with at least two antagonistic groups, even when there was no active fighting in their area.

Even though their support of Peláez was relatively open, it was by no means always a comfortable collaboration. The payoffs to Peláez were high, and the methods used to extract them bordered on extortion. Later, these sums formed a large portion of the claims that U.S. companies brought against the Mexican government for revolutionary damages. According to one report, in 1917 the Pan American Petroleum Company of Los Angeles, a Doheny enterprise, was paying Peláez as much as $40,000 a month, while the Texas Company paid him $10,000.[20]

The various bands of men working for Peláez also frequently helped themselves to supplies and food from the camps. After 1918, Peláez became particularly uncooperative and began to cap some of the wells and destroy installations. By this time, the government of Venustiano Carranza was well established in other parts of the country, and he was turning his attention to control of the oil regions, the area of major economic activity. His ability to exert pressure on the companies and on Peláez was increasing. Peláez's demands on the companies were increasing, as well. It seems likely that Peláez was trying to force U.S. intervention to "save" the oil fields, as his only chance for survival faced with the challenge of the new revolutionary government.[21] Moreover, as Carranza's military efforts against Peláez were stepped up, Peláez's people extended their guerrilla activities, burning railroad bridges and cutting water lines, causing substantial problems for the oil camps. Carranza's men began confiscating draft animals, money, and commissary supplies, without offering payment or receipts of any kind. The companies were particularly incensed about the activities of the chief of military operations in the Tampico district, Gen. César López de Lara, who habitually helped himself to the launches and other craft belonging to the companies and returned them only when they were too damaged to be of further use.

By this time, the oil companies were principally interested in an end to the fighting, but were very pessimistic about the government's ability to clear out the Pelaecistas. In fact, the North Americans would have preferred for the authorities to concentrate on the bandits instead. The consul at Tampico even asserted that the Peláez movement was "infinitely more moral and sincere in its treatment of foreign interests than is the recognized government itself."[22]

Other major difficulties were caused by the administrative rather than military actions of new revolutionary President Carranza as he tried to assert control over all portions of the country and economy after his election in 1917. Yet even before that date, Carranza, when he was First Chief of the Constitutionalists, had taken steps to restore all subsoil rights to the nation. In 1914, he had ordered his Ministry of Development, Colonization, and Industry to devise measures to achieve this end. In the same year, Cándido Aguilar—at that time the governor of the state of Veracruz, a major oil area—had levied a tax on oil production and enforced payment by threatening to cut off the pipelines that delivered the combustible to the tankers in the port. Carranza himself issued a decree on September 19, 1914, asking that all owners of land and industries register an assessment of their holdings with the government. Obviously, Carranza wished to use this material to arrive at a better understanding of national resources and development, but the main purpose for the decree was to furnish the government with the necessary information for taxing the oil industry and for applying other legal and administrative measures. In 1914, however, Carranza was in no position to enforce the decree, and the companies refused to comply.

Other measures followed at intervals, including one issued at Veracruz in January 1915, when Carranza's forces were deeply embroiled fighting Pancho Villa in a new phase of the Revolution. In this decree, he called for the suspension of all work in progress and threatened to destroy any installations that were undertaken without the permission of his government. Further, any oil wells that were brought in in contravention to his decree were declared to be the property of the nation, raising the specter of confiscation that was to haunt the oil companies until the end of the decade.[23] On August 15, 1916, an additional decree caused great concern to the foreign oil proprietors. This circular informed them that if they intended to operate in Mexico in the future, they would have to "consider themselves Mexicans, waiving their rights as foreigners and privileges of appeal for protection or claim to their respective Governments," a decree that raised a storm of protest and called forth an immediate refusal to accept such conditions from U.S. Secretary of State Lansing.[24]

Of even more concern to U.S. businessmen and diplomatic personnel was Article 27 of the Constitution, promulgated on May 1, 1917, which clearly returned all subsoil rights to the state and in effect canceled all previous concessions. Finally, in the decree of February 19, 1918, Carranza reiterated the nation's right to all oil deposits; asserted that all those wishing to exploit such rights must apply to the government for permission; and indicated that in the event of noncompliance, the landholder or company involved would lose its rights and third parties could claim the land in question after a certain date. In effect, Carranza was declaring that land titles granted to oil companies by earlier governments were actually only temporary concessions.[25]

Fortunately for the oil companies and unfortunately for Carranza, various circumstances prevented him from putting these measures into effect. First, Carranza did not control the entire oil area. As noted before, much of the territory in question was dominated by Manuel Peláez during most of the period from 1914 to 1920. Second, Carranza could not even closely control his own state governments. Third, confusion reigned even in the areas in which he might have enforced his decrees, and of course the oil companies—supported firmly by Washington—cooperated as little as possible, although they did begin to pay some taxes.

The problem with the various states was a serious one. In order for the national government to obtain sufficient revenues to function, oil company resources had to be tapped, but state governors such as Cándido Aguilar of Veracruz, Carranza's own son-in-law, had been making their own laws to control the industry since 1914. In August 1916, Carranza issued a decree indicating that the state governors had "invaded the proper and exclusive sphere of the Federal Government" by such actions. He then clearly stated that the governors were precluded from issuing laws and decrees in a number of areas, including banking and mining, but particularly designating the "exploration, exploitation and commerce" of minerals, coal, and petroleum. All state government decrees on this topic were thus declared null and void. Unfortunately, or perhaps fortunately, for the companies, Carranza was frequently unable to control state and local officials, and the situation remained chaotic until the end of the decade. Some of these officials were merely self-interested and took as much from the companies in the form of taxes and bribes as they could get. Others, such as Aguilar, had real practical and philosophical differences with Carranza in regard to his oil policies.[26]

Aguilar maintained the position that the nation did not have the right to confiscate oil deposits without indemnification of the companies and individuals involved. He felt, however, that the nation could reasonably claim "direct dominion" over these deposits and thus had the right to nonconfiscatory royalties, probably about 6 percent, on the gross output. He further believed that tampering with the legal status of the industry was dangerous. In November 1917, after Carranza's decree, Aguilar submitted a proposal to the state congress of Veracruz that expressed these ideas. Had they been adopted at the national level, they would have basically altered the oil policy of the Revolution. The proposal, though, was never discussed thoroughly in the national congress, and high officials in Carranza's Ministry of Industry were opposed to it.[27] Nevertheless, it is significant that an individual as close to Carranza as Aguilar, serving as his own governor in one of the major oil regions, differed so radically and so publicly from the president.

Another significant, complicating element for Carranza was the international situation in the later part of the decade and the importance of Mexico's oil supply, given the accelerating conversion of the navies of the world from coal to oil power. Aguilar himself became Carranza's special representative in Paris during the peace conference. Aguilar, in a long letter to his father-in-law on the eve of his departure from New York for Paris, pointed out that Mexico had no hope of pressure from other nations as a counterbalance to the power of the United States, indicating that country was regarded by Europe as responsible for the affairs of Mexico. Moreover, the Great Powers had come to regard world supplies of oil as a military matter, and therefore their positions on the oil industry had become far more important and less negotiable than they might have been in other circumstances. He then made several suggestions for future Mexican oil policy. First, enforcement of the new Constitution should shift to other social areas such as land reform, leaving the most difficult and complicated issue—oil—for a later time, as a long as the companies continued to pay their taxes. Second, instead of pretending that the current oil legislation, which was obviously directed toward the enforcement of Article 27, was tax oriented, the government should deal frankly and honestly in this area in order to avoid misunderstandings and "twisted interpretations". Third, the government must face the fact that it could not take away wells in production, and instead concentrate on the problem of whether it would tolerate the companies' holding enormous reserves in a kind of "oil latifundism," thus focusing on a more manageable problem and giving the opposition less ammunition. Last, a commission should be established of persons both inside and outside the administration to study oil questions carefully and determine policies and criteria for judgment on oil issues.[28]

Unfortunately, it is not known whether these reasonable suggestions were ever seriously considered by Carranza, as his hold on the country, never entirely secure, was already beginning to crumble in the face of an effective political campaign by his former minister of war, Alvaro Obregón. The entire question faded when Obregón and his Sonoran supporters, frustrated by Carranza's unwillingness to give up power within the framework of a legitimate political campaign, revolted against him and drove him from office in May 1920. The problems between U.S. oil companies and the Mexican government were left for the Obregón administration to consider after this date.

It is easy to see why the oil companies, faced with all these difficulties of operation in Mexico, began to turn their attention to other areas, particularly Venezuela, in the early 1920s. Nevertheless, oil had fueled the Mexican Revolution economically and sometimes literally, and oil revenues became the backbone of the institutionalization of the Mexican Revolution in the following decade. Although the relationship between the oil companies and the revolutionaries was never comfortable, it is interesting to speculate that the Revolution and its subsequent institutionalization might never have succeeded if American Southwesterners had not sought their fortunes, despite the dangers and political difficulties of the Revolution, in the oil fields of Mexico.

7

Mining and Revolution: A Losing Proposition

Although the petroleum industry in Mexico was able to survive the ten years of violence during the Mexican Revolution with high profitability and rising production, the mining industry suffered serious damage. Most of the mines were located in the northern part of the country, particularly in the area that was controlled and frequently ravaged by the most dangerous of all the major revolutionary leaders, Pancho Villa. Sonora and Chihuahua were the two principal mining states on the border and were the scenes of serious conflict during the early phase of the Revolution when Francisco Madero was fighting Porfirio Díaz; the middle phase, when the Constitutionalists fought Madero's assassin, Victoriano Huerta; and the final period, when factional fighting between Villa and his major military opponent, Alvaro Obregón, determined ultimate control of Mexico.

As the petroleum industry had furnished money, supplies, and support for the various revolutionary forces, so did the mines, but the margin of profitability in the mines was far lower, and many mining operations could not stand the strain. Closing mines even briefly frequently caused extensive damage and flooding, necessitating repairs that were both costly and time-consuming.

Moreover, North Americans in the mining areas could not easily be evacuated in case of violence, as they had no relatively quick outlet to the sea as did foreigners in the oil-drilling areas. These logistical difficulties applied as well to supplying the products of the mines to markets. Although the mines were close to the U.S.-Mexican border, the terrain was frequently mountainous, and transportation depended on the railroads, which were being used by the various revolutionary factions as their most important form of conveyance for troops and materiel. The oil companies, on the other hand, could use pipelines and boats.

Finally, many mining operations were deliberately destroyed and their Mexican and foreign employees harassed and sometimes killed, particularly in the outbreak of antiforeign violence perpetrated by Villa in late 1915 and early 1916 after the United States' de facto recognition of Carranza's Constitutionalists in October 1915.

Before the Revolution, U.S. involvement in Mexican mining had been extensive. So many North Americans and British were involved that a major journal, *The Mexican Mining Journal*, was published in English in Mexico City. Some of the dangers inherent in mining exploration and production in Mexico were highlighted in the advertisements in this publication.

Dangerous chemicals were used in the extraction of ores, "regular cyanide and cyanide of sodium from the Roessler and Hasslacher Chemical Company" being available from the Mexican Gold and Silver Recovery Company, Ltd. Blasting was perilous as well, as can be gleaned from the announcement of the Eagle Fuse Ligther [sic] which was promoted as "the greatest device ever perfected for the elimination of the uncertainties of blasting and the protection of life and limb." Malaria and dysentery debilitated many, despite the availability of medication from Píldoras Nacionales "contra calenturas," ("against fevers"). The company announced that "these Pills are Chemical food. Quinine, Calomel, Arsenic are antiqquities. We do not purge or poison you. Our little pills go in and malaria and debility go out, and you get stronger and more robust every day"—provided, of course, that you survived the treatment.[1]

Moreover, foreign capital was constantly under intellectual attack during the course of the Revolution. *The Mexican Mining Journal* felt compelled to respond editorially as early as 1910:

> Foreign capital is not to be looked on as a necessary evil in the development of our natural resources, but rather as a great help to progress and stimulus to development and production along every line. . . . It is true that we are paying a high rate of interest on the foreign capital invested here; but as an investment we are far from violating what has proven to be sound business policy in the development of other countries that have and are at present passing through the same stage that Mexico is in today.

The United States, Canada, Argentina, South Africa, Australia, and Japan were listed as examples of this phenomenon. Interestingly, the editorial closed by proclaiming that "the amount of foreign investment is a true index of the state of prosperity or depression in which a nation exists."[2] Still, even at the best of times during the decade, mining was a dangerous business, and the climate of revolutionary thought was so opposed to foreign investors that they were forced to defend themselves. As in the case of the oil industry, the revolutionary tenet of Mexican resources for the Mexicans became part of the Mexican Constitution of 1917, when Article 27 declared that all subsoil rights belonged to the Mexican state and natural resources were to be used in the social interest of the Mexican people. As a result, mining as well as oil interests had to face many difficulties with changing laws throughout the decade, particularly after 1917, although the Carranza government was much less rigorous in its attempts to control and tax the mining industry than it was in the case of oil.[3]

The Revolution took a tremendous toll on mining operations through its violence, disorganization, and legislation. U.S. direct investment in Mexican mining and smelting fell from $302,000,000 in 1914 to $222,000,000, a significant drop that might be considerably larger if the starting date were earlier in the decade. At the same time, U.S. direct investment in petroleum was soaring from $85,000,000 to $200,000,000.[4] Although production figures indicate that mining had recovered to a large degree by 1920, the years 1913–16, the period of heaviest fighting, show disastrous decreases in silver, gold, lead, zinc, and copper, with recovery only beginning in 1917.[5]

Silver production in Mexico in 1922 was already 39.32 percent of the world's supply (followed by the United States with 26.91 percent), but Mexican capital was far more important in the recovery than North American. The Revolution was a significant deterrent to future U.S. investment in Mexico, as evidenced by the fact that of 1,728 mining titles granted in 1922, only 176, 10.2 percent of the total, were North American, with four more including recognizable U.S. partners, while Mexicans held 79.6 percent of the total. Mining remained a border industry, however. Of 201 permits for exploration issued in 1922, Chihuahua had the highest number with 69, followed by Sonora with 35. Coahuila had 40, Nuevo León 58, and Tamaulipas 7.[6]

The mines suffered in various ways from the needs of revolutionary groups. First, many of the miners joined revolutionary forces. For example, Giuseppe Garibaldi, grandson of the famous Italian revolutionary, found that in 1910 and 1911 the workers in his gold and silver mining operations were more interested in revolution than in mining. As he shared their predilections, this problem was not as serious for him as it was for mineowners more interested in profits. Garibaldi closed his works and took his men to join Abraham González, one of Madero's most trusted aides, who was gathering forces in El Paso.[7] The mines furnished many troops, some of whom were attracted by the wages that were being paid by revolutionary forces, and even some leaders, notably Esteban Baca Calderón and Manuel M. Diéguez, both former employees of the Cananea Copper Company. The atmosphere of the Revolution itself encouraged discontent among the mine workers, leading to an outbreak of strikes in June 1911 at smelters as widely scattered as Chihuahua, Monterrey, and Torreón, and many mining camps such as Santa Eulalia, Parral, Naica, and Cananea.

Mineowners on the U.S. side were also not immune from labor problems at an early stage. In 1911, there were already revolutionary recruiters in the Arizona mining towns of Clifton, Globe, and Morenci.[8] By 1912, recruiting efforts for the forces of by-then revolutionary President Madero were going on all along the border, and the Mexican consul in Clifton indicated to his counterpart in Douglas that he had arranged for those who took temporary duty to be given their jobs back when they returned.[9]

Even more serious for the operation of the mines were the constant demands made on them by the various revolutionary forces. Most mineowners tried to follow the same pragmatic policy that the oil companies did: to cooperate with the groups in the area at the time, to the degree that they could, so they could stay in operation. In practice, however, this approach proved difficult, and owners were not always given a choice. The explosives necessary for all mining operations proved a particularly important lure for the revolutionaries, and equipment of all kinds could be turned to various war-making purposes. Many of the mines were actually forced to suspend operations early in the decade because of the violent conditions.

Typical was the Santa Matilde Mining Company of Dolores, Chihuahua, which was owned by the Tennessee Corporation. The company reported to the U.S.-Mexican Claims Commission in 1926 that Mexican revolutionary groups and "other forces" had attacked the mine several times during the preceding decade, taking bullion and other property. During April 1911, the corporation had been forced to abandon all property and equipment and seek safety elsewhere. The Mollie Gibson Oil and Mining Company of Parral, Chihuahua, was unable to ship the machinery for a 100-ton stamp mill beyond El Paso, where it had to be sold for storage charges, and the property of the company in Mexico was destroyed or confiscated by several different forces at various times after 1910. North American holdings abandoned usually became targets for theft and looting. El Paso customs inspector Zach Cobb commented, after arresting a Mexican smuggler carrying 531 troy ounces of silver in a canvas vest under his shirt, that "all bullion that is smuggled is presumed to have been stolen . . . from the property of absentee Americans."[10]

Sonora also suffered serious problems. La Libertad Mining and Milling Company, owned by the Arizona Corporation, reported the abandonment of its works in 1911, when the lives of its fifty workmen were threatened and the property of the company stolen. La Libertad had for some time had difficulty because all supplies had to be brought in by mule from the nearest railroad point, the trek amounting to 120 miles through country infested by bandits and revolutionaries. An officer of the company had been attacked by bandits and his life threatened. When an appeal had been made to the civil authorities, they had recommended that he leave the country. Similar was the case of the Candelero Mining company near Hermosillo. Between November 1910 and November 1920, many armed Mexican forces had entered its property, destroyed buildings, and taken away large quantities of machinery, supplies, mining equipment, and personal property. The company loss was estimated at $500,000. The mine had, in fact, not really been functional since 1910, when it had suffered an armed attack by the Madero faction. All the company's workers had been drafted into the rebel group. The response of the judge of the municipality to the concerns of the foreman, J. R. Brown, was to urge him to leave the district and return to the U.S., advice which he took.[11]

One North American who lasted until 1914 reported that in the three years between 1911 and 1914, "a fierce and bitter war [was] raging in said State of Sonora," and that the adherents of Victoriano Huerta, president during the later part of the period, were "exceedingly bitter against all Americans" and "never lost an opportunity to apply to President Wilson and the people of the United States, the derisive and insulting epithet 'Gringo.'" This was by no means the only epithet applied to North Americans, however. As Dr. Francis Nicholas, manager of the Copete mines east of Carbo, Sonora, reported indignantly, he frequently heard Mexicans "who were careful to keep out of my sight" express the following sentiments: "We have insulted your flag, we have looted your stores, we have killed your men and we have ravished [using the vulgar word] your wives. What can we do to make you Gringo sons of bitches fight?"[12]

Probably the greatest threat to mining operations were the forces that were, nominally or in fact, associated with the revolutionary leader, Pancho Villa. Villa's relationships with the mining industry varied between administrative extortion and outright violence. Villa badly needed money and thus attempted to get mining operations resumed. ASARCO, the Guggenheim mining and smelting enterprise, seems to have made loans, forced or otherwise, to the Villistas as early as 1913. In 1914, Villa's governor of Chihuahua, Fidel Avila, ordered that all mines in the state be reopened or face forfeiture. Villa himself, defying U.S. Secretary of State Bryan's warnings, issued his own Decree No. 5 in early 1915, threatening to confiscate any unworked mines. Some mines were, in fact, confiscated, although the Villistas seem to have had great difficulty running them themselves.

Another problem for the companies was railroad transportation. Lázaro de la Garza, one of Villa's financial advisors, wrote to him several times in 1914, indicating the willingness of several companies, including ASARCO, to resume operations if transportation facilities could be assured. The smelters, particularly, were unwilling to start up if transportation for their supply of coke and coal to keep their ovens stoked was not guaranteed. As Villa needed the railroads himself for troop movements and coal for the trains was difficult to come by, he was unable to cope with this logistical and supply problem. By September 1915, he was desperate for funds for his campaign and tried to extract a forced loan of $300,000 in gold from the mineowners, on threat of confiscation. Apparently Gen. Hugh L. Scott of the U.S. Army managed to forestall Villa at this time by supplying coal for the Villista engines.[13]

As Villa's military situation worsened, he became both more vindictive and more desperate. Particularly after U.S. de facto recognition of Carranza, he turned his ire on North Americans, although his cruelty was by no means confined to any one national group. Kidnapping became a major fund-raising device. In late 1916, Enrique Salas, administrator of a mine in San Pedro, wrote to De la Garza that Villa's "barbarities" in the region had made communication impossible and that the mine had completely flooded. He also reported that he himself had been a victim of Villa, who had kidnapped him and his son, later releasing him in Parral, but carrying off the child. Fortunately, the son had been able to escape and return to the family, whom Salas had removed to San Buenaventura to "save my family from that region infested with terrible people."[14]

The case of the Erupción Mining Company illustrates the difficulties of starting a mining business during this period. The company, founded in January 1917, began operations at a site about eighty miles south of El Paso and forty-five miles east of Villa Ahumada, Chihuahua, and operated until October 1918 under constant harassment by revolutionary parties claiming to be Villistas. These troops robbed the commissary; kidnapped Mexican employees, for whom they charged small ransoms; and drove the freighters who supplied the mine with water away from the camp, sometimes making it necessary to stop operations entirely. On October 22, 1918, the president, the general manager, and the mine superintendent themselves were kidnapped on the road to Villa Ahumada. The leader of the band, after two days of traveling around the countryside and many heated discussions with the prisoners, announced that he had direct orders either to collect $50,000 gold as ransom or take the men directly to General Villa. When they were unable to produce this amount, they traveled for several days until they were brought to Villa's camp, where Villa "threw himself into a rage and threatened us with death, simply because we were Americans. . . . " Later, Villa said that he had no charges against any of the men, but that his hatred of the U.S. President Wilson was so great that he would execute them anyway and that no amount of money could save them. Later, he "changed his tactics" and asked $30,000 for permitting them to live. Finally, he dropped the price to $20,000, saying "Shut up, quit talking about it, go get the money." Eventually the men were ransomed, but not until there had been several attempts to get the payment in the only acceptable currency, gold. The liberated men left the country.[15]

The most famous incident with Villistas occurred in early 1916, very shortly after they had been decisively defeated by the Constitutionalist forces under Alvaro Obregón. Obregón had urged North American mining operators to return to Mexico and had assured them that their safety would be guaranteed by the Constitutionalist forces. Unfortunately, though the Villistas had lost the capability of mounting a major attack against another organized armed force, they were still able to make smaller but spectacular strikes against civilians. One of the first groups to attempt a resumption of operations was the Cusi Mining Company, which operated several mines in the state of Chihuahua. All the North American employees and many of the Mexicans had spent the dangerous, preceding months in the United States, but in early January, despite or perhaps because of reports of the looting of their property, they began to plan for a return to Mexico. Gen. Alvaro Obregón was requested to send troops to protect the mine and punish the looters, and on January 4, three troop trains carrying a total of one thousand men, including several Mexican employees of the company, were sent to Cusi. This action apparently satisfied the officials of the company that it was safe to start the mines up again.[16]

On the morning of January 9, 1916, seventeen of the Americans and twenty Mexicans gathered at El Paso to return to Mexico together to reopen the mines. The American engineers, mine officials, and technicians traveled in one train car, the Mexicans in another. The trip proceeded without incident until a barrier laid across the track forced the train to stop about five miles west of a cattle-loading station called Santa Ysabel. Several of the North Americans stepped out, only to discover twelve or fifteen men firing at them. All the men ran, but only Thomas B. Holmes managed to escape by seeking shelter in a clump of bushes and then crawling away until he reached the relative safety of another group of bushes on the river bank one hundred yards from the train. A group of armed men, led by Villista Pablo López, entered the train and herded the rest of the North Americans off, calling to the Mexicans, "If you want to see some fun, watch us kill these gringos." Each of the Americans was then shot at the side of the train. After listening to the gunfire signaling these executions, Holmes waited for about half an hour and then waded farther down the steam away from the train to a more concealed place, where he waited another forty-five minutes. Later he cautiously approached several ranch houses, finally meeting an "unknown Mexican" who gave him directions to Chihuahua City. He arrived there early in the morning of January 11. Later information, gathered principally from the Mexican survivors, indicated that there were approximately eighty-five men in the firing squad, backed up by about five hundred armed men who were stationed farther up the hill.[17]

This massacre had three important consequences. First, the resumption of mining in all areas potentially threatened by Villistas was delayed. North American companies, such as ASARCO, the Alvarado Mining Company, and the Potosí Company, ordered their employees to leave Mexico. Second, the incident stirred up a great deal of anti-Mexican feeling in the United States, particularly along the border. Gen. John J. Pershing reported from Fort Bliss, Texas, that the funeral of several of the victims had engendered "considerable talk of revenge" and had almost led to a mass meeting called by the friends of the victims. Although that assembly was forestalled by the action of the civil authorities, disturbances erupted after the closing of the bars at 9:30 that evening, and several Mexicans were beaten. Pershing rather strangely characterized the mood of the crowd as one of "revelry," although he went on to indicate that the incident had been potentially much more dangerous. He also pointed out that the responsible citizens of El Paso were doing what they could to avoid "outbreaks against Mexicans," and that the leaders of the mobs were "outsiders, nonproperty-owners, and irresponsibles." Finally, the raid shook the confidence of North Americans in the ability of Carranza forces to control the country, thus encouraging the mood leading to American intervention in Mexico. (See Chapter 5). Pershing commented that "there is little confidence in Carranza among Americans coming out of Mexico and many Mexicans are of the same mind. Practically all Americans think him powerless to establish anything like a stable government." Interestingly, Pershing added that many people regarded Obregón, Carranza's principal military chief, "as the ablest man of them all." There was also considerable feeling that little was being done to apprehend those responsible for the Santa Ysabel killings.[18] By the time that Pablo López was apprehended, the United States had already sent the Pershing Expedition into Mexico.[19]

The relationship between the revolutionaries and the mining companies in Sonora can be followed through the correspondence of Dr. James Douglas, the mining genius who had developed many of the Arizona copper mines and had become president of Phelps Dodge, and his elder son, James S. Douglas, an engineer who worked for Phelps Dodge for a time as builder of the Nacozari Railroad and manager of the Moctezuma Copper Company at Nacozari. He later engaged in various other related enterprises in the Arizona-Sonora border region. Even before the Revolution had begun, the Douglases were aware of and concerned about the abuses of the Díaz government. As father wrote to son, the Yaqui deportations were a "horrible picture of inhumanity and brutality," and any denial of these activities would be a "tissue of lies if it exonerates the government from Díaz downwards from responsibility for the Yaqui barbarities." He went on to explain, however, that if any group stood "stubbornly in the way of the onrush of modern progress, they are liable to be exterminated, or at any rate driven into a corner." Ultimately he reserved judgment, indicating that the Yaquis could have been fighting to retain tribal institutions and property.[20]

By January 1911, Dr. Douglas was sufficiently concerned about the political situation in Mexico that he requested that James, though not an employee of Phelps Dodge, "take command of the political situation in Mexico as far is it is liable to affect us." Young Douglas was to act through agents that he happened to know in "the affected district, in Hermosillo or the city of Mexico" and give counsel to the manager of Phelps Dodge holdings in Mexico. He was to do so on behalf of its two major enterprises, the Moctezuma Copper Company at the Pilares de Nacozari and the Nacozari Railroad. Although the son would have no involvement in the management of either business, he was to be paid $5,000 for three month's work. James answered his father very formally, agreeing to hold the powers of attorney for the allotted time, but indicating that he would return these to J.S. "Sid" Williams, Phelps Dodge's Mexico manager, after the three months ended. He also stated that "it should be understood that I will advise with Mr. Walter Douglas, General Manager for Phelps Dodge and Company, and will keep you both fully informed." Walter Douglas was his brother.[21]

The situation in Sonora was particularly difficult at this time, and on February 27, Sid Williams' train was stopped by a band of three hundred "revolutionists" under Arturo López. The brakeman escaped and returned to Izabal, sending news back to Williams that all wires were cut north of that point. Williams was able to communicate with James in

Douglas, Arizona, through Cumpas, with his wire arriving at 11:30 A.M. the next day. James immediately left by car to try to meet the train, arriving in Fronteras at 5:30 in the evening. There he found the insurrectos had pulled out several hours earlier, so he wired Williams to bring equipment up to repair damage to a burned-out bridge on the railroad line. Williams arrived at midnight, and by 9:30 the next morning the damage was repaired, with the trains running normally by 1:00 in the afternoon. Douglas added in his report that "Sid and I had a satisfactory chat this morning, and he is sure of the situation," although he neglected to say what he meant by "sure."[22]

That the trouble continued is evidenced by a letter from Walter Douglas to his father. In April 1911, Agua Prieta was attacked by the revolutionaries. When Walter arrived there, he found that the insurrectos had taken the town and were patrolling about twenty paces from the line, facing a troop of United States soldiers on the other side. Douglas attempted to cross the border to obtain word about one of his employees who had entered Mexico earlier in the day to take arms and ammunition down to Fronteras. While waiting, Walter witnessed the murder of a man he described as "poor, old Julián García," who was the chief of the customs house force and whom he and Dr. Douglas had visited the previous Saturday. The man had been captured and was being taken to the guardhouse when a crippled young man, who was a resident of Agua Prieta, walked up to him and shot him through the heart, apparently because of a personal grudge.

After this jarring incident, Douglas discovered with relief that his employee was at the train depot and was miraculously uninjured, though several of his companions had been killed or wounded, including a North American employee of the Pilares de Teres mine. They had been unfortunate enough to be passengers on the train or waiting at the depot when it was occupied by the revolutionaries, who had drawn Federales' fire by shooting out through the windows. Douglas's employee and the other noncombatants had protected themselves by crouching behind the safe, which was not much protection since the bullets were coming from all sides of the building. He had survived by pure luck. Walter ended by warning his father that even if the Federales were able to control the insurgents, they would in all likelihood cross over to the U.S. side, constituting a "very considerable disorderly element," and a "great menace to property and life." He therefore requested that his father persuade the Department of War to reinforce the border to prevent such entry.[23]

James wrote his father six weeks later, after the resignation of President Díaz, that the situation had calmed somewhat, but that an old friend was still in jail at Agua Prieta and he was worried about his safety. By this time the Maderistas were firmly in control. He was also concerned about changes in the city government in Nacozari, which could affect the operation of the mine there. He indicated that conditions were becoming quieter in the local area, but that "I cannot but expect that there will be more or less trouble for some time to come."[24]

By July 5, the Douglases had come completely to terms with the new government, partly through the good offices of Manuel Calero, who had been their attorney in Mexico. Calero, the new minister of development under the revolutionary government, had written to Dr. Douglas to inform him that all his legal practice was being taken over by Jorge Vera Estañol, his former partner. (Calero later became foreign minister when Francisco Madero assumed the presidency. Vera Estañol served as minister of education under Victoriano Huerta.) Calero had also brought Dr. Douglas up-to-date on Mexican political developments, indicating that Gen. Bernardo Reyes, former governor of Nuevo León who had himself plotted against the Díaz government, had joined Madero, and Douglas indicated his approval. (Reyes, however, would later revolt against Madero.)

Douglas's letter to Calero expressed his understanding that Calero's interest in national affairs must have absorbed a great deal of time and interest, but hoped that "more settled conditions will allow of closer attention to business."[25] The opposite occurred, however, as Calero in July arranged for a third party to handle Phelps Dodge interests, and Dr. Douglas wrote to James that "we are at the beginning of trouble, instead of at the end of trouble, in Mexico."[26]

Indeed, his observation was correct, and the Douglases continued to correspond on the ins and outs of Mexican politics and the civil war. In March 1912, Dr. Douglas again wrote his son James in regard to acting as an advisor for Phelps Dodge interests and included his hope that as few North Americans as possible would travel or reside in Mexico until the period of "restlessness—possibly of violence" was over. James continued to spend a great deal of his time south of the border, and soon became involved in the management of the other great Sonoran copper company, Cananea.[27]

Pascual Orozco's Chihuahuan rebellion was spreading into Sonora, and the state was deeply involved both in the movement against Victoriano Huerta, who had taken over the presidency after the assassination of Francisco Madero, and in the ensuing struggles between Pancho Villa and the Constitutionalists under Carranza and Obregón. On July 8, 1912, young Douglas was anticipating with concern the arrival of a group of revolutionists from Chihuahua. By April 1913, according to James, the operation of Cananea was severely cut back, largely because of the difficulty of getting reliable supplies of combustibles. His father responded that the Mexican situation was puzzling and that forming an opinion was difficult. He hoped for strong action from Ignacio Pesqueira, the governor of the state, but unfortunately Pesqueira had neither men nor money and had been unsuccessful in controlling the violence. By this time, the Phelps Dodge works at Nacozari were threatened by a typhoid epidemic that revolutionary conditions had helped to spread. Still, he warned that a shutdown of other plants might be undiplomatic, as "starvation sometimes acts as an irritant instead of a sedative," presumably a reference to the copper company workers.

By May 13, James was more optimistic, as Cananea had a new prefect who was reasonable and able. Nevertheless, he was concerned that Cananea would be vulnerable until a military commander was appointed for the area. Meanwhile, the idle workers had begun whitewashing the company's fences, and copper production stood at 2.5 million pounds a month, despite his judgment that "general conditions in Mexico could hardly be worse than they are at present." James was living on the U.S. side at this time, a choice his father approved as rational given the circumstances. He urged his son to remember that, from a national rather than a personal point of view, his safety was important. Dr. Douglas pointed out that on a previous occasion the son had almost been killed by a mob, and "the chances are that had that happened it would have involved a war with the United States, and at a critical period like this, I think that every American ought to be very cautious lest any act on his part should aggravate the present delicate relations of the two countries."[28]

The Douglas interests in Nacozari and Cananea continued to suffer from the political problems involving various Sonoran groups. As James put it, "The trouble is amongst our Sonora friends, that they are jealous of each other and each of them have [sic] their own personal axe to grind. . . ." The situation at Cananea was worse than that at Nacozari, and Dr. Douglas commented to his son after a temporary shutdown of the concentrator at the latter operation: "The trouble in Nacozari was probably fomented by political agitators, but fortunately we have very few of that ilk at Nacozari compared with what you have in Cananea." When Constitutionalist troops took control of the state, conditions temporarily became better. The younger Douglas reported to his father a net profit of $276,000 in October 1913, and James bought heavily in Green Cananea stock in late 1913, only to sell some of it, at a profit, in early 1914. James wrote to his stockbroker that, despite good production, "we have no government to lean upon," and "the whole business is liable to blow up any time. . . . " Dr. Douglas was also pessimistic, feeling that Carranza, even if he were able to drive Huerta from the country and become president, would still face a serious challenge from Villa. He commented presciently that "I am afraid peace will not reign." By August 1914, the Cananea operation was shut down again, and by November 1914, young Douglas, after difficulties with the upper management of Cananea, had resigned his position.[29]

James S. Douglas continued to reside in Arizona and keep his father informed of conditions on the border. His letters detailed the buildup of U.S. troops in the area and the deterioration of the Mexican political situation. In April 1916, his father commented unfavorably on the potential war between the two countries, saying that "a war with Mexico would be very ignominious, and very difficult to conduct; and the result in no case could be greatly to either the credit or the advantage of this country." At the time he wrote this last letter to his son, the Pershing Punitive Expedition was already in northern Mexico.[30] The Douglases' business enterprises continued to thrive despite the border situation, and they moved their interests more and more to the Arizona side of the border. Dr. Douglas resigned as president of Phelps Dodge in 1916 and was succeeded by Walter; James became involved in the development of the United Verde Extension in Jerome, Arizona, and in December 1914 struck a five-foot vein of copper tested at 45 percent, leading to profits over the next few years of $50 million.[31]

The Douglas interests not only included copper and railroads, which were particularly important to the development of mining, but also banks and utility companies. James S. Douglas was the president of the Bank of Douglas at the time and also led a planning group that incorporated the Douglas Improvement Company "for the purpose of operating and maintaining an electric light and power plant, telephone system, ice plant and water works." The dependence on the mining industry and other related industries is illustrated by the loans outstanding in the Bank of Douglas in July 1911. Of fifty-four loans outstanding, twelve were secured by Phelps Dodge stock, and five more by other mining stocks. Twelve others were land mortgages, and the remainder were divided among stocks of various kinds such as oil, meat, insurance, and drugstores, with two secured by warehouse commodity holdings. Douglas, Arizona, was indeed a family and company town.[32]

The Douglas family was able to survive and thrive in this situation for several reasons. They had the support of a powerful and well-established company behind them, they were associated with the two most important and most profitable copper mining interests in Sonora, and they were able to shift their interests to the Arizona side when conditions became particularly difficult in Mexico.

As mentioned before, many more marginal operations had been paralyzed earlier in the decade, and most of the larger enterprises were finally destroyed in the struggle between Villa and Obregón in 1915 and the disorders that followed in 1916. Consul Simpich in Sonora wrote to Secretary of State Lansing that several major mines, including La Colorada, La Cobriza, and El Plomo, and some smaller operations that had managed to survive had closed in the early months of 1916. Problems resulting in this outcome included the high export tax on bullion, the constant raids by various factions and bandits, insecure working conditions, and difficulties in transporting supplies. Threats against the American employees and vandalism of company properties were also significant. The Washington mine had closed in June after the killing of W. R. Dickinson. The San Xavier mine, operated by Laughlin and Schrater, was finally closing because the goods in the company store had been seized not by revolutionaries, but by the de facto military authorities who paid in fiat money, which, at ten cents on the dollar, was virtually worthless. It had been the only major mine still operating except for Cananea, Nacozari, and El Tigre. Mining in the state, except in the largest and most profitable operations, was virtually paralyzed.[33]

Despite these problems, the relationship between the revolutionaries and the mining companies in Sonora was considerably different from the open antagonism that prevailed in the Villista areas from late 1915 on. As governor of the state, Plutarco Elías Calles made great efforts to keep at least the large mining operations at Cananea, Nacozari, and El Tigre functioning. All the companies seem to have made an effort, at least up to this point, to accommodate whoever happened to be in control. In May 1915, for example, the Cananea Consolidated Copper Company was cooperating with the forces of José María Maytorena, Sonora governor during the Madero regime, who by this date had affiliated himself with Pancho Villa and temporarily held control of a large part of the state. A report from a U.S. military intelligence officer indicated that Maytorena's forces were using the Cananea foundry for making three-inch artillery shells. According to him, "They do not pay for anything, they simply present an order on the Copper Company for all the materials required for the manufacture of the shells and the work is done by the Mexican soldiers under the supervision of their officers." The Mexicans produced one hundred shells per day, despite the fact that the workmen were unskilled. The company itself, however, was barely operational at this time; of a normal work force of four thousand only four hundred men were then at work, keeping the mines from flooding or caving in. Smaller operations were usually already closed by 1915 and 1916, and many of these never reopened.[34]

The breakdown of the Mexican mining industry had consequences all along the border, illustrating the interrelationship of the economies of the two regions. Coal mines on both sides of the line had problems as various metal smelters closed down and used less of their product. In 1915, Ernesto Madero, a relative of Francisco, was trying to sell his coal mines near Eagle Pass, Texas, to a compatriot who was already purchasing large amounts of coal for his zinc smelter in the same location. Madero indicated that the mines had been idle because of the "Mexican situation," as most of his product was formerly sold to metal smelters in Monterrey and Torreón that were now idle. His acquaintance turned him down, as his own business was also in difficulty because of existing conditions.[35]

El Paso, Texas, was particularly affected. The city had developed as a rail center serving major mining areas on both sides of the border and was an advantageous location for smelting as well as for a supply center for the mining camps. Local firms did a booming business in personal items, both necessities and luxuries, for miners and mineowners and sold large amounts of mining supplies. Much of the North American interest in Mexican mines was directed through this border city. Mexican miners used it as a point of transit when they crossed the line between the two countries and frequently were recruited for jobs while they were in the city. Moreover, many jobs within El Paso were mining-related as well. In 1910, 29 percent of the labor force was employed in industry, 17 percent in trade, and 15 percent in transportation. These jobs served to support the outlying mining areas of West Texas, Arizona, and New Mexico on the U.S. side, and Chihuahua and Sonora on the Mexican side, and even the more distant states of Durango, Baja California, and Coahuila.[36]

Smelting was the major industry in El Paso, and the El Paso Smelter was the town's largest employer, especially of workers from Mexico. Owned by ASARCO, it purchased all classes of copper, silver, lead, and gold ores. As early as 1903, it was reported to have employed 1,500 workers and ranked as one of the largest in the world, contributing $1 million dollars each month to the economy of the city. During the Revolution, ore supplies from Mexico were greatly reduced, leading to a shift to lead shipments from Colorado, Arizona, and New Mexico, although these could not be maintained at the same high level. As a result, the smelter increased its proportion of copper smelting since it had a supply of ore from its own Santa Rita Mines in New Mexico. In spite of the fact that the smelter was having difficulty with its supplies and that El Paso was an important point of refuge for many Mexicans fleeing the violence of the Revolution, the smelter was not immune from labor problems during the decade. In 1913, Mexican workers went on strike for a pay raise of $.35 a day, to a total of $1.75, and some asked for a reduction of daily hours from twelve to eight. Eventually 650 Mexicans left their jobs along with 5 Anglo carpenters. Their efforts were thwarted, however, as the company brought in Texas Rangers to help put down the strike and imported black workers from Louisiana and east Texas. Some of the Mexicans eventually returned to their jobs, but the smelter refused to rehire many of them.[37]

All along the border, mining men and companies tried to salvage their businesses by turning their attention to the U.S. side. Fortuitously, World War I had stimulated the demand for copper and had caused a significant price rise, leading to increased activity in the Arizona mines. In fact, copper had become so important by April 1917 that the U.S. secretary of the interior wrote to the secretary of state indicating that in a conversation with Walter Douglas he had learned that Phelps Dodge was considering closing down all of its Mexican mines, which were yielding 125 million pounds of copper a year. The interior secretary had urged Douglas, a member of the Council of National Defense, to inform him before taking such action. He also worried about the political effect of such a closing; fifty thousand men would be put out of work and would thus be available for a revolution against President Carranza. The secretary recognized the difficulties, however; costs per pound of production had doubled in the last year and especially in the last two months, and the conditions of labor were described as "almost impossible."[38]

Besides banditry and revolutionary problems, social disorganization in the camps had caused great difficulties. In 1916 at Cananea, for example, the governor of the state had found it necessary to decree the death penalty for ordinary robbery. Lest his warning go unheeded, he ordered the military commander of the town to go ahead and carry out the penalty in the first two or three cases that came up.[39]

Many Mexican miners, faced with these severe revolutionary conditions, migrated across the border, some of them permanently. In some cases, the miners were from farther south and had come first to northern Mexico. Then, confronting the violence and disruption of the area, they crossed the border in search of safer conditions. A report in the mid-1920s indicated that 43 percent of Arizona's copper mining force was Mexican, and undoubtedly many of them had gained their experience in Mexico.[40]

Both businessmen and many laborers found it safer to move to the U.S. side of the line, although World War I gave a tremendous boost to mining everywhere. Cananea and Nacozari worked at full capacity through much of 1917 and 1918 despite the frequently dangerous conditions, and the Mexican government from 1917 on generally tried to stimulate the revival of industry and the return of foreign managers and technicians.

Copper mining had been a major activity in Arizona from the 1880s on, total production ranging from 250 million to 290 million pounds per year from 1906 to 1910. The most significant producers were the Copper Queen at Douglas, the nearby Calumet and Arizona mine, and the United Verde in the Clifton district. The Arizona industry was very closely tied to the Mexican copper mines, even at this time, with Arizona smelters processing a large part of the Sonora output, particularly from Greene Cananea and the Phelps Dodge holdings at Nacozari. Although Phelps Dodge was never a major stockholder in Cananea, the interrelationship of this border industry is indicated by the fact that, in 1904, William Greene asked James Douglas to join the board of directors of Cananea. By 1908, Greene himself was out; the company had been taken over by Amalgamated Copper (later Anaconda); and Douglas's friend and colleague, Louis D. Ricketts, had assumed the management of the company. In 1913, Ricketts in turn had brought in James S. Douglas as manager.[41]

The war in Europe, which had begun in 1914, brought a tremendous surge of prosperity to the copper companies. As *Fortune* magazine stated in a 1931 article about Phelps Dodge, "If copper is electricity, it is likewise war." The demand for copper began to grow, and the Arizona companies produced at a high level. Even Cananea, despite a slump resulting from military and political problems in 1917, maintained a high level of production in 1916 and 1918 (See Table 7.1). The year 1917 was the high point for both total demand and prices. Copper reached $.37 cents a pound, and the highest level of exports of the five-year period from 1915 through 1919 was achieved in that year. The industry geared up for yet higher production, but demand ended suddenly, along with the war, in 1918.[42]

An unstable market was not the only problem concerning the copper companies at this time. Labor unrest was also widespread throughout the Arizona mines as the International Workers of the World fought the less radical Western Federation of Miners for control of the area. The most extreme example of management action came when a strike at Bisbee was broken in 1917 by deporting the strikers from the community and leaving them stranded in the desert (See Chapter 3).

Other measures taken were less severe. Management tried to pacify labor by explaining to the workers, through the local newspapers, that conditions were actually very good compared to other places. A newspaper article announced that "Food Cheap as Elsewhere, Wages Higher in Douglas" and went on to compare prices with New York, showing that only fresh vegetables, especially perishables, were significantly higher. It also explained that wages were much higher in Douglas than in New York or on the Pacific Coast.[43] In 1918, Mexican mine and smelter employees in the Verde area were mailed copies in Spanish of an editorial that had

Table 7.1
Copper Production (lbs.) in Selected Companies, 1916–19

Company	1916	1917	1918	1919
Phelps Dodge	189,435,138	204,783,530	209,097,262	110,000,000
Anaconda	307,305,092	239,014,880	272,923,031	150,000,000
United Verde Extension	36,378,010	63,237,000	55,527,916	27,745,564
Arizona Copper	34,100,000	42,482,000	40,442,000	33,400,000
Calumet & Arizona	74,898,783	62,397,017	51,537,154	46,348,000
Greene-Cananea	63,250,067	30,496,487	53,349,009	41,500,000

Source: *Arizona Mining Journal* (Mar. 1920), 16.

appeared in the Verde Copper News, explaining to them that conditions in the district were better than in any other part of the United States. This situation prevailed, according to the article, because construction had continued at a high rate, despite the expense of freight and labor; wages were as high as and sometimes higher than those paid by any other mining company in the West; and the Verde mines had continued to operate despite the softness of the copper market since the end of World War I. Furthermore, the cost of living was not high in comparison with prices in other parts of the country. Given these favorable conditions, it was optimistically predicted that all involved in the copper mining enterprises could resolve their differences, keeping in mind the necessity of economizing as much as possible. The editorial ended by reminding the workers that in recent years some of them had found themselves unemployed, and that "it is not necessary to advise those who have good jobs to retain them."[44]

In fact, with the end of the war, the whole mining industry suffered a period of adjustment, unlike the oil industry, which was undergoing a boom. The price of copper, for example, dropped precipitously, plunging from $.26 per pound in January 1919 to $.1475 the following March. Production for 1919 dropped significantly in the Arizona and Sonoran mines, as copper exports from the U.S. plummeted (See Tables 7.1 and 7.2). Moreover, in the copper industry, the Arizona-Sonora mines were faced with increased competition from Chilean mines, which began significant production in the following decade. The situation in 1920 was so serious that the Cananea mines, smelter, and concentrator were ordered to close at the end of the year, with the men leaving to seek work in the Arizona cotton fields. The U.S. consul in the area informed his government that twenty-five thousand men would be adversely affected and might "commit anti-American acts." He viewed with alarm the potential

Table 7.2
Copper Exports from the United States, 1915–19

Year	Total Exports in Tons
1915	276,344
1916	327,310
1917	493,256
1918	328,844
1919	226,611

Source: *Arizona Mining Journal* (Mar. 1920), 17.

Table 7.3
Metals Production in Mexico

Year	Silver (Kgs.)	Gold (Kgs.)	Lead (Metric tons)	Zinc (Metric tons)	Copper (Metric tons)
1910	2,416,669	41,420	124,292	1,833	48,160
1920	2,068,938	22,864	85,518	15,651	49,192

Source: Marvin D. Bernstein, *The Mexican Mining Industry, 1890–1950* (Albany: State University of New York, 1965), 101.

entrance of these workers into the United States, as they might be of the "radical or 'agitator' class, which has been very active at Cananea." Problems were by no means confined to Sonora, but extended throughout the country. Mines and smelters in many areas, most of them recently reopened, were closing again.[45]

By the end of the decade, metal markets and the Mexican Revolution had taken a tremendous toll on mining. Between 1910 and 1920, of the five major mining products, all but zinc and copper suffered significant drops in production (See Table 7.3). Thus, the new Mexican president, Alvaro Obregón, would have to shift the economic basis of his government from one of its traditional mainstays, the mining industry, to the newly booming oil industry. Because of the close interrelationship of the border economies, both sides were profoundly affected.

8

The Refuge: Mexican Migration to the United States

During the revolutionary decade, Mexicans flooded north across the border into the relative safety and stability of the United States. This population movement, which has continued to the present day, had permanent consequences, setting the future patterns that such migrations would follow by establishing large Mexican communities that served as support networks for newcomers. In addition, the seeds of the social problems that would be faced in later years, such as the impact on social services and the need for bilingual education programs, were planted at this time. The migration was largely a flight from the conditions of violence and social disorganization in Mexico that resulted from the events of the Mexican Revolution. This decade marked the beginning of the enormous flow of Mexicans to the United States, a migration that has continued, with only brief setbacks, up to the present time.

The devastation, chaos, danger, and economic disaster during the period from 1910 to 1920 led to the widespread migration to the safety, if not necessarily comfort, of the United States. Mexicans by the thousands came across the border as legal immigrants, "temporary" workers, refugees, or illegal aliens. Nearly 1.5 million of them spent at least a part of the revolutionary years in the U.S., and many stayed permanently, particularly in Arizona and Texas. The official figure for legal migrants crossing the Mexican border into the United States between July 2, 1910, and July 1, 1920, is 890,371, a figure that includes both legal immigrants and

Table 8.1
Registered Legal Migration across the Mexican Border into the United States 1910–20

Year	Legal Immigration	Nonstatistical Aliens	Total
1911	24,527	32,000	56,527
1912	26,573	27,852	54,425
1913	15,285	66,360	81,645
1914	14,897	51,500	66,397
1915	15,695	49,553	65,248
1916*	17,198	82,766	99,964
1917*	16,438	123,484	139,922
1918*	17,602	69,244	86,846
1919	44,668	56,679	101,347
1920	68,816	69,234	138,050
Total	261,699	628,672	890,371

Source: *Reports of the Commissioner General of Immigration, 1911–1920* (*CGI*, 1911–20).
*Only the total figures and the figures for legal immigration are given in these reports for the years indicated. Column I gives the figures for legal *Mexican* immigration for these years, and the figure for nonstatistical aliens is derived from Columns I and III.

temporary workers, who at that time were called "non-statistical aliens" by border authorities, although they were in fact counted but not included in immigration figures (See Table 8.1).[1] Many others came as uncounted refugees and, when immigration laws became stricter toward the end of the decade, as illegal migrants.

The reasons for migration were many, but separating political from economic motives would have been extremely difficult. In most cases, the economic advantages afforded by employment in the U.S. pulled Mexicans across, just as the violence and social and economic disorganization occasioned by the Revolution pushed them out of Mexico. In many instances, an additional reason was adventure, an opportunity to seek one's fortune in a strange land. Thus danger, on the one hand, and economic opportunity and excitement on the other, propelled large numbers of Mexicans across their northern frontier.[2]

As a result of the record-keeping practices of the Bureau of Immigration and Naturalization, far more is known about legal immigrants, that is, Mexicans coming into the country with the explicit intention of remaining permanently, than about any other group. For reasons not entirely clear, the figures for *legal Mexican immigrants* differ rather widely from the number of *legal immigrants coming across the Mexican border*. In any case, the number given by the Department of Labor for *legal Mexican immigrants* during the decade is 206,945 (See Tables 8.1 and 8.2).[3]

As the figures show, legal migration started with significant numbers of Mexicans coming across during 1911 and 1912, but increased considerably toward the end of the decade. The increase was irregular, however, as migration rose and fell as a result of conditions and events in both countries. Nineteen eleven and 1912 were years of revolution and confusion, but they were also years of hope and change for the common people, since major economic dislocation had not yet taken place. The year 1913, however, marked a severe increase in violence, as President Madero was overthrown by usurper Victoriano Huerta and later killed. The north of Mexico erupted and furnished the leaders and troops who defeated Huerta. Throughout this important year, the border saw military action, even though it was not always the focus of major fighting. Thus, though *legal immigration* dropped significantly during 1913, total migration increased 50 percent over 1912.

The following two years, 1914 and 1915, saw a slight decrease in migration, as revolutionary battles continued in the interior of the country rather than in the border area. In fact, during this period the major railroads were controlled by revolutionary factions, and it was difficult for many individuals to reach the border at all. The violence slowed down in 1916, however, as the Constitutionalists extended their control through many areas. Rail service was resumed, economic and social dislocations were at their postrevolutionary peak, and many men accustomed to earning their living as soldiers were put out of work, causing the tide of migration again to surge northward. Despite new immigration laws in 1917, migration continued at a high and increasing level, except for a setback in 1918, when the U.S. entrance into World War I caused many Mexican nationals to fear being drafted into the U.S. Army. By 1920, the total was again very high and still rising.

The character of the migration is particularly interesting. Legal immigrants were recorded in the statistics according to occupation. The professional category included actors, architects, clergymen, lawyers, physicians, teachers, and even musicians. The second category, skilled, included bakers, barbers, carpenters and joiners, miners, metal workers, tailors, weavers, and photographers. The miscellaneous category was made up almost entirely of unskilled laborers of various kinds, mostly unspecified, although an occasional hotel keeper was included.

Three years during the decade have been selected for comparative study: 1912, 1916, and 1920 (See Table 8.3.).[4] The professional category was increasing every year, but hovered around 1 percent of the total. Teachers were the largest group in this category in all three of these years,

Table 8.2
Legal Mexican Immigration into the United States
July 1, 1910–July 1, 1920

1911	18,784
1912	22,001
1913	10,954
1914	13,089
1915	10,993
1916	17,198
1917	16,438
1918	17,602
1919	28,844
1920	51,052
Total	206,955

Source: *CGI,* 1911–20.

Table 8.3
Skill Levels of Entering Mexican Immigrants
July 1910–July 1920

Year	Professional	Skilled	No Profession	Total
1912	186 (.8%)	1,203 (5.5%)	20,612 (93.7%)	22,001
1916	220 (1.3%)	1,474 (8.8%)	15,008 (89.9%)	16,702
1920	588 (1.2%)	3,912 (7.7%)	46,542 (91.1%)	51,042

Source: *CGI,* 1912, 1916, 1920.

followed by musicians, actors, electricians, lawyers, and engineers. All five of these latter groups were approximately equal. Physicians represented a small percentage, and an assortment of architects, clergymen, sculptors and artists, and "literary and scientific persons" accounted for the rest. Interestingly, bankers were not counted among the professionals, but were lumped in with common laborers in the miscellaneous category.

In the skilled category, clerks and accountants furnished the largest number of immigrants. Miners formed a substantial portion of the total, and many were probably heading for the developing copper mines in Arizona. Mechanics and carpenters and joiners also accounted for from 5 to 10 percent each of the total immigrants during these years.

It is striking that for the years available, even in the category of *legal Mexican immigrants*, by far the largest number either were unskilled workers or listed no occupation. In 1916, unspecified laborers accounted for 29.2 percent of total immigration. In 1920, the percentage had risen to 41.8 percent. The number of immigrants with no occupation (usually women and children) made up 53.1 percent of the total in 1916 and 42.6 percent in 1920. Through the decade, more and more unskilled workers were coming in, while the number of nonworking family members declined.

In the early part of the decade, U.S. immigration officials noted that the "quality" of the immigrants was declining. In 1912, the commissioner general's report indicated that Mexican immigrants had "not measured up to the standard of previous years."[5] One disgruntled inspector commented in 1913, a year of considerable fighting and disorganization in northern Mexico, that "the immigration over this border during the past year has not averaged up in quality with that of the previous year."[6] However, during the fighting, the socioeconomic status of the immigrants seems to have risen somewhat. In 1914, perhaps the time of the Revolution's heaviest fighting, the border inspector reported that the "so-called 'better classes'" had been immigrating in particularly large numbers. He theorized that the war had deprived the "peons of the means wherewith to travel," whereas the wealthier sections of society were still able to flee to the United States.[7]

Of course, legal immigrants formed by far the smallest category of migrants. The so-called "non-statistical" aliens, migrants who entered legally and were counted, but did not register their intent to stay permanently, numbered 628,672. No record was kept of their occupations, but it seems fair to assume that their socioeconomic status was lower than that of Mexicans who entered intending to become residents. According to the commissioner general's report in 1911, most of the nonstatistical workers admitted up to that time were coming in to work in railway construction and maintenance.[8]

In addition to the migrants, permanent or temporary, thousands of refugees were pouring across the border in response to war conditions in northern Mexico. It was not unusual for an entire town to cross the border en masse either before or during military clashes in the area.

As early as 1911, immigration officials were reporting that large numbers of Mexican aliens were seeking refuge in the United States. The attitude of U.S. officials was generally sympathetic. As one report detailed, aliens were given asylum as a "measure of humanity," especially as the "unusual and oftentimes harrowing circumstances influencing their applications justified a more than ordinarily liberal interpretation of the law."[9] Many of these early refugees seem to have been of the upper socioeconomic classes, and concern was expressed that although they were running out of money and seeking jobs, many were "unfit to perform hard manual labor."[10]

The problem increased considerably during the extensive violence of 1913 and 1914. For example, in October 1913, eight thousand inhabitants of Piedras Negras abandoned the town just ahead of a force that was about to attack the city, crossed the line, and entered Eagle Pass, Texas. Despite "heroic efforts by the Marine Hospital Service and the Army" to prevent them from "scattering aimlessly over the country," it proved impossible to keep them together and return them to Mexico. Only those found "excludable," probably by reason of disease, were returned to Mexico.

Another problem involved the entrance of defeated military forces crossing to the U.S. side rather than surrendering to the victors. In January 1914, some five thousand Federal troops crossed the border at Presidio, Texas, accompanied by camp followers and "hundreds of civilian refugees." Although attempts were made to contain these entrants as well, many did make their way into the interior of the country.[11]

By 1916, U.S. border officials were defining refugees somewhat more broadly. Noting that the number of political refugees had fallen off drastically because of reduced violence near the border, they nevertheless reported that migrants continued to pour into the Southwest as a result of "industrial depression and its attendant evils" in Mexico. It is unclear whether the individuals indicated had been counted or not. In any case, immigrant officers explained that industrial activity in the Southwest and even more remote regions had fortunately created a large demand for unskilled labor and the acute economic distress suffered by the migrants in the border region in 1915 had thus been considerably reduced.[12]

A somewhat more bizarre group of refugees followed General Pershing's troops out of Mexico in 1917. These were the civilians who had been employed by the U.S. military during Pershing's expedition into Mexico in search of Pancho Villa. They numbered 2,755, of whom 197 were North Americans, 2,030 Mexicans, and 528 Chinese. They all feared reprisals at the hands of angry Mexicans who viewed them as collaborators. Immigration officials immediately took charge of the foreigners, reporting that most of the Mexicans had sufficient funds for their immediate needs and many had "friends to whom they proceeded." Most of the Chinese remained with the army, which initially guaranteed that they would leave the country if they could not provide proof of their status as admissible Chinese. Since this status had been difficult to attain since the Chinese Exclusion Act of 1882, most would normally have been returned to Mexico or eventually to China, but the army prevented their forced departure. The grateful Chinese, after arriving in San Antonio, gave their protectors an elaborate chop-suey dinner at the Menger Hotel, the entertainment being furnished by a "celestial quartet." As late as 1919, 401

Chinese who otherwise would have been deportable were still working for the Quartermaster Corps of the army. Evidently many of them remained under the protection of the Corps and settled in San Antonio, the headquarters of the army's Southern Department, despite continuing efforts by the local immigration office to have them deported.[13]

Even toward the end of the decade, whole towns were still periodically migrating across the border as the revolutionary activity in the north degenerated into banditry. The Immigration Service noted that these mass migrations took place whenever there was a rumor of an attack by "Mexican outlaws which denominate themselves as revolutionaries." One harried official added that most of these refugees returned to Mexico if the attack did not materialize or after order had been restored, but that in the "hurly-burly of congested traffic" some of those who would not otherwise qualify for entrance were able to escape the attention of the immigration officers and remain in the United States.[14]

In addition to these categories of migration, there was also a substantial amount of unrecorded movement along the border. Large numbers of people, even before 1917, simply walked across the border at points where there were no immigration officials. The Immigration Service itself, of course, was totally inadequate to the task of controlling the flow, and the Border Patrol was not established until 1924.[15] Until 1917, however, the Immigration Service was not greatly concerned with the Mexicans coming into the country, as most Mexicans were not excluded by law and crossing was largely a formality. Only the diseased, the criminal, the insane, and those under labor contracts had been excluded by the Immigration Act of 1884.[16] The great concern was with the Chinese, whose entrance had been highly restricted by the Chinese Exclusion Act of 1882, as mentioned above. The Immigration Act of 1917, however, imposed a literacy test and a head tax of $8.00 on Mexican migrants and reiterated the prohibition against contract labor.[17] This act had the immediate effect of removing much of the migration, which might otherwise have been legal, from the control of the Immigration Service, as Mexicans, not understanding the new regulations or fearful of exclusions, began to come in illegally. The problem was ameliorated by the fact that immigration briefly became less attractive, since many Mexicans feared conscription into the U.S. armed forces for service in World War I. In fact, Gov. James E. Ferguson of Texas was inspired to write the following panicky letter to President Woodrow Wilson:

> A very serious situation confronts me. From a large portion of Texas come pressing reports to me that Mexican laborers are leaving the fields and going to Mexico to escape registration. The idea has gained much credence among them that they are

> to be conscripted and taken to France immediately. On account of a greater portion of the Mexican population being unable to understand English, it is almost impossible to explain to them the registration laws. In fact we have some difficulty explaining them to our own people. If the exodus continues, I am afraid the yield from the crops in this state will be greatly diminished. I would appreciate very much if you could see your way clear to issue a proclamation at once exempting all Mexicans from registration and selection during the year 1917. This will remove our most serious danger at this time and will in the meantime enable us to educate more thoroughly the Mexican population just what selective draft means. Our situation is indeed serious.[18]

By 1918, even the Immigration Service was bemoaning the new difficulties caused by this act. In 1918, a border official reported that "the suppression of countless illegal aliens of the Mexican race, exluded or excludable under what they deem to be the harsh provisions of the immigration act of 1917, has constituted one of the most difficult problems with which this district has had to contend in the past year." Hundreds of aliens were reported to have arrived at the border, lacking both money and food and badly needing work on the U.S. side. The desperation of these people had led to the "creation of a new and thriving industry" of smuggling Mexican aliens across the frontier. Those elements previously engaged in smuggling Chinese, sometimes along with opium, shifted their attention to the potentially much larger client population of Mexicans desiring to cross the frontier. As the immigration officer pointed out, these "parasites" frequently misrepresented the requirements of the act so as to gain customers who actually could have entered legally.[19]

The numbers of those entering illegally are impossible to determine with accuracy, but the officer in charge of one border port estimated that sixty thousand illegals entered in 1920 in that vicinity alone.[20] Unquestionably, large numbers of Mexicans were now coming in surreptitiously. Given the fact that the total number of entrants who were actually counted by the Immigration Services was 890,371 and that refugees and illegals were *not* counted, it seems probable that the number of Mexicans who spent at least a part of the decade 1910–20 in the United States would reach 1.5 million. This figure gives a far different picture than the one usually used of 206,945 legal immigrants.[21]

The pull across the border, despite the temporary setback in 1917, continued to be strong. In fact, the Immigration Act of 1917 was scarcely in effect when the Bureau of Labor began to reduce its restrictions under pressure from labor-short employers in the U.S. Southwest. Railroads in particular felt a drastic pinch in the supply of maintenance and construction workers, while farmers needed labor to harvest their crops.

World War I itself had exacerbated the problem, as many potential workers were fighting in Europe just as the demand for farm products was rising and railway shipping was becoming ever more crucial to the war effort. In addition, the flow of immigrant workers coming in from Europe through the eastern part of the United States had almost completely stopped.[22]

The situation was so problematical that as early as May 21, 1917—only three months after the passage of the Immigration Act and coincident with the spring arrival at the border of the usual flood of temporary Mexican workers—the commissioner general of immigration sent a memorandum suggesting that exceptions to the literacy test, head tax, and contract labor provisions of the act should be made in the case of farm laborers. The literacy test was singled out as a particular stumbling block. These exceptions were justified by a shortage of labor near the Mexican and Canadian borders that was likely to become "embarrassing, if not disastrous." The commissioner general's suggested guidelines for admission were approved by the secretary of labor on May 22, 1917, and circulated a few days later. It is an interesting sidelight to note that only *Mexican* laborers were to be exempted. The original draft had included Puerto Ricans, but the secretary had pencilled them out since their status as admissible migrants changed in the same year.[23]

The secretary of labor and prominent politicians were besieged with complaints, requests, and explanations of the problems caused by the act, principally from farmers and railroad executives. One cotton company executive, somewhat relieved by the circular permitting Mexicans to enter for agricultural purposes, wrote to President Wilson approving the new interpretation of the law and saying that:

> Personally, I believe that the Mexican laborers are the solution of our common labor problem in this country. Many of their people are here, this was once a part of their country, and they can and they will do the work. . . . I personally find them, especially those with families, to be appreciative of fair treatment and to be deserving of it.

He went on to mention that the Southwest Cotton Company's manager of construction was a "high-minded, educated Mexican," who was drawing a large salary and earning it.[24]

Letters from Texas and California described and confirmed for these areas a pattern of migration that had become customary. The railroads brought the Mexicans, who usually did not pay for their transportation, in the early spring. The migrants would work on the railroads in section gangs until it was time for the crops to be harvested. They would then leave to work temporarily for the farmers and ranchers at slightly higher wages. After the harvest, they would return to the railroads and complete the work there. This system worked well as long as the supply of laborers could be replenished from Mexico in case of any drop in the numbers in the U.S., but with the change in the law, the incoming Mexicans could work *only* in agricultural pursuits, and the railroads were left shorthanded. All the Mexicans shifting over from agriculture could be deported. Railroad executives urged that laborers be permitted to work for them as well, pointing out that a reliable, well-maintained railroad system was critical to the war effort. The Bureau of Labor was concerned, but made no further change in the regulations until June 1918, when exemptions for railway workers were permitted.[25]

Most of the letters of complaint came from Texas, Arizona, and California, areas to which Mexican migration had become established. All had communities of Spanish-speaking individuals within almost every town.[26] As one observer noted, "It is all but natural that these communities should draw unto themselves from the neighboring Republic aliens in whose veins the same blood flows and who are possessed of the same ideals and aspirations, aliens speaking the same language, having the same customs, and professing the same religion."[27]

While the only reliable statistical information is restricted to the category of legal immigrants, the figures are clear and probably reflect a tendency for migrants in general (See Table 8.4). The astonishing fact is that 71.1 percent of Mexican immigrants intended to settle in Texas, and, of course, most of these would have been bound for San Antonio or points in south Texas that already had sizeable Mexican populations. Arizona was the next largest area of intended settlement, accounting for 12.4 percent of total immigration, and California was third with 8 percent. All other states combined totaled only 8.3 percent. By the end of the decade, California was beginning to overtake Arizona as the second choice for residence. In both 1919 and 1920, more chose the West Coast state, with its railroads and booming agriculture, than Arizona.

The impact on border communities and the border states in general was considerable. In many areas, local women's groups were among the first to come to grips with the problems both caused and faced by the migrants. For example, women in Pasadena, California, called on the mayor of that municipality to improve the living conditions of the town's Mexican residents. As the Los Angeles *Times* reported in 1913, Pasadena, one of the most prosperous communities in the country, had a teeming Mexican slum, where the people were said to be "packed like sardines." Children frequently had no sanitary facilities at home and had to be bathed by teachers when they came to school. People were jammed in ten to twelve to a room in little houses, which usually had no sewer connec-

Table 8.4
Intended Destination of Legal Mexican Immigrants into the United States

Year	Texas	Arizona	California	All Other States
1911	15,218	1,737	968	861
1912	18,494	1,784	894	829
1913	6,749	2,465	874	866
1914	9,180	2,171	811	927
1915	7,703	1,659	811	820
1916	12,060	2,607	952	1,579
1917	7,981	4,307	1,454	2,696
1918	11,661	2,067	1,666	2,208
1919	20,952	2,187	2,743	2,962
1920	37,210	4,767	5,691	3,374
Totals	147,208	25,751	16,864	17,122
		Percent of Total Legal Immigration		
	71.1%	12.4%	8.1%	8.3%

Source: *CGI,* 1911–20.

tions. According to the report, the Mexicans, who for the most part had been brought in by the railroads, were being herded like cattle, or perhaps worse. The mayor, responding to the women's complaints, replied that sewer connections would be put in and the streets paved. In a statement reflecting the confusion of local authorities in other localities faced with the same problems, he commented, "I do not know how it got that way; it just grew from bad to worse."[28]

San Antonio was one of the cities most affected during the decade. Refugees of all social classes streamed into the city from the first rumblings of the Revolution. Francisco I. Madero, the Apostle of the Revolution, had gone there to issue his Plan of San Luis Potosí in 1910. Most of the rest of the Madero family had migrated there during the factional violence that followed his death, hiring an entire train in 1916 to take them, their many retainers, and most of their movable property to the Texas city.[29] As early as January 1914, the San Antonio *Express* reported that refugees were pouring into the city and settling in the "corrals," or shacks, along South Laredo Street. San Antonians were concerned about the problem not only for humanitarian reasons, but also because of the public health hazard these settlements presented. One writer, protesting the attitude of some Anglos that "they don't have any connection with us," pointed out:

> If you could go down there into those filthy hovels and see men and women and children, ragged, uncombed, unwashed, sitting about dirty tables in smoke laden, foul coops, called rooms, cracking and picking out pecans by the quart for the local market, you might begin to realize that those people who live in such degradation may come in close touch with you. For how do you know that the big pecans in your nut cake, your fruit cake, your salad or ice cream have not been handled by those same dirty fingers and left standing for days in rooms where the air is so bad it staggers one just about to enter?[30]

Again, it was the women's groups that rallied to deal with the problem. They first began to work in an eight-block area that surrounded the Navarro School. Estimates were that between six and eight thousand Mexicans lived in this tiny area and that at least one thousand of these were "helpless refugees from Mexico." To aid the people of this neighborhood, the Women's Board of Missions of the Methodist Episcopal Church South had instituted the Wesley Community home. The Home helped provide the necessities of life to the migrants and established a free kindergarten for at least a few of the children.[31] A short time later, the Christian Women's Board of Missions, headquartered in Indianapolis, opened the Mexican Institute, noted as "one of the finest and best equipped plants for settlement work to be found in the South."[32]

Migration was also changing the character of the city. In January 1915, the *Express* reported that the thousands of refugees from the fighting in northern Mexico were bringing their culture with them and also contributing to the economy of San Antonio. A pottery works to provide the immigrants with their accustomed earthenware had been established, and three or four tortilla factories were reported in operation. The Mexicans, according to the *Express*, smoked constantly, contributing a haze to the entire area of settlement. The favorite tobacco was said to be "Black Horse," a product reported to be as strong as its name indicated. Factories to produce Mexican cigarettes had also been established, and the Mexican women and children employed there could each produce thousands daily. The same article listed what the economic impact was believed to be:

> Two to three thousand of the rich class.
> Five to eight thousand of the middle class.
> Twenty thousand of the laboring class.
> Permanent investment of possibly half a million dollars.
> Tenants in from 2,500 to 3,000 houses that might otherwise be vacant.
> A greater guest list at all big and family hotels and boarding houses.
> The establishment of two new newspapers, a pottery works,

> mills where tortilla meal is ground, three cigarette factories, a new movie house and theater, more grocery shops and bakeries and new restaurants on almost every street in little Mexico.
>
> A daily expenditure at the lowest estimate of $10,000.[33]

In addition, at least some Texans were concerned with the provision of public education for the migrants, and a campaign to provide schooling for the Mexican children was started by Mr. J. A. Phillips of San Antonio. In February 1915, he addressed the state superintendent of public intruction on this question, pointing out that an uneducated citizenry was a danger to society and an injustice to those deprived of education. He stated: "The general effect of the public school is to create wealth, material as well as moral and intellectual. Conversely crime is prevented. The wealth of the wealthy is not due to their own self efforts, but to peace, intelligence and harmony among people generally." Phillips appealed to the superintendent to educate children of all nationalities and presented a petition from himself and other concerned citizens. This petition pointed out that there was an almost universal indifference among both Mexicans and "Americans" in Texas to the education of Mexican children and that only about sixteen thousand of the sixty-six thousand Mexican children in Texas were receiving any sort of education at all. Specific recommendations were put forward, many addressed to the problems of making the children feel welcome in the schools and of recognizing and providing for the special administration of programs designed for their benefit. The result of this petition, however, seems to have been insignificant.[34]

Unfortunately, the large size of Mexican migration during the decade, in combination with World War I and the resulting concern about a potential fifth column in the substantial German settlements in Texas, stimulated a strong Americanization movement in the schools. In 1920, a report on the teaching of the social sciences in the Texas high schools warned that:

> The Great War . . . revealed to America its weakness of unassimilated aliens, native and foreign-born, and set in motion the various agencies for counteracting this weakness. Now that that titanic struggle has ceased, the heedless may think that there is no longer a need for this phase of patriotic activity. But such is not true: Americanization is active patriotism.[35]

The report went on to point out that Texas, with a total population of almost 4 million, had 241,938 residents who were foreign-born. Of these, 67,295 were illiterate, and some 29,710 children of foreign-born parents could not read and write. This figure, combined with the figures for the native-born, both black and white, gave a total of 282,904 illiterates in the state, "a mass of ignorance that offers a most vulnerable broadside to the machinations of the enemies of the nation."[36] It seems clear, given the emphasis placed on public schools by the German residents of Texas, that most of the illiterates with foreign-born parents were Mexican.

In 1923, the argument went on to include even those private and parochial schools in the state that gave instruction principally in a foreign language. These schools, of course, were those serving the Germans and Spanish-speaking communities. The call for a law against such schools came from the Texas State Department of Education, which argued in its *Handbook of Information as to Education in Texas* that "a state may, with safety, admit as residents only those capable of being assimilated—those who can adopt its standards of living, its language, and its ideals of citizenship and of government." The law proposed would require that all private and sectarian schools and private tutors make English the medium of instruction, so that the child would "grow, from childhood, into the habits, customs, and ideals for which our state should stand. The child of foreign parentage must learn in Texas schools the lessons which we would teach to every future Texan."[37]

Migration also had an effect on Arizona. Substantial social problems were developing from migration and the mixture of peoples in Arizona, even at the beginning of the decade. In a report on admissions to the state mental institution at the beginning of the decade, of 141 admissions, 26 were of Mexican origin, and only one of these was a native of Arizona. These figures no doubt reflect that most persons with emotional problems were treated at home, if at all possible. They also reflect, though, the profound mental stresses that accompany migration.

The state reform school, with ninety-six admissions, reported that eleven were Mexican-born, but of the native-born forty-eight had Mexican parents and four had Mexican American parents. Sixty-four of those entering were Catholic. Again, Anglos were probably much less likely to wind up in reform school after committing an offense, but the figures are still striking.

Even more striking is the fact that of 493 prisoners in the state prison in June 1911, 273 were Mexican, as opposed to 152 whites, 31 Indians, 34 blacks, 1 Chinese, and 1 Japanese. Of the 277 prisoners admitted during that fiscal year, 138 were foreign-born and at least 117 of those were Mexican. Four more were listed as being from Lower California.[38]

The situation in Texas was somewhat different. The Mexican proportion of the prison population was only slightly higher than its official representation in the Texas population as a whole. The 1910 census shows that 3.87 percent of the residents of Texas were Mexican nationals; in 1920, the figure had risen to 5.35 percent. It is also important to realize that these figures were probably considerably lower than the actual number of Mexican nationals in the population. This underreporting would be particularly acute in 1920, after the new immigration law had taken effect and Mexican nationals accurately reporting their place of birth might be fearful of deportation. On September 1, 1910, the penitentiary population of the state showed only 5.17 percent Mexican nationals, and this figure had risen only slightly to 6.1 percent by January 1, 1912. Mexicans were also listed *by race* in these prison reports, and these figures were considerably higher. On September 1, 1910, 10.14 percent of the prisoners were Mexican by race, as compared to 11.17 percent on January 1, 1912.[39] It is important to note that the term Mexican applied to both Mexican nationals and persons who were Mexican in appearance and language, but who had been born in the United States. In the Texas of this period, even native-born persons of Mexican culture were not really thought of as "Americans," much less citizens.

The Mexicans in the Texas prison system were segregated by race, sometimes with the blacks and sometimes alone. One of their camps at the Sugarland prison farm was reported by an observer to be "ship-shape," and the convicts, who called their supervisor C. L. Jones "padre mío," were "getting along splendidly." According to the report, this situation was in marked contrast to the camps of other prisoners, both black and white, which were described as dismal. Nevertheless, the miserable conditions even for the clean and resourceful Mexican convicts at Sugarland were reflected by the fact that in one calendar year, 77 of the men with Spanish surnames were reported as having had malaria attacks, and 29 others were suffering from other maladies ranging from injuries to Paris-green poisoning, which resulted from the use of a common insecticide. Thus, at least 106 Mexicans and Mexican Americans, of no more than 388 in the entire prison system, were seriously ill in a one-year period. The proportion was probably much higher, as the report of illness was restricted to only one part of the system. Still, the camp reportedly had no doctor, though remedies were said to be administered by a "competent man."[40]

Refuge on the U.S. side of the border was far from ideal, and social problems that have persisted until the present were already developing. North Americans were not always welcoming, and the different culture and language of the migrants were perceived as irritants or even dangers to American institutions. Problems of education for the migrants and their children were beginning to be discussed, although the major remedy contemplated involved the assimilation, or "Americanization," of the new arrivals. Nevertheless, the migration was seen by many groups, especially Southwestern employers, as both beneficial and necessary to the economy of the region, and they were outspoken in their criticism of the laws that would restrict the free flow of Mexicans northward. Even the San Antonio *Express* recognized the economic significance, as both producers and consumers, of the migrants from the south. Women's groups and especially church groups, then as now, made an effort to ameliorate the suffering of the uprooted. During most of the decade, however, movement by Mexicans across the border was both legal and virtually unhindered. Only after restrictions were placed on immigration in 1917 did Mexicans begin to have difficulty in entering, leading immediately to the growth of the illegal activity of alien smuggling, and the development of negative attitudes toward Mexicans on the part of immigration authorities. Still, Mexican migrants did not lack supporters on the U.S. side of the border who spoke strongly about their good character as well as their importance to the economy. The massive migration stimulated by the violence and socioeconomic dislocation during the Mexican Revolution from 1910 to 1920 formed a foundation for continuing movement northward.

9

Trade, Arms, and Revolutionaries

Throughout the years of the Mexican Revolution, trade on the U.S.-Mexican border continued at a high level despite the violence and insecurity, the economic disorganization south of the border, and the difficulties of shipment as well as payment. Goods and people continued to flow back and forth, although circumstances changed, laws and proclamations in both countries attempted to impose restrictions, and the kinds of merchandise involved shifted toward the requirements of the various revolutionary forces operating in the border area. The economic relationship on the border was symbiotic as it is today, and both sides adjusted to the necessities imposed by the times. Trade, both legal and illegal, was changed, but certainly neither stopped nor even diminished by revolutionary conditions. In fact, as revolutionary leaders sold off cattle and other moveable items of value from confiscated ranches, purchasing power probably increased in northern Mexico, providing money principally for arms. Certainly the magnitude of trade between the United States and Mexico increased significantly between 1910 and 1920. Only during 1915, the year of bloody struggle between revolutionary leaders Francisco Villa and Alvaro Obregón, did the figures for legal trade dip significantly from preceding years. From 1915 on, trade continued upward until the end of the decade (See Table 9.1).

Much of the trade occurring in the border area was not registered in official figures. Smuggling had long been a way of life in the region and

Table 9.1
Official Statistics for U.S.-Mexico Trade, 1911–20 (U.S. dollars)

Year	Imports into the U.S. from Mexico	Percent of Total Imports into the U.S.	Exports to Mexico from the U.S.	Percent of Total Exports of the U.S.
1911	57,450,111	3.76	61,281,715	3.00
1912	65,915,313	3.98	52,847,129	2.40
1913	77,543,842	4.28	54,383,424	2.21
1914	92,690,566	4.89	38,748,793	1.64
1915	77,612,691	4.64	34,164,447	1.24
1916	(97,676,544)	(4.44)	47,945,519	(1.11)
	105,065,780		54,270,283	
1917	(112,138,677)	(4.22)	(79,004,597)	(1.26)
	130,526,935		110,829,375	
1918	(140,659,542)	(4.78)	(107,077,033)	(1.81)
	158,643,427		97,788,736	
1919	148,926,376	3.81	131,455,101	1.66
1920	179,331,755	3.40	207,858,497	2.53

Source: *Commercial Relations of the United States, 1911–1920.*

The figures for 1911–15 are for fiscal years, running July 1 to June 31.

For 1916 through 1918, the figures for the fiscal year, July 1 to June 31, are given in parentheses. The figures without parentheses are for the calendar year, January 1 to December 31.

For 1919 and 1920, figures are for the calendar year only.

continued at what may be assumed to be a high level throughout the Revolution. One of the offending groups most regularly recorded was the Yaqui Indians, who went in and out of Arizona, clandestinely purchasing arms and returning with them to perpetuate their struggle against the Mexican government in Chihuahua and Sonora. Enrique Creel, the Chihuahuan who served as Mexican ambassador to the United States in 1907, protested in that year to the United States government that the practice of smuggling arms to the Yaquis had been resumed and that it was causing great difficulties in the areas in which they operated. He appealed for assistance from the United States to "end this war of the savage against humanity and civilization," emphasizing that the Yaquis did no harm without arms, but became fanatical fighters and grim menaces as soon as they had obtained them. Mexican forces had been unable to contain them, and they had continued to maraud despite the arming of civilians to pursue them. The governor of Arizona responded to a subsequent inquiry from the U.S. secretary of interior on this matter that he had notified the border counties to exercise the "utmost diligence" to stop the trade in arms to the Indians. In spite of the efforts of authorities on both sides of the line and a peace treaty signed in 1909, the trade continued throughout the years of the Mexican Revolution.[1]

The difficulties of border enforcement may be seen in the report from Del Rio customs agent D. R. Dowe in December 1910, in which he pointed out that the entire Big Bend area from San Francisco Creek at Sanderson, Texas, to El Paso, a distance of four hundred miles, had only eight men to guard the border. Further, the U.S. side was sparsely populated, while the Mexican side had many small settlements occupied, according to Dowe, by a "class who are by nature inclined to lawlessness." Dowe further reported that several officers had lost their lives already in their attempts to stop illegal trade. The border agents received little help from state or local authorities, as the county seats of most areas fronting on the river were actually located eighty to one hundred miles from the river and only rarely did sheriffs or state rangers visit the border region.[2]

Of course, the first and most crucial trade problem during the revolutionary decade was that of arms and ammunition. As early as November 16, 1910—only a few weeks after Madero had escaped from prison in Mexico and arrived on North American soil, and four days before the date he had set for a mass uprising against Díaz—federal officials in San Antonio discovered a cache of one hundred rifles and seventy-five thousand rounds of ammunition ready for shipment to rebels in Mexico. According to the San Antonio *Express*, never before had such a large quantity of arms been purchased in the United States for presumed use in revolutionary Mexico. The *Express* concluded that "so many rifles being uncovered gives color to the belief that San Antonio has again been selected as one of the revolutionary headquarters and that efforts are being made to concentrate a great quantity of arms here."[3] Indeed, as noted before, San Antonio *was* a center of revolutionary activity as well as a major supplier of all kinds of goods to Mexico and would continue to be so throughout the course of the violence (See Chapter 2).

A few weeks later, several large shipments of air rifles destined for Mexico from a St. Louis manufacturer were held up at the border after the Porfirian government declared them contraband. According to the shipper, the rifles were toys destined for the Mexican Christmas trade. In January 1911, the Del Rio customs agent, Dowe, reported to the collector of customs in Eagle Pass that he had observed three Mexicans who came down regularly on the train from San Antonio, always arriving with one to four heavily loaded trunks. After disappearing for an hour or so, they would return with empty trunks and catch the train back to San Antonio. He assumed that they were smuggling weapons across the border. Dowe also, at the urging of customs officials, tracked a suspected smuggler named Gabriel Herrera and discovered the recently abandoned camp where Herrera had met with fourteen presumed revolutionaries. Later he discovered the cave where Herrera was storing the arms.[4]

Naturally, this influx of weapons was viewed with alarm and indignation by the government of President Díaz. The Mexican ambassador informed the U.S. secretary of state on January 19, 1911 that Madero and his supporters were "boldly and flagrantly" violating U.S. neutrality laws in their revolutionary activities conducted on the U.S. side of the line. The secretary maintained that there had been no such violations, although he promised future vigilance. Under continuing pressure, the secretary on January 24 again wrote the Mexican ambassador, informing him that the "mere fact that a man is engaged in revolutionary undertakings in another country does not render his presence in the U.S. illegal" and that the "sale of arms and ammunition to individuals does not constitute unneutral conduct." Two weeks later, the U.S. acting secretary of state added that the United States intended to enforce the neutrality laws, but that commercial trading in arms and ammunition was forbidden neither by international law nor by U.S. neutrality laws. He added, probably correctly, that it was not possible for the Federal executive to prohibit such transactions and, somewhat less plausibly, that almost all of the reports of such violations had turned out to be "groundless rumors."[5]

Meanwhile, U.S. troops were dispatched to Brownsville, Laredo, Del Rio, and Eagle Pass to aid civil authorities in enforcing neutrality laws, although they were cautioned not to cross into Mexico, as there was no agreement authorizing such action.[6] The problem was illustrated by the U.S. acting secretary of war, who wrote to the secretary of state on February 23 that 80 percent of the Mexican population on both sides of the river and most of the Americans sympathized with the rebels. He added that most residents of the area agreed on the desirability of the patrol system that had been set up by the U.S. forces, as it seemed to have had some success in preventing violations of the law. The troops of the Mexican government, he noted, did virtually no patrolling of the border.[7] Meanwhile, Oscar B. Colquitt, governor of Texas, indignant at the potential danger to Texans posed by fighting on the border of his state, ordered the Texas Rangers to arrest Madero for violating U.S. neutrality laws. The governor informed President Taft on February 23, 1911, that such action would be taken, and he requested permission to send his men across the Rio Grande in pursuit of rebels and bandits. Permission was denied (See Chapter 2).[8]

The government in Washington, however, was beginning to realize that the Díaz government was unable to contain the rebellion, although the Maderistas had won no major battles. By March 17, 1911, the Department of Justice had concluded that perhaps it could control the shipment of arms on a case-by-case basis, but acknowledged that there was no specific statute that directly forbade the shipment of arms. By March 23, the U.S. ambassador to Mexico, Henry Lane Wilson, was informing the secretary of state that Díaz and the most powerful man in his government, José Yves Limantour, were unable to develop a plan to unite against the rebels and that "if the situation is to be saved at all, it will be by the military precautions of President Taft almost exclusively."[9] The possibility that Díaz would prevail became even slimmer when Madero's forces, commanded by Pancho Villa and Pascual Orozco, took Ciudad Juárez on May 10, 1911, thus affording the rebels a major international port across the frontier from El Paso, one of the most important border trading cities.

Madero's victory led to speculation in the border states about future trade regulations. On May 12, the San Antonio *Express*, concerned, no doubt, about that city's major role in Mexican commerce, noted that the State Department was taking no position on trade, indicating that the administration of neutrality laws was in the purview of the Department of Justice, while the control of the exportation of arms and supplies was the responsibility of the Department of the Treasury. Meanwhile, the Department of War continued to follow its original instructions to "execute the neutrality laws as they understood them" and to conform to any change in practice suggested by either State or Treasury.

Trade in regular supplies was continuing between Juárez and El Paso, but no decision had as yet been made on arms since there had been no effort to transport them. The assumption was that the past rule would be maintained: regular dealers could continue in the arms trade. Meanwhile, the Madero government had taken control in Juárez, and Madero himself would appoint his own customs officials.[10] By May 13, the *Express* was reporting with relief that Madero had opened the customs house at Juárez the previous day and that the U.S. government had decided that there need be no interruption in trade provided such commerce did not violate the neutrality laws. Military commanders would let all materials pass that had cleared U.S. customs. It was made clear, however, that this action on the part of the U.S. government in no way implied official recognition of the Madero belligerency.[11]

The El Paso Morning *Times*, even more concerned with the events directly across the river, reported that the rebels had interpreted the government position to mean that arms and ammunition could be passed freely through El Paso-Juárez and were making arrangements for large purchases.[12] Apparently passage was not altogether free, however, for by November of the same year federal authorities had to ban "international funerals" after discovering that many coffins contained rifles instead of bodies. At Laredo, for example, five to ten such funerals were taking place daily until the deception was discovered.[13]

The internal situation in Mexico had altered substantially by 1911. On May 21, Madero had signed a treaty with the Mexican government that ended the immediate fighting. Although Díaz was not completely aware of what the agreement included, his own resignation as well as that of Limantour, his minister of finance, had been promised. Finally, after large demonstrations in Mexico City that Díaz ordered put down by the army and that entailed great loss of life, the president resigned on May 25 and left for exile in Paris. After the interim presidency of Francisco León de la Barra, Madero came to office on November 6, 1911. At that time, Madero himself, soon faced by local insurgencies of various kinds, began to request the strict enforcement of neutrality laws. Again, the United States was eager to avoid direct involvement in Mexican internal affairs. The Department of State pointed out in a memo to the attorney general that a "clear distinction" should be drawn between "a vigorous enforcement of our neutrality statutes and activities such as are seemingly desired by the Mexican Government which if carried out would amount in effect to cooperation in putting down revolution."[14] Several days later, Madero issued his own decree for a three-month embargo on arms, munitions, and war matériel, exempting only explosives for mining and industrial purposes. The decree was indefinitely extended on May 5, 1912.[15]

Meanwhile, on March 13, 1912, the U.S. Senate, indicating that the unrest in northern Mexico was leading to a serious and potentially dangerous situation in the state of Texas, authorized President Taft to prohibit the exportation of coal or any other war matériel from any point in the United States. On March 14, Taft embargoed arms shipments to Mexico.[16] Originally, it seemed that the order would apply to the Madero government as well and might include foodstuffs, clothing, and regular hardware. However, by the end of the month it was clear that the less lethal items could be shipped freely and that the Madero government could order war matériel on a case-by-case basis.[17]

War matériel had also been more strictly defined by the attorney general in a note to the president, in which he indicated that prohibited goods should be "articles primarily and ordinarly used for military purposes in time of war, such as weapons, projectiles, cartridges, ammunition of all sorts, parts used to repair such arms, raw materials used to manufacture ammunition, all explosive substances, implements used to manufacture or repair arms and war materials."[18]

By April 1912, arms were flowing again in large quantities to the Madero government.[19] When Woodrow Wilson became president of the United States on March 4, 1913, the embargo was still in place, but President Madero of Mexico was not. He had fallen victim to Huerta's coup the previous month, and the violence of the Revolution was again on the upswing. Nevertheless, Wilson continued the embargo, although this decision helped Huerta, the new president of Mexico, and worked to the detriment of the Constitutionalists, former supporters of Madero who were trying to overthrow Huerta. Carranza, leader of the Constitutionalists, wanted the United States either to lift the embargo or to enforce it on all sides in the Mexican conflict, but it was not rescinded for almost a year.[20]

Meanwhile, the smuggling of arms continued at a high level. The enforcement of the neutrality laws in the United States was not initially rigid, and many cases of neutrality violations involving arms shipments were dismissed on the grounds that the shipments had not actually been delivered on the Mexican side. In May 1913, however, the Supreme Court ruled that any attempt to carry arms from the United States into Mexico was a violation of both the congressional resolution and the presidential proclamation on the arms embargo. Many new arrests were anticipated as a result of this new interpretation.[21]

Despite the law, smuggling continued. Even children were involved in the trade, two being apprehended by authorities in El Paso when they attempted to cross the line with ten thousand rounds of 30/30 ammunition loaded in wagons. Although they were detained, the San Antonio *Express* noted that they would not be charged. The commanding general of the Southern Department, Tasker Bliss, reported that it was impossible for him to enforce neutrality laws completely along the international boundary, even though most of the troops of his command were engaged in this effort. Violations continued, "notwithstanding the employment of all legal and perhaps some extra-legal means" to prevent them. The border remained "perfectly open," as the region was sparsely populated, and what population there was sympathized with one or another of the revolutionary movements. Moreover, smuggling was a profitable activity in an economically devastated region and in addition offered the local population some protection against more dangerous bandit activity. Bliss went so far as to suggest that since the Mexicans could not or would not police their side of the line, the United States ought to do the job for them. He proposed that the army take over a "few border towns," while leaving the control of the courts and the municipal government in Mexican hands.

A few months later the situation seemed no better to him, and he protested the vagueness of the law, which placed too much responsibility on the junior officers and troopers who were called on to interpret it. He forecast that a "considerable proportion" of the U.S. Army would have to remain on the border for an indefinite period of time because of the Mexican situation.[22] Meanwhile, Governor Colquitt of Texas wrote to the secretary of state reporting on smuggling activities near Eagle Pass and complaining that, although Texas authorities had attempted to aid the federal government in the enforcement of the neutrality laws, they were no longer doing so because "the Secretary of War (had) stated that it was none of our business" and "I did not wish to have any conflict with the Federal agents or authority."[23] He later indicated that despite the fact that President Taft had asked for help from Texas in enforcing these laws, he had asked state officials to desist until a direct request came from President Wilson. He added that there was "absolutely no doubt" that violations of the laws by both the Constitutionalists and the Huertistas occurred daily.[24]

Huerta, moreover, was attempting to control future traffic in explosives to the Constitutionalists, whom he considered rebels, by requesting that all U.S. exports of this nature be passed through the Mexican War Department. The acting secretary of state replied that arms exports were "a domestic matter" and that exceptions to the arms embargo could not be contingent on the opinion of the Mexicans. He added in a note that was no doubt supposed to be reassuring that "no exception is granted when there appears to be any probability of its being used in any way to promote domestic disorder in Mexico."[25] Meanwhile, a lack of understanding of what actually constituted war matériel led to an occasional absurdity. In August 1913, the Constitutionalists were reported to be on the U.S. side cutting the brass buttons off a shipment of khaki uniforms that had been stopped by U.S. authorities, hoping to get them admitted as "clothing."[26]

Finally, by the end of January 1914, President Wilson, eager to extricate himself from the "irregular position" the United States had taken with regard to the contending forces in Mexico, was ready to end the embargo. As U.S. Secretary of State Bryan wrote to one of his ambassadors, this stand was taken with regret, since "settlement by civil war carried to its bitter conclusion is a terrible thing but it must come now, whether we wish it or not, unless some outside power is to undertake to sway Mexico with its armed forces from end to end, which would be the beginning of a still more difficult problem."[27] Unfortunately, the U.S. did not maintain a hands-off attitude for long, occupying Veracruz in April of the same year.

In any case, on February 3, 1914, Wilson lifted the embargo in the hope that Huerta, whom Wilson had come to loathe, would be overthrown. Huerta reported that he was not concerned since he believed, probably correctly, that the "rebels" were already receiving all the arms for which they could pay. Pancho Villa, however, was overjoyed and was reported to have placed large orders for military goods with several arms merchants who had called on him on February 3. He confidently predicted that Huerta would be overthrown within six months as a result, a prediction that turned out to be overly generous, since Huerta had fled the country by the end of July. The Constitutionalists also asked for the release of 1.5 million rounds of ammunition and five hundred rifles that U.S. authorities had seized during the previous months.[28] Unfortunately for them, however, yet another embargo, applicable to both Federales and Constitutionalists, was put in place by Wilson when the United States occupied Veracruz in April and was not canceled again until September.

Still, as the violence of the struggle between Huerta and the Constitutionalists escalated from April through the end of July, smuggling continued at a high level.[29] The Washington *Post* reported that there was a hardware store in El Paso that had sold enough Winchester rifles and cartridges in the two previous years to kill every person in Mexico, and Senator Lippett of Rhode Island publicly abhorred the "carnival of crime and carnage . . . whose confetti has been flying bullets . . . sent across the American border and put into the hands of Mr. Villa and his associates with the consent and approval of the President of the United States."[30]

Aiding the smugglers was a Treasury Department ruling that contraband war matériel could be confiscated, but those engaged in the illegal trade could not be arrested, since the Taft embargo had had the authority of a congressional resolution, while Wilson's embargo did not have congressional sanction. As a result, the El Paso Morning *Times* anticipated a big increase in arms traffic.[31] Military officials estimated arms traffic at twenty thousand rounds of ammunition a day and added that the army could neither arrest the miscreants nor use firearms in preventing them from carrying out their intentions. The officers and troopers would be able to use "only their fists in case of conflict."[32]

The legal arms trade continued to open and close throughout the decade, subject principally to political considerations, with the U.S. attempting to help those it supported and handicap those it opposed. Nevertheless, as Huerta had pointed out earlier, if any faction had the money, arms from the United States were available, and the length of the U.S.-Mexican border and the lack of enforcement worked in favor of smugglers and revolutionaries bent on circumventing U.S. policies.

It was, of course, the northern revolutionaries who were most greatly helped by the easy availability of arms. Border newspapers reported the sales of cattle and other goods from Mexico, and it seems likely that a substantial proportion of the proceeds were used to buy arms and other needed items. Some revolutionary needs were filled in other ways, however. The Douglas *Oasis* reported in March 1913 that a large number of horses had been stolen in the area of the Arizona border, that they had been tracked south, and that they were believed to be in use by the "volunteers" in the Mexican struggle. One group who benefited from the trade in arms were the Sonorans, who were able to raise revenues from the continued mining and exportation of copper from that state (See Chapter 3).

The usual source of the arms were the many sporting goods merchants and hardware stores in the border area. One such source was Penney and Robinson of Phoenix who wrote to Sonoran revolutionary governor Plutarco Elías Calles that they were sending along a catalog of baseball goods, as they had previously done a good business in his area, but announcing that they also had available for delivery between May 1 and May 15 (probably 1916) two hundred thousand rounds of Winchester soft point cartridges, F.O.B. Phoenix at the cost of $40.00 per case of one thousand, and fifty to one hundred Winchester carbines. They urged haste in replying, as they intended to close out the lot within ten days. The alternative purchasers, though not mentioned in the letter, were probably the Constitutionalists' opponents and various leaders on the right.[33] In fact, the amount of war matériel Villa was purchasing led Carranza to order his consul in San Francisco, R. P. Denegri, not to approve any arms shipments to Mexico because most of them were going to "our enemies." The traffic, Denegri reported to his friend Calles, was heavy.[34]

As the papers of Lázaro de la Garza, one of Villa's purchasing agents, make clear, Villa was engaged in constant trade across the border during the revolutionary years. During 1914, the period of the major struggle against Huerta, this trade was particularly active. A look at a few of the transactions during one week in February gives a sense of the nature of the trade.

On February 24 of that year, De la Garza reported to Villa that Felix Sommerfeld, a ubiquitous figure on the border who had close ties with the German secret service, had available for purchase a three-inch cannon (equivalent to 75 millimeters, according to the report), for $5,500, with five hundred to one thousand projectiles for $15 apiece. He further reported that he had already shipped a car of ammunition in charge of Alfonso Madero with 160 cases of 30/40 ammunition from the firm of Shelton-Payne and a rifle order from Sommerfeld. Villa replied quickly, urging him to send along two thousand pounds of black powder immediately, in addition to two thousand 38-calibre short cartridges and five rolls of steel wire. He further encouraged him to get Sommerfeld and José Sepúlveda, another agent, moving on the purchases of powder and other materials. The next day, Villa wired that the powder was in El Paso consigned to Raúl Madero and that it should be sent immediately. De la Garza replied efficiently that he had many boxes there for Madero and for Sepúlveda, and that he would send them immediately if they contained the powder.[35]

The goods were being paid for largely by the proceeds from the sales of cattle and to a smaller degree ixtle and cotton, which Villa was taking from confiscated ranches in his area, although for a few days he ordered that sales of cattle be stopped because such export had been prohibited by the Constitutionalists. When de la Garza protested that expenses had far exceeded the value of the cattle sold up until that time, however, Villa sent him 100,000 pesos in gold by his brother, Hipólito, to cover the deficit and then resumed cattle sales. Villa added, however, that De la Garza was not to buy anything that was not essential.[36]

Villa's agents became fearful later in the month, when Sommerfeld reported that "enemies and interventionists" in the United States were lobbying the government of that country to embargo arms and ammunition. De la Garza urged haste in purchasing. He went on to add that he was "working hard with Carothers and the head of Customs Zach Cobb," who, he reported, were "good friends of the administration," in order to persuade them to use their influence to prevent such a prohibition. He added that a million cartridges had recently been confiscated, but that fortunately they had come C.O.D.[37]

On February 28, De la Garza delivered to the Villista Cuartel General in Ciudad Juárez one hundred rifles and fifty boxes of 30/40 shells as well as two hundred rifles from Shelton-Payne, and a Colt 7-mm. machine gun, along with twenty-four belts for the gun and a machine to fill the belts. These would serve for the defense of that border city. The big excitement on that day, though, was the arrival of Villa's recently purchased airplane, which had already made "two magnificent flights" over the city.[38]

The trade did not always go smoothly since De la Garza was not always able to find the articles that Villa needed. The black powder Villa requested, for example, could only be located in New York. De la Garza was requested to scout for sources in Dallas, San Antonio, and other, closer points. When he inquired whether the thick black powder that was available in El Paso would work, Villa replied testily that he needed fine powder and that the machine-gun parts he had ordered from Shelton-Payne had not arrived. De la Garza kept looking for the powder and informed Villa that Shelton-Payne had to know exactly *what* parts were required before they could ship. Villa—at that time preparing for the major battle of Torreón, the center of the agriculturally important Laguna region—was understandably impatient. A further problem was the differing calibres of the arms and ammunition being sent. Villa plaintively asked De la Garza on March 12 to tell Sommerfeld to purchase *only* 7-mm. and 30/40 Mausers because his men's confusion when many different sizes were received was "terrible."[39]

Villa purchased more than arms, however. One of his largest orders during 1914 was for hats, uniforms, and slickers. De la Garza authorized payment from his account at the cooperative Rio Grande Valley Bank and Trust in El Paso, in which institution he deposited almost $100,000 between July 31 and November 20, 1914, and from which he withdrew only $50,000 for purchases. The size of the U.S. trade with Villa can be imagined, as this account was only one of several used. The Rio Grande Valley Bank also helped De la Garza by receiving a "sporting goods" order for him from A. G. Spaulding of Massachusetts and F.A.O. Schwartz and paying the shipping charges, which amounted to between $300 and $400.[40]

Another important item in the trade were banknotes, which were printed in the United States. In March 1914, 21,480,000 pesos in Villista banknotes were received, 2,000,000 pesos of which were given to De la Garza and Sepúlveda as commissions, although, of course, their value was far less than the value of a peso in gold. Nevertheless, being a Villista purchasing agent seems to have been a very good business.[41]

Villa was further concerned with the well-being of the civilian populace, as indicated in his order to De la Garza on March 27, 1914, when Villa was in Gómez Palacio. Aware of the suffering caused by the lack of food supplies in the state, he asked De la Garza to acquire "the elements of first necessity": coffee, sugar, rice, and lard. He also indicated his awareness that border merchants were taking advantage of the revolutionary situation and urged him to look further north from El Paso for goods, as the Texas border suppliers were "abusing our situation." He added that this purchase was of "great importance," as "in this region there is much hunger."[42]

Villa's well-known anti-Spanish attitudes were tied to his need to finance arms and other purchases. On April 8, a large number of Spaniards, whom he had driven from the Laguna region and whose property he had confiscated, arrived at the border, but even before they had completed the trip to the international boundary, Villa was committing the money he would make on the sale of their cotton. Villa, a cockfight enthusiast, had ordered the "entire available supply of fighting fowls" from a professional breeder of gamecocks near Pensacola, Florida. The birds were to be forwarded express to Villa's relatives at Ciudad Juárez to await his arrival from the front. A few days later, Villa himself was reported to be headed to Juárez to expedite the sale of the cotton confiscated in the Laguna area, and the San Antonio *Express* claimed that he was "anxious to sell." Villa also indicated that he would not pursue the federal army further until his men had had time to rest and had been reprovisioned with food, new uniforms, and new equipment, all, presumably, to be purchased from U.S. suppliers.[43]

Trade on the border continued to boom as long as revolutionaries had the money to make purchases. However, as the tide turned against the Villistas and with the dwindling of the available supply of moveable goods on the haciendas which he had provided to his subordinate leaders and to the Chihuahua state Administración General de Confiscaciones, his purchasing power declined sharply. Particularly during 1915, when the Sonoran leader Alvaro Obregón began to defeat Villa on the battlefield, Villa's credit in the U.S. dropped significantly, and the prices quoted to him rose precipitately.[44]

Meanwhile, the Sonorans were able to finance their own purchases with revenues from the state's copper mines, which operated more or less continually during that period, and from revenues from the oil regions of Tampico, which the Constitutionalists were able to control. Thus, trade, purchasing power, and access to war matériel from the United States significantly affected the eventual preponderance of the Constitutionalist military effort over the Conventionists under Villa, in turn affecting the outcome of the Mexican Revolution.

Illegal trade was by no means confined to arms and ammunition, however. As noted before, large numbers of horses, both purchased and stolen, crossed the U.S. border going south to the cowboy cavalries of the northern revolutionaries. Beef and cattle on the hoof, again both stolen and purchased, made their way in the opposite direction. The smuggling of aliens, especially the Chinese and later Mexicans themselves, into the United States was also common, as was smuggling mescal and other liquors into Arizona, nominally a dry state. Two Mexicans were even apprehended attempting to cross the border illegally carrying 1,448 pounds of garlic. Authorities on the Mexican side also tried to cut down on smuggling, as customs revenues were a major source of financing the revolutionary effort as well as local and state governments. Enforcement on both sides remained difficult, however, and corruption was common.[45]

Legal, recorded trade continued high as well. The figures for the U.S.-Mexican border ports were always a significant portion of the total trade between the two countries, although the port of New York maintained its position as the leader in both import and export trade with Mexico throughout the decade. During most years, though, the Arizona border district was the next largest in total import-export trade with Mexico, with the San Antonio area showing an enormous jump, particularly in exports, by the end of the decade. The El Paso customs district, which had been the leader on the Texas border in the late nineteenth century, was also significant (See Tables 9.2 and 9.3). Indeed, El Paso's trade can be seen to vary directly with border conditions during the decade (See Table 9.4). Dropping almost 50 percent in 1912–13, a period in which much fighting was taking place along or close to the border, it recovered to a

Table 9.2
U.S. Imports from and Exports to Mexico in Mexican Border Districts

	1910		1911	
	Imports	Exports	Imports	Exports
Arizona	10,012,562	5,756,095	9,122,499	5,345,572
Brazos de Santiago, TX	96,143	152,095	216,561	511,520
Corpus Christi	1,960,691	11,581,111	1,481,229	12,876,106
Paso del Norte	4,383,444	6,990,549	3,091,728	6,914,094
Saluria, TX	6,362,062	4,626,250	6,324,909	4,749,619

Source: *Commercial Relations of the United States, 1910–1911.*

Table 9.3
U.S. Imports from and Exports to Mexico by Customs Districts, Year Ending June 30, 1915
(Value in U.S. Dollars)

	Imports	Exports	
		Domestic	Foreign
New York	20,453,123	8,239,344	614,704
Galveston	5,186,218	2,108,135	72,147
New Orleans	16,872,049	4,253,030	44,112
El Paso	9,372,082	7,961,447	527,684
Arizona	5,039,728	3,273,129	163,998
San Francisco	2,421,237	1,295,170	292,512
Southern California	1,992,494	1,422,087	69,896
Eagle Pass	2,120,814	648,967	58,603
Laredo	4,129,471	2,067,883	99,023

Source: *Commercial Relations of the United States, 1915.*

new high in 1914–15, when the purchasing power of northern revolutionaries was increasing as a result of their control of the copper mines in Sonora and the cattle ranches and cotton resources of Chihuahua. However, in 1915–16, the period in which Villa was defeated by Obregón and he began marauding in the frontier area, trade again dropped almost 50 percent, not recovering to its 1914–15 levels until the end of the decade. At that time, exports to Mexico through El Paso had a value more than double that of imports, reflecting El Paso's importance as a commercial center supplying considerably more of Mexico than just the then economically devastated northern region.[46] Indeed, although conditions in various parts of Mexico affected trade with the United States in various ways,

Table 9.4
Dollar Value of Trade through El Paso, 1910–20

Year	Imports	Exports
1909–10	4,453,689	6,990,549
1910–11	3,156,024	6,914,094
1911–12	4,680,366	6,172,436
1912–13	3,422,768	2,555,772
1913–14	6,689,572	3,379,702
1914–15	9,392,626	8,849,891
1915–16	5,564,398	3,785,470
1916–17	3,381,138	4,790,179
1918	2,034,366	5,777,208
1919	2,699,307	7,938,122
1920	5,113,839	13,656,502

Source: Oscar J. Martínez, *Border Boom Town: Ciudad Juárez Since 1848* (Austin: University of Texas Press, 1978), 48.
*1909–17 are fiscal years; 1918–20 are calendar years.

total trade in general continued upward during the decade, and many Mexican exports seem to have been more affected by the U.S. business cycle than by the violent conditions of the Revolution.

The nature of the trade is of considerable interest. An examination of selected U.S. exports to Mexico indicates that legal trade fell considerably in particular products during the most violent years of the Revolution (See Table 9.5). In the case of firearms, obviously changes in the legal status of such exports greatly affected what was reported, and no figures for these items are available for 1916 through 1918; but still the figures for 1915, one of the most violent years of the Revolution, show an enormous increase. By 1920, as the violence was coming to an end, the figure for firearms and cartridges drops precipitously. In addition, Mexico had by this time developed some capacity to produce its own weapons and ammunition (See Chapter 7).

The demand for mining machinery also reflects the events of the Revolution. Between 1915 and 1917, when much of the fighting was taking place in the mining areas of northern Mexico, close to the border, such machinery came into Mexico at a very slow rate. By 1918, however, improving conditions led to rising investor confidence, and the figures jumped considerably. The increase by 1920 was even more dramatic. The figures for dynamite, which was used heavily in the mining industry as well as for revolutionary purposes such as blowing up bridges and railroads, showed a brief decline in 1915, reaching a high at the end of the

Table 9.5
Selected United States Exports to Mexico
(Value in U.S. Dollars)

Year	Firearms	Mining Machinery	Oil Well Machinery
1911	270,832	1,804,522*	——
1912	354,533	1,325,354*	——
1913	269,014	1,671,724*	——
1914	488,274	1,316,017*	——
1915	1,280,442	368,846	not available
1916	not available	346,854	215,613
1917	not available	732,518	217,543
1918	not available	1,336,378	468,407
1919	204,863	1,489,191	632,470
1920	31,285	2,144,929	1,600,521

Source: *Commercial Relations of the United States, 1911–1920.*
*Category including oil and "all other" mining machinery.

decade. Likewise, less violent conditions led to a rapid increase in the Mexican importation of oil field machinery in 1920. Steam engines, however, showed a slow, but relatively steady rise throughout the decade, leading to a big jump in 1920, indicating an increasing level of industrial development. In most categories, however, U.S. exports to Mexico were considerably affected by the specific course of the Revolution in particular areas.

Strikingly, however, Mexican exports to the United States during the same time period seem to have responded far more to the U.S. business cycle than they did to revolutionary conditions. During the period of time between December 1914 and August 1918, the U.S. economy was in a period of expansion stimulated by World War I. From March 1919 through January 1920, it was again contracting.[47] In most cases, specific Mexican exports to the U.S. were high during the expansion and dropped considerably during the contraction (See Table 9.6). Copper, one of the most important exports paying for the financing of the revolutionary armies during the decade, reflects this decline, as the demand for this metal dropped after the end of World War I. The decline is also quite noticeable, however, in coffee, cattle hides and sisal as well. Only cotton and particularly oil among major products continued dramatic rises as the North American economy contracted. Oil became the mainstay of the Mexican economy during the immediate postrevolutionary years. Were it not for the tremendous expansion in oil exports to the United States, the responsiveness of the Mexican economy to business conditions in the U.S.

Table 9.6
Selected Imports into the United States from Mexico
(Value in U.S. dollars)

Year	Coffee	Copper	Copper (pigs, ingots, etc.)	Cattle hides	Cotton	Oil	Sisal
1911	2,982,693	2,136,917	9,643,832	1,011,189 dry 1,778,111 gr.	9,472	60,058	11,465,854
1912	5,211,629	1,761,127	14,632,685	1,231,777 dry 2,312,522 gr.	15,802	2,142,715	10,733,880
1913	4,090,909	2,092,559	17,316,966	1,362,775 dry 2,857,797 gr.	97,680	7,062,174	15,495,574
1914	8,028,186	2,287,875	12,061,619	2,786,475 dry 3,492,426 gr.	3,989,669	10,975,611	22,980,480
1915	6,898,161	1,365,101	799,293	2,820,618 dry 4,187,964 gr.	3,662,172	8,614,858	19,236,410
1916	6,222,326	1,120,139	9,850,198	combined 7,450,377	1,549,810	11,364,828	24,696,743
1917	6,382,845	999,824	15,003,927	combined 7,785,653	2,623,421	13,677,102*	23,190,796
1918	3,336,131	854,002	11,621,389	combined 4,586,316	4,431,478	17,901,639*	47,933,760
1919	5,434,884	175,388	9,932,742	combined 5,496,673	10,168,237	29,584,587	36,659,716
1920	3,873,217	162,716	12,885,356	combined 1,704,547	10,235,905	60,732,838#	29,200,666

Source: *Commercial Relations of the United States, 1911–1920.*
*Figures given are for crude oil only.
#Another figure also given is $65,276,798.

would be quite marked in the aggregate figures. Thus, despite the strains of the Revolution and the destruction of production facilities, Mexico's production was highly influenced by U.S. demand.

Mexico's responsiveness to changes in U.S. demand calls into question the negative impact of the Mexican Revolution on the economy. Although certainly the violence of the times caused great destruction, and in some cases decapitalization, particularly in the mining industry and in agriculture, the Revolution may have had the effect of making the Mexican economy more flexible. It certainly forced significant changes in the economic structures of the country. In any event, trade with the United States during the revolutionary decade was considerably changed, but not diminished.

10

Conclusion

The 1910–20 Revolution left the border area profoundly changed. Trends already in progress were accelerated, and significant shifts in direction were put into motion. In the economic realm, the mining business never fully recovered from the violence and devastation in northern Mexico, though oil continued to increase in importance and to become the mainstay of the Mexican government through the taxes paid by the oil companies. The arrangements under which foreign, and particularly U.S., oil companies operated in Mexico became a major issue between the two countries in the 1920s. In trade, the United States continued to be Mexico's principal and most powerful partner.

Migration from Mexico into the United States continued as well and was an additional area of concern and controversy during the 1920s as Mexicans, responding to economic conditions on both sides of the border, continued to travel relatively freely back and forth across the line. Further, the massive migration of the decade from 1910 to 1920 had put in place permanent networks of Mexicans in the southwestern United States, particularly in Texas, that would furnish support for future arrivals. Although much of this migration was seen as temporary, especially by the migrants themselves, many Mexicans stayed permanently as children were born in the United States and as other ties to the new land of residence grew. The social and economic changes wrought in the United

States by this population movement have continued in increasing significance to this day.

A further legacy was the ill-will caused on both sides of the border by the violence of the Revolution. Anger was engendered from the earliest days of the fighting, as shells from the battles for Mexican border cities fell on the U.S. side, killing and injuring individuals and sometimes destroying property. Another cause of friction was the violence done to U.S. citizens and to their property in Mexico. This damage was particularly extensive in the mining regions relatively close to the border in the states of Chihuahua, Sonora, and, to some extent, Coahuila. Americans and other foreigners fleeing from these regions and from the interior of Mexico emerged with tales of danger, hardship, and even atrocity which fed the fires of indignation on the border. The so-called Plan of San Diego, which led to a number of violent incidents in South Texas, was yet another stimulus to the growth of racist anti-Mexican sentiment on the border and to the abuse of Mexicans and Mexican Americans resident on the U.S. side. Finally, the Santa Ysabel massacre, in which sixteen North American employees of the Cusi Mining Company died at the hands of Villistas led by Pablo López, and the Villista raid on U.S. territory into Columbus, New Mexico, led a reluctant but exasperated Woodrow Wilson to send troops into northern Mexico. Needless to say, Mexicans at all social and political levels were unimpressed with Wilson's distinction between a limited action to "help" the Mexican forces destroy the Villista threat and a military invasion, and thus refused to cooperate with the expedition. Had the Mexican nation not been weakened by years of civil war and had the United States not been threatened with possible entry into the war in Europe, the two might have been drawn into serious hostilities. In any case, passions ran high on both sides of the border.

Innocent Mexicans and Mexican Americans in the border area had, of course, suffered at the hands of hostile Americans during this period of time. As many as three hundred Mexicans and Mexican Americans in South Texas may have lost their lives as a result of summary executions stemming from raids linked to the Plan of San Diego in 1915 and 1916. The American occupation of Veracruz in 1914 and the introduction of American troops onto Mexican soil with the Pershing Punitive Expedition in 1916 and 1917 additionally angered Mexicans and led to increasing border tensions. Moreover, the Punitive Expedition had the unintended effect of restoring the military reputation of the largely discredited revolutionary leader and bandit Pancho Villa, whose defiance of the gringoes in the Columbus raid and whose successful evasion of American troops returned him to the heroic status he had enjoyed before the destruction of his forces in his 1915 battles against Obregón. In fact, the Punitive Expedition led to increased status for Obregón as well, as President Carranza was forced finally to accord him the status of Secretary of Defense, a portfolio he had previously reserved for himself. Carranza was forced to recognize that only Obregón possessed the military capabilities and internal support to rally the Mexican people against both the United States forces and his old adversary, Villa.

However, despite the animosities that developed between the residents of both nationalities on both sides of the border, familiarity may breed understanding as well as contempt. In the period of the early 1920s, while many U.S. interests sought to use the recognition of the post-revolutionary Obregón government as a bargaining chip in maintaining the privileged position of American capital in Mexico, U.S. border interests by and large pushed for recognition and regularization. These interests understood that a stable Mexico under Obregón's leadership would be the best insurance against the restoration of the hostilities from which residents on both sides of the border had suffered during the preceding decade. In addition, a politically stable Mexico would be most likely to develop as an economically prosperous trading partner. Therefore, border merchants were far more eager that Mexico reestablish a viable internal economy than were U.S. oil interests, who were jockeying for continued dominance of an industry that they could operate as an enclave without reference to the general economic well-being of the nation.

Another consequence of the importance of the border area during the Revolution was the closer integration of the northern periphery of Mexico into the mainstream of Mexican political life. Indeed, it was the northern revolutionaries who came to power after the Revolution, first with Coahuilan Carranza's highly nationalistic government and then in the 1920s with the presidency of the Sonoran, Obregón. Obregón, who maintained his ties both with his home state and with associates in the U.S. border states, was acutely conscious of the significance both of the border area and of Mexico's relationship with the United States. Sonorans continued to control the Mexican national government until 1934, and at least until that time, the border area remained a major focus of national concern. Since then, however, the border region again has drifted from the center of the interests of the Mexican national government and has recently become the area of major opposition to the official government party.

Finally, the Revolution, despite its antiforeign aspects, left the United States as the preeminent foreign influence in Mexico. Economically, when the United States caught cold, Mexico continued to get pneumonia. Increasingly, the ups-and-downs of the Mexican economy have come to influence the well-being of the United States as well. Politically, during the

1920s, the United States had a major effect on the institutionalization of the Mexican state, withholding foreign loans and recognition until satisfactory arrangements could be made with regard to the repayment of the Mexican foreign debt and the circumstances under which foreign oil companies could continue to operate in Mexico. These U.S. pressures ultimately led to the Mexican expropriation of the oil companies in 1938. Ironically, the weakening of the oil market in the 1980s and Mexico's now enormous foreign debt have led to a new era of dependence on the United States and its lending institutions.

Thus, though significant changes have taken place in Mexico since 1920, many of the problems and relationships of the Revolution persist to the present. As long as the United States remains economically powerful and Mexico economically vulnerable, their location side by side along thousands of miles of border will continue to foster problems strikingly similar to those faced by the two countries during the era from 1910 to 1920.

ABBREVIATIONS

AGES	Archivo del Gobierno del Estado de Sonora
AGO/VR	United States, National Archives, Villa's Revolution #2212358
ASRE	Mexico, Archivo de la Secretaría de Relaciones Exteriores
BP	William F. Buckley Papers, University of Texas at Austin
CGI	Report of the Commissioner General of Immigration
CPD	La Colección General Porfirio Díaz
CP:UT	Colquitt Papers: University of Texas at Austin
DLG	Lázaro de la Garza Archive, University of Texas at Austin
EMJ	*Engineering and Mining Journal*
EPMT	El Paso Morning *Times*
FO	Great Britain, Foreign Office Archives
FR	Papers Relating to the Foreign Relations of the United States
FRC-FW	Federal Records Center, Fort Worth
FTC	Archivo de Fernando Torreblanca
HLS	Hugh Lenox Scott Papers, Library of Congress
HMM	*Historia Moderna de México*
IMA	*Investigation of Mexican Affairs*, Senate Document 285, 66th Congress, 2nd Session
LWD	Lewis W. Douglas Papers, University of Arizona
MD 165	United States, National Archives, Military Intelligence Division, Record Group 165

NA RG 76, USMC:125	United States, National Archives, Record Group 76, Records of United States and Mexican Claims Commission, Records of the Agency of the United States
PHS	Mexico, Museo de Antropología, Patronato de la Historia de Sonora
RDS-IA	*Records of the Department of State Relating to the Internal Affairs of Mexico, 1910–1929*
SAE	San Antonio *Express*
SGS-Pemex	Mexico, Archivo Histórico de Pemex, Sistema General Sinclair
TBSOH	Trinity Border Studies Oral History Project
TSA, AG:GC	Texas State Archives, Adjutant General, General Correspondence
TSA, GP:JEF	Texas State Archives, Governors' Papers, James E. Ferguson
TSA, GP:OBC	Texas State Archives, Governors' Papers, Oscar Branch Colquitt
USDL/BI	United States, Department of Labor, Bureau of Immigration
WP	Washington *Post*

NOTES

Chapter 1

[1]Bernardo Reyes to J. G. Carbó, May 31, 1981. *La colección General Porfirio Díaz*, Legajo VI, Document 780. [Hereinafter cited as CPD, followed by legajo number and document number.]

[2]Charles W. Hackett, "The Recognition of the Díaz Government by the United States," *Southwestern Historical Quarterly*, 28 (July 1928):41. In effect, the policy was to recognize anyone controlling Mexico City. See Karl M. Schmitt, *Mexico and the United States, 1821–1973* (New York: John Wiley & Sons, 1974), 92–94. Daniel Cosío Villegas, ed., *Historia moderna de México* (9 vols.; Mexico City: Editorial Hermes, 1955–72), VI, 8–20. Hereinafter cited as *HMM*. Foster reported that the delay in recognition was construed as "proof of hostility towards Mexico." See Foster to Evarts, February 15, 1879, *Dispatches from United States Ministers to Mexico, 1823–1906*, vol. 66. Luis G. Zorilla, *Historia de las relaciones entre México y los Estados Unidos de América, 1800–1958* (2 vols.; Mexico City: Editorial Porrúa, 1965–66), I, 537–38, 556–58, 546–47, 556. Robert D. Gregg, *The Influence of Border Troubles on Relations between the United States and Mexico, 1876–1910* (Baltimore: Johns Hopkins Press, 1937), 58–80. For a complete review of the recognition controversy, see Daniel Cosío Villegas, *The United States versus Porfirio Díaz*, trans. by Nettie Lee Benson (Lincoln: University of Nebraska Press, 1963).

[4]César Sepúlveda, "Historia y problemas de los límites de México, I. La frontera norte," *Historia Mexicana*, 8 (julio–septiembre, 1958):20.

[5]Gregg, *Border Troubles*, 83–87. See also Cosío, *HMM*, VI, 34–37; César Sepúlveda, *La frontera norte de México* (Mexico City: Editorial Porrúa, 1976), 81–84.

[6]Gregg, *Border Troubles*, 12–13, 169–78. Sepúlveda, *La Frontera norte*, 82–83. Cosío, *HMM*, VI, 40–42.

[7]México, Ministerio de Relaciones Exteriores, *Correspondencia diplomática cambiada entre el gobierno de los Estados Unidos Mexicanos y los de varias potencias extranjeras* (4 vols.; Mexico City: Tip. de Gonzalo A. Esteva, 1882–87), II, 1–2.

[8]Clarence C. Clendenen, *Blood on the Border* (London: Macmillan Company, 1969), 10.

[9]Despite the decline in revolutionary activity, Mexican officials still kept close watch on anything resembling antigovernment activity or a filibustering movement. One Díaz agent reported that "Quijote Dalrymple" was trying to organize a 50,000-man "army of occupation" to attack Mexico from Texas and that "the excitable Texans who are always ready for anything relating to a piratical war against a neighboring country have received with visible enthusiasm the call of Dalrymple." See CPD, V, 3166–68, 3188.

[10]Gregg, *Border Troubles*, 12–16.

[11]Clendenen, *Blood on the Border*, 77. Gregg, *Border Troubles*, 51–61. Zorilla, *Historia*, II, 543–59.

[12]David to Morgan, Aug. 18, 1882, *Papers Relating to the Foreign Relations of the United States, 1882*, 396–97. Hereinafter cited as *FR*, followed by year and page numbers.

[13]Cosío, ed., *HMM*, VI, 227–32. Gregg, *Border Troubles*, 180–86. Sepúlveda, *La frontera norte*, 90–91.

[14]Foster to Evarts, Aug. 16, 1879, *FR, 1879*, 826–33. Luis Pombo to J. G. Carbó, Mar. 9, 1882, CPD, VII, 889.

[15]Jorge Espinosa de los Reyes, *Relaciones económicas entre México y Estados Unidos, 1870–1910* (Mexico City: Nacional Financiera, 1951), 77–84. Romero to Frelinghuysen, Mar. 14, 1884, May 20, 1884, *Notes from the Mexican Legation in the United States to the Department of State, 1821–1906*, vol. 33. Morgan to Frelinghuysen, May 17, 1884; May 18, 1884; May 20, 1884, *U.S. Ministers to Mexico*, vol. 82. Morgan to Bayard, May 8, 1886, *U.S. Ministers to Mexico*, vol. 89. Annual Message of the President, December 8, 1885, *FR, 1885*, xii–xiii.

[16]Espinosa de los Reyes, *Relaciones*, 52–54.

[17]*Ibid.*, 50–54, 64–65. Cosío, ed., *HMM*, VII, 637–38, 688–711. For most of the Porfirian period, Mexico enjoyed a favorable balance of trade. See Raymond Vernon, *The Dilemma of Mexico's Development* (Cambridge, Mass.: Harvard University Press, 1963), 45.

[18]Vernon, *Dilemma*, 42–43. French and British investment followed a similar trend, with total French investment quadrupling between 1902 and 1911.

[19]Zorilla, *Historia*, II, 89–90, 127–31.

[20]George McCutchen McBride, *The Land Systems of Mexico* (New York: American Geographical Society, 1923), 73–74. Lucio Mendieta y Núñez, *El*

problema agrario de México (9th ed.; Mexico City: Editorial Porrúa, 1966), 124–39. Jesús Silva Herzog, *El agrarismo mexicano y la reforma agraria* (Mexico City: Fondo de Cultura Económica, 1959), 112–17. Roger D. Hansen, *The Politics of Mexican Development* (Baltimore: The Johns Hopkins Press, 1971), 23–27.

[21]Vernon, *Dilemma*, 50.

[22]The extent of this decline has still not been completely determined. See Hansen, *Politics*, 20–23 and Friedrich Katz, "Labor Conditions on Haciendas in Porfirian Mexico: Some Trends and Tendencies," *Hispanic American Historical Review*, 54 (February, 1974):1–47.

[23]Cosío, ed., *HMM* VI, 321–52. Zorilla, *Historia*, II, 178–94. Alberto María Carreño, *La diplomacia extraordinaria entre México y Estados Unidos, 1789–1947* (2 vols.; 2d ed.; Mexico City: Editorial Jus, 1961), II, 232–33.

Chapter 2

[1]Mario T. García, *Desert Immigrants: The Mexicans of El Paso*, (New Haven and London: Yale University Press, 1981), 155–71. Roscoe Martin, *The People's Party in Texas: A Study in Third Party Politics* (Austin and London: The University of Texas Press, 1970), 98–99. Arnoldo de León, *The Tejano Community, 1836–1900* (Albuquerque: University of New Mexico Press, 1982), 23–49. Evan Anders, *Boss Rule in South Texas: The Progressive Era* (Austin: University of Texas Press, 1982), 15–18.

[2]W. Dirk Raat, *Revoltosos: Mexico's Rebels in the United States* (College Station: Texas A & M University Press, 1981), 20–21. James D. Cockcroft, *Intellectual Precursors of the Mexican Revolution, 1900–1913* (Austin and London: The University of Texas Press, 1968), 117–18.

[3]Raat, *Revoltosos*, 32. Interview with Flores de Andrade in Manuel Gamio, *The Life Story of the Mexican Immigrant* (New York: Dover Publication, 1971), 29–40.

[4]Raat, *Revoltosos*, 167, 235.

[5]The basic work on Colquitt is George P. Huckaby, "Oscar Branch Colquitt: A Political Biography," (Masters Thesis, University of Texas at Austin, 1946). Huckaby devotes only marginal attention to Colquitt's border policy. For the importance of the Mexican American vote in securing Colquitt's election, see Huckaby, 203, 213, and Charles H. Harris III and Louis R. Sadler, "The 1911 Reyes Conspiracy: The Texas Side," *Southwestern Historical Quarterly*, 83 (Apr. 1980):331–32, 346–47.

[6]Díaz originally honored his no reelection pledge by stepping down from the presidency in 1880; see Don M. Coerver, *The Porfirian Interregnum: The Presidency of Manuel González of Mexico, 1880–1884*. (Fort Worth: Texas Christian University Press, 1979). Díaz was subsequently reelected in 1884, 1888, 1892, 1896, 1900, 1904, and 1910.

[7]W. Dirk Raat, "The Diplomacy of Suppression: Los Revoltosos, Mexico, and the United States, 1906–1911." *Hispanic American Historical Review*, 56 (Nov. 1976):529–33.

[8]Raat, "Diplomacy of Suppression," 547–50. Charles C. Cumberland, "Mexican Revolutionary Movements from Texas, 1906–1912," *Southwestern Historical Quarterly*, 52 (Jan. 1949):306–307.

[9]Charles C. Cumberland, *Mexican Revolution: Genesis Under Madero* (Austin: University of Texas Press, 1974), 121–23.

[10]Cumberland, "Mexican Revolutionary Movements," 308–309.

[11]Michael Dennis Carman, *United States Customs and the Madero Revolution* (El Paso: Texas Western Press, 1976), 19–23, 40–44. Dorothy Pierson Kerig, *Luther T. Ellsworth: U.S. Consul on the Border during the Mexican Revolution* (El Paso: Texas Western Press, 1975), 35–45.

[12]Cumberland, *Mexican Revolution*, 124–28; "Mexican Revolutionary Movements," 309–12.

[13]Adjutant General Hutchings to C. W. Dawson, Mar. 8, 1911, Texas State Archives, Adjutant General: General Correspondence. Hereinafter cited as TSA, AG:GC. Hutchings served as adjutant general throughout Colquitt's two terms as governor.

[14]San Antonio *Express*, Feb. 3 and 4, 1911. Hereinafter cited as SAE.

[15]A copy of the proclamation is in *Records of the Department of State Relating to the Internal Affairs of Mexico, 1910–1929*, 812.00/809. Hereinafter cited as RDS-IA, followed by file number.

[16]Edward Haley, *Revolution and Intervention: The Diplomacy of Taft and Wilson with Mexico, 1910–1917* (Cambridge, Mass.: MIT Press, 1970), 25–28. Washington *Post*, Mar. 8, and 10, 1911. Hereinafter cited as WP. SAE, March 8, 1911. Texas, Adjutant General, *Biennial Report of the Adjutant General of Texas from January 23, 1911 to December 31, 1912*. (Austin: Von Boeckmann-Jones Co., 1913), 3–8. Colquitt to Taft, Mar. 20, 1911, Texas State Archives, Governor's Papers: Oscar Branch Colquitt, Letter Press Books. Hereinafter cited as TSA, GP:OBC.

[17]Peyton J. Edwards, sheriff of El Paso County, to state adjutant general, Feb. 14, 1911, TSA, AG:GC. Cumberland, "Mexican Revolutionary Movements," 314. WP, Apr. 22, May 9, 1911. El Paso *Morning Times*, May 8, 1911. Hereinafter cited as EPMT. Michael C. Meyer, *Mexican Rebel: Pascual Orozco and the Mexican Revolution, 1910–1915* (Lincoln: University of Nebraska Press, 1967), 28–37. City clerk of El Paso to Col. E. Z. Steever, May 12, 1911 in acting secretary of war to secretary of state, May 22, 1911, RDS-IA, 812.00/1961.

[18]WP, Sept. 16, 1911. Colquitt to Taft, Nov. 17, 1911, Colquitt Papers: University of Texas at Austin. Hereinafter cited as CP:UT.

[19]The best account of the role played by Reyes in the closing years of the Díaz era is Anthony T. Bryan, "Mexican Politics in Transition, 1900–1913: The Role of General Bernardo Reyes," (Ph.D. diss., University of Nebraska, 1969). See also SAE, Oct. 3, 8, and 26, 1911. Vic Niemeyer, "Frustrated Invasion: The Revolutionary Attempt of General Bernardo Reyes from San Antonio in 1911," *Southwestern Historical Quarterly*, 67 (Oct. 1963):213–17, 219–221. Adjutant general to Colquitt, Dec. 1, 1911, TSA, AG:GC. Harris and Sadler, "The 1911 Reyes Conspiracy," 332–33. Colquitt to Hutchings,

Nov. 19, 21, and 22, 1911, TSA, GP:OBC, Telegrams. Hutchings to Colquitt, Nov. 19, 1911, TSA, GP:OBC, Adjutant Generals Department. Adjutant general, U.S. Army, to General Duncan, Nov. 21, 1911, RDS-IA, 812.00/2533. SAE, Nov. 19, 21, 24; Dec. 12, 31, 1911; Jan. 6, 9, 10, 11, Feb. 3, Apr. 15, 1912. State Department Memorandum to acting secretary of state, Dec. 2, 1911, RDS-IA, 812.00/2540.

[20]SAE, Jan. 13, 1913. Colquitt to Hutchings, Jan. 25, 1912, Colquitt to Taft, Jan. 25, 1912, TSA, GP:OBC, Letter Press Books. EPMT, Feb. 1, 1912, extra edition; Feb. 4, 1912. Colquitt to Hughes, Feb. 2, 1912, Colquitt to Taft, Feb. 2, 1912, Colquitt to Taft, Feb. 25, 1912, TSA, GP:OBC, Telegrams. Army chief of staff to adjutant general, Feb. 2, 1912, RDS-IA, 812.00/2857. Meyer, *Mexican Rebel*, 50–52.

[21]Secretary of war to secretary of state, Feb. 16, 1912, RDS-IA, 812.00/2807. SAE, Feb. 16 and 17, 1912; EPMT, Feb. 16, 1912. Acting secretary of state to Mexican ambassador, Feb. 26, 1912, *FR, 1912*, 726–27. WP, Feb. 24 and Mar. 25, 1912.

[22]SAE, Feb. 2, and 3, 1012. EPMT, Feb. 27, 1912. Meyer, *Mexican Rebel*, 67.

[23]Colquitt to Wilson, Dec. 27, 1912; Wilson to Colquitt, Jan. 3, 1913; Colquitt to Wilson, Jan. 7, 1913, CP:UT. The best source on Wilson's personal representatives in Mexico is Larry D. Hill, *Emissaries to a Revolution: Woodrow Wilson's Executive Agents in Mexico* (Baton Rouge: Louisiana State University, 1973).

[24]SAE, Feb. 25, 1914. Walter Prescott Webb, *The Texas Rangers* (2d ed.; Austin: University of Texas Press, 1965), 486–91.

[25]SAE, Feb. 27, Mar. 1, 4, 1914. WP, Feb. 27, Mar. 9, 11, 1914. Sanders to Colquitt, Mar. 8, 1914; Cook to Colquitt, Mar. 11, 1914; Hutchings to Colquitt, Mar. 13, 1914, CP:UT.

[26]The basic work on the Tampico incident and the Veracruz occupation is Robert E. Quirk's *An Affair of Honor: Woodrow Wilson and the Occupation of Veracruz* (New York: W. W. Norton & Company, 1962). Casualties among the Mexican defenders may have been as high as five hundred. The Americans suffered nineteen dead and forty-seven wounded. See Quirk, *An Affair of Honor*, 103. The diplomatic correspondence relating to the affair is in *FR, 1914*. SAE, Apr. 21, 1914. The governor's opposition to a special session was based on financial as well as political considerations; it would cost more to call a special session than to increase state defenses along the border. See SAE, Apr. 26, 1914. Gen. A. L. Mills, chief of militia affairs, U.S. Army, to Hutchings, Apr. 28, 1914, TSA, AG:GC.

[27]Charles H. Harris III and Louis R. Sadler, "The Plan of San Diego and the Mexican-United States War Crisis of 1916: A Reexamination," *Hispanic American Historical Review*, 58 (Aug. 1978):385–87. Douglas W. Richmond, "La guerra de Texas se renova: Mexican Insurrection and Carrancista Ambitions, 1900–1920," *Axtlan*, 11 (Spring 1980):17–18. SAE, Aug. 14, Sept. 7, 25, Oct. 1, 1915. WP, Aug. 13, 15, Sept. 7, 1915. Funston to adjutant general, Sept. 28, 1915, RDS-IA, 812.00/16326. U.S. v. Basilio Ramos, Jr. et al., U.S.

Commissioner, Brownsville, no. 249, Federal Records Center, Fort Worth, Texas. Hereinafter cited as FRC-FW. James A. Sandos, "The Plan of San Diego: War and Diplomacy on the Texas Border," *Arizona and the West*, 14 (Spring 1972):8–13.

[28]SAE, July 18, Aug. 6, 7, 17, 18, 1915.

[29]Secretary of war to secretary of state, Sept. 11, 1916, RDS-IA, 812.00/19142. SAE, Aug. 15, Sept. 9, Oct. 20, 1915. Normally, there was little effort made to distinguish between Mexicans and Mexican Americans. Charles C. Cumberland, "Border Raids in the Lower Rio Grande Valley—1915," *Southwestern Historical Quarterly*, 57 (Jan. 1954:300–302. Funston to adjutant general, June 7, 1916, RDS-IA, 812.00/18364.

[30]The most comprehensive work on Huerta is Michael C. Meyer's *Huerta: A Political Portrait* (Lincoln: University of Nebraska Press, 1972). For the German connection, see Meyer's article, "The Mexican-German Conspiracy of 1915," *The Americas*, 23 (July 1966):76–89. Kenneth J. Grieb, *The United States and Huerta* (Lindoln: University of Nebraska Press, 1969), 182–87. Allen Gerlach, "Conditions along the Border—1915: The Plan de San Diego," *New Mexico Historical Review*, 43 (July 1968):195–97. Meyer, *Mexican Rebel*, 115–29. SAE, June 28, July 3, 1915.

[31]SAE, June 14, 1915.

[32]Grieb, *United States and Huerta*, 186. Commander, Southern Department, to secretary of war, Apr. 21, 1915 and May 5, 1915, RDS-IA, 812.00/14899 and 812.00/14971. Cobb to secretary of state, June 27, 1915, *FR, 1915*, 828–29. Meyer, *Huerta*, 222-25. The charge against Huerta is outlined in U.S. v. Victoriano Huerta et al., District Court, San Antonio, no. 2185, FRC-FW. SAE, July 3, 1915.

[33]Ferguson to secretary of state, June 30, 1915 and July 7, 1915, Texas State Archives, Governors' Papers: James E. Ferguson, Letter Press Books. Hereinafter cited as TSA, GP:JEF. WP, July 2, 4, 9, 1915. SAE, July 4, 18, 1915.

[34]Meyer, *Mexican Rebel*, 130–32; *Huerta*, 227–29. George J. Rausch, Jr., "The Exile and Death of Victoriano Huerta," *Hispanic American Historical Review*, 42 (May 1962):133–51. Both deaths provoked controversy. Many claimed that Orozco had been summarily executed, while others maintained that Huerta had been poisoned or deliberately killed by improper surgery.

[35]Friedrich Katz provides an excellent analysis of Germany's attempt to use the Mexican Revolution to achieve its broader global policies in *The Secret War in Mexico: Europe, The United States, and the Mexican Revolution* (Chicago: University of Chicago Press, 1981). See especially 326–339, 346–350. James A. Sandos, "German Involvement in Northern Mexico, 1915–1916: A New Look at the Columbus Raid," *Hispanic American Historical Review*, 50 (Feb. 1980):83–88. German involvement in the Plan of San Diego is disputed. Gerlach and Sandos see a definite German connection, while Katz and especially Harris and Sadler maintain that German involvement is unproven. The complete text of the telegram is in James B. Scott, ed., *Diplomatic Correspondence between the United States and Germany, August 1, 1914–April 6, 1917* (New

York: Oxford University Press, 1918), iv. The basic work on the incident is Barbara Tuchman, *The Zimmermann Telegram* (New York: Viking Press, 1958). SAE, Mar. 8, 26, 27, 28 and Apr. 1, 1917.

[36]Mexico, Presidente, *Un siglo de relaciones internacionales de Mexico a través de los mensajes presidenciales* (2d ed.; Mexico City: Editorial Porrúa, 1970), 270, 276–77, 308–309. EPMT, Apr. 3 and 6, 1917. WP, Apr. 4 and 14, 1917. Pershing to Scott, Apr. 7, 1917, Hugh Lenox Scott Papers, Library of Congress. Hereinafter cited as HLS. Texas, adjutant general, *Biennial Report of the Adjutant General of Texas from January 1, 1917 to December 31, 1918* (Austin: Von Boeckman-Jones Co., 1919), 63–70. Hanson to adjutant general, Feb. 1 and 28, 1918, TSA, AG:GC. Carrancista officials had expelled Hanson from Mexico in 1914 because of his support for the Huerta regime. He was later accused of being connected with the Plan of San Diego, which he allegedly hoped to use as a device for embarrassing the Carranza administration. See Harris and Sadler, "Plan of San Diego," 382.

[37]Commander, Southern Department, to secretary of war, June 21, 1919, RDS-IA, 812.00/22752. The civilian casualties in El Paso that provoked the crossing were two killed and four wounded. SAE, June 26 and 27, 1919. EPMT, Aug. 17, 1919.

[38]SAE, Oct. 8, 1920.

Chapter 3

[1]Jay J. Wagner, *Arizona Territory 1863–1912: A Political History* (Tucson: The University of Arizona Press, 1970), 383–95. Marshall Trimble, *Arizona: A Panoramic History of a Frontier State* (Garden City, N.Y.: Doubleday and Company, 1977), 321–27.

[2]Wagner, *Arizona Territory*, 384–92. Héctor Aguilar Camín, *La frontera nómada: Sonora y la Revolución Mexicana* (Mexico City: Siglo Veintiuno Editores, 1977), 119–21. Antonio Rivera, *La Revolución en Sonora* (Mexico City: Imprenta Araña, 1969), 142–60.

[3]Cumberland, *Mexican Revolution*, 92–93, 111, 117–18. Rivera, *La Revolución*, 200.

[4]Rodolfo Acuña, *Occupied America: The Chicano's Struggle Toward Liberation* (San Francisco: Canfield Press, 1971), 94.

[5]Penney and Robinson to Calles, 1916, Archivo de Gobierno del Estado de Sonora, Tomo 3809. Archive hereinafter cited as AGES, followed by tomo number.

[6]Alvaro Obregón, *Ocho mil kilómetros en campaña* (Rpt.; Mexico City: Fondo de Cultura Económica, 1970), 35–36.

[7]Eyewitness account by Mrs. Ada E. Jones, "The First Battle of Nogales," manuscript, Mar. 14, 1913, Arizona Historical Society.

[8]"Toma de la villa de Nogales," written Mar. 15, 1913, in Obregón, *Ocho mil*, 36–39.

[9]Charles C. Cumberland, *Mexican Revolution: The Constitutionalist Years* (Austin and London: The University of Texas Press, 1972), 25.

[10]Dallas *Morning News*, Oct. 7, 1914.

[11]Arizona *Daily Star*, Oct. 12, 1914; Oct. 13, 1914; Oct. 15, 1914; Oct. 20, 1914; and Nov. 26, 1914. Dallas *Morning News*, Oct. 13, 1914.

[12]Hugh L. Scott, *Some Memories of a Soldier* (New York and London: The Century Co., 1928), 509.

[13]See Villa to Maytorena, Jan. 9, 1915, and copy of accord signed by Calles and Maytorena, Jan. 11, 1915, in National Archives, Villa's Revolution #2212358, Box 7644. Archive cited hereinafter as AGO/VR, followed by box number. For a more detailed discussion of the Naco incident, see Linda B. Hall, "The Mexican Revolution and the Crisis in Naco, 1914–1915," *Journal of the West*, 16 (Oct. 1977):27–35.

[14]See commanding officer, 12th Infantry, to department engineer, Southern Department, Apr. 23, 1915, in National Archives, Military Intelligence Division, Record Group 165, #8536-7. Archive cited hereinafter as MD 165, followed by document number.

[15]Calvin W. Hines, "The Mexican Punitive Expedition of 1916," (Master's thesis, Trinity University, 1961), 45–47.

[15]Clendenen, *Blood*, 187–89.

[17]Hines, "The Mexican Punitive Expedition," 47–48.

[18]Hines, "The Mexican Punitive Expedition," 49–50.

[19]Clarence C. Clendenen, *The United States and Pancho Villa* (Ithaca: Cornell University Press, 1961), 224.

[20]Vice-consul, Douglas, Arizona, to Foreign Office, Archive of the British Foreign Office, 371/2699, #68777. Archive hereinafter cited as FO, followed by document number.

[21]For Villista sympathies, see Ricketts to Scott, Dec. 1, 1916, HLS.

[22]Calles to presidente municipal, Cananea, June 18, 1916, HLS.

[23]Kingdon to Allen, June 18, 1916, HLS.

[24]Scott to Slocum, June 20, 1916, HLS.

[25]Ricketts to Scott, June 20, 1916, HLS.

[26]Ricketts to Scott, June 21, 1916, HLS.

[27]Scott to Ricketts, June 21, 1916, HLS.

[28]Douglas to Scott, June 27, 1916; Ricketts to Scott, June 26, 1916, HLS.

[29]Ricketts to Scott, June 27, 1916, HLS.

[30]Scott to Ricketts, June 28, 1916, HLS.

[31]Douglas to Davis, June 27, 1916; Douglas to Scott, July 3, 1916, HLS.

[32]Ricketts to Scott, Dec. 6, 1916, HLS.

[33]Calles Decree #3, Aug. 20, 1915, Roll Number 60, Patronato de la Historia de Sonora. Archive hereinafter cited as PHS, followed by roll number.

[34]Ricketts to Scott, Dec. 1, 1916, HLS. Moreno to U.S. Consul, Nogales, June 5, 1916; Simpich to De la Huerta, June 5, 1916; and Acuña to Huerta, June 13, 1916, PHS/63.

[35]Huerta Decree #71, Dec. 10, 1916, PHS/65.

[36]Mexico, *Diario de los debates del Congreso Constituyente* (Mexico City: Cámara de Diputados, 1917), 1:719.

[37]See lists of unions in Cananea in gobernador del Estado de Sonora to

presidente municipal, Cananea, Nov. 14, 1918, PHS/70. A more general but incomplete list is in "Las sociedades existentes en el estado de Sonora, 1918," PHS/71.

[38]Commanding officer, Yorktown, to commander, Division II, Pacific Fleet, Aug. 18, 1917, RDS-IA, 812.00/21271. Lawton, Report on Conditions in Sonora, Sept. 12, 1917, RDS-IA, 812.00/21282.

[39]Calles to Aguirre, July 11, 1917; Calles to administrador de bienes intervenidos, July 9, 1917, PHS/66.

[40]Calles to Aguirre, July 11, 1917; Calles to Carranza, July 11, 1917, PHS/67.

[41]Commanding officer, Yorktown, to commander, Division II, Pacific Fleet, Aug. 18, 1917, RDS-IS, 812.00/21271.

[42]Lawton, Report on conditions in Sonora, September 12, 1917, RDS-IA, 812.00/21282.

[43]Military report of conditions along the border, Sept. 29, 1917, RDS-IA, 812.00/21312.

[44]David Pletcher, *Rails, Mines and Progress: Seven American Promoters in Mexico, 1867–1911* (Ithaca: Cornell University Press, 1958), 254.

[45]Pamela Mayhall, "Bisbee's Response to Civil Disorder," *The American West*, 9 (May 1972):22–31. Military report of conditions along the border, Sept. 29, 1917, RDS-IA, 812.00/21312. Presidente municipal, Agua Prieta, to gobernador interino, Oct. 4, 1917, PHS/67.

[46]De la Huerta to Echeverría, June 4, 1916, and July 5, 1916; secretario de gobierno de Sonora to Cruz, June 5, 1916; De la Huerta to Acuña, July 5, 1916, PHS/63. Calles to Carranza, Feb. 28, 1916, PHS/61. Claudio Dabdoub, *Historia de El Valle del Yaqui* (Mexico City: Librería Manuel Porrúa, S.A., 1964), 193–235, 293–327. Luis L. León, Interview with Linda B. Hall, July 30, 1974.

[47]SAE, June 18, 1915, and June 20, 1915. Dabdoub, *Historia*, 320–21.

[48]Congreso de Sonora a sus comitentes, Oct. 24, 1917, PHS/67. Washington to Carranza, Dec. 1, 1917; Castro to Carranza, Jan. 6, 1917, PHS/68. Sage to commanding general, Southern Department, May 28, 1915, MID 165, 8536/18.

[49]Colonel H. B. Wharfield, "Yaqui Border Incident," manuscript, Arizona Historical Society. Colonel H. B. Wharfield, "The Yaqui Indian Fight," in *The Black Military Experience in the American West*, ed. John M. Carroll, (New York: Liveright, 1973), 367–74.

[50]Clendenen, *Blood*, 346–74.

[51]Goff, *George W. P. Hunt*, 82. *El Heraldo de Mexico*, Oct. 12, 1920; *Excelsior*, Oct. 9, 1920; *El Demócrata*, Dec. 1, 1920; *El Monitor Republicano*, Oct. 17, 1920, in *Campaña política del c. Alvaro Obregón*, ed. Luis N. Ruvalcaba, (Mexico City: n.p., 1923), 5:261, 270, 297, 513–15.

Chapter 4

[1]Secretary of war to secretary of state, Jan. 26, 1916, RDS-IA, 812.00/17207. The secretary of war was reviewing a policy established on November 21, 1910.

[2]Adjutant general to commanding officer, Department of Texas, Nov. 19, 1910, RDS-IA, 812.00/436 1/2.

[3]SAE, Mar. 8-18, 1911. EPMT, Mar. 8-18, 1911. WP, Mar. 8-18, 1911.

[4]Taft stated these views in a letter to Secretary of State Knox on March 11, 1911. See Haley, *Revolution and Intervention*, 26–27.

[5]Meyer, *Mexican Rebel*, 25–37.

[6]WP, May 8, 1911.

[7]Corral to Díaz, May 4, 1911, CPD, XXXVI, 8227–28. In the same letter, Corral became one of the first to state that Madero could not control the revolution, bringing the risk of U.S. intervention.

[8]See *Congressional Record*, 62nd Congress, 1st Session, vol. 47, pt. 2, 1131–36.

[9]Wilson to secretary of state, May 23, 1911, RDS-IA, 812.00/1981.

[10]SAE, Aug. 8 and Sept. 7, 1911. WP, Aug. 8, 1911. Despite the mobilization, the number of troops actually patrolling the border was only about three thousand. See Carman, *United States Customs and the Madero Revolution*, 48–50.

[11]Meyer, *Mexican Rebel*, 62–63. Orozco to Taft, Apr. 15, 1912, RDS-IA, 812.00/3538.

[12]Haley, *Revolution and Intervention*, 39–44. Meyer, *Mexican Rebel*, 70–88.

[13]Wilson to secretary of state, Aug. 22, 1912, *FR, 1912*, 826.

[14]Wilson to minister of foreign affairs, Sept. 15, 1912, *FR, 1912*, 842–46.

[15]Haley, *Revolution and Intervention*, 49–50.

[16]President's annual message, Dec. 3, 1912, *FR, 1912*, xiv, xxvii.

[17]Wilson to secretary of state, Feb. 4, 1913, *FR, 1913*, 696–99. Also in RDS-IA, 812.00/6068.

[18]Wilson to secretary of state, Feb. 11, 1913, *FR, 1913*, 704. Secretary of state to Wilson, Feb. 12, 1913, *FR, 1913*, 706. There is extensive coverage of the diplomatic correspondence during the February 9–18 period (the Decena Trágica) in *FR, 1913*.

[19]Haley, *Revolution and Intervention*, 64–69. WP, Feb. 11–14, 1913.

[20]Wilson to secretary of state, Feb. 23, 1913, *FR, 1913*, 731–32. WP, Feb. 24, 1913. By his own admission, Wilson played a central role in bringing together Reyes and Huerta. Wilson defends his much-criticized tenure as ambassador in his *Diplomatic Episodes in Mexico, Belgium, and Chile* (Garden City, N.Y.: Doubleday, Page and Company, 1927). For the best discussion of Huerta's role in the death of Madero, see Meyer, *Huerta*, 70–82.

[21]Secretary of state to Wilson, Feb. 21, 1913, *FR, 1913*, 728–29. Also in RDS–IA, 812.00/6325a.

[22]Secretary of state to chargé, Aug. 4, 1913, *FR, 1913*, 817–18.

[23]Haley, *Revolution and Intervention*, 101–11. Mark T. Gilderhus, *Diplomacy and Revolution: U.S.-Mexican Relations under Wilson and Carranza* (Tucson: University of Arizona Press, 1977), 2–7.

[24]The term "watchful waiting" is a composite of two phrases used by the president in a message to Congress in late August 1913; Wilson told Congress that he would "wait" and "vigilantly watch" political developments in Mexico. See, *FR, 1913*, 820–27.

[25]From the diary of Josephus Daniels, Apr. 18, 1913, in Arthur S. Link, ed., *The Papers of Woodrow Wilson* (Princeton: Princeton University Press, 1966–1979), 17:331–32. Hereinafter cited as POWW.

[26]From the diary of Colonel House, May 2, 1913 in Link, ed., *Papers*, 17:383.

[27]Moore to Woodrow Wilson, May 15, 1913 in Link, ed., *Papers*, 17:437–40.

[28]Report by Hale, July 9, 1913, Link, ed., *Papers*, 28:33.

[29]The lengthy letter from Bliss was enclosed in secretary of war to secretary of state, Aug. 14, 1913, RDS-IA, 812.00/9122. The central feature of intervention under the "Alternative Plan" was a landing at Veracruz, followed by a march to Mexico City that would require most of the regular army.

[30]Secretary of war to secretary of state, Aug. 18, 1913, in president to secretary of state, Aug. 20, 1913, RDS-IA, 812.00/8679. Garrison euphemistically referred to intervention as "the efforts of our government to bring about an improvement in the national affairs of the Republic of Mexico."

[31]Secretary of war to secretary of state, Aug. 19, 1913, RDS-IA 812.00/8487.

[32]Secretary of state to consular officers in Mexico, Aug. 27, 1913, *FR, 1913*, 895–96.

[33]RDS-IA, 812.00/8679. WP, Aug. 26, 1913.

[34]Lind to Bryan, Sept. 19, 1913, POWW, vol. 28, 199–200. Lind, close friend of Secretary of State Bryan and a former governor of Minnesota, had been dispatched to Mexico to secure Huerta's agreement to hold early elections and refrain from being a candidate. When Huerta balked, Lind offered assistance in getting a loan and later threatened intervention, but failed to influence Huerta. See *FR, 1913*, 821-22.

[35]Diary of Colonel House, Oct. 30, 1913, in Link, ed., *Papers*, 28:447–78.

[36]Bacon to Wilson, Nov. 4, 1913, in Link, ed., *Papers*, 28:488.

[37]Bryan to chargé, Nov. 24, 1913, *FR, 1914*, 443–44. Wilson to Bryan, Nov. 23, 1913, in Link, ed., *Papers*, 28: 585–86.

[38]Sir Cecil Spring Rice to Sir Edward Grey, Jan. 23, 1914, in Link, ed., *Papers*, 29: 168–69. The British government had recognized the Huerta regime in May 1913 and often found itself at odds with the Wilson administration over Mexican policy.

[39]WP, Feb. 4, 1914.

[40]Larry D. Hill, "The Progressive Politician as Diplomat: The Case of John Lind in Mexico," *The Americas*, 27 (Apr. 1971): 355–72. Lind had earlier suggested a plan in which American officers would lead a Constitutionalist force in the seizure of Huerta's gunboats in the Gulf. The gunboats would then have been used in an attack on Veracruz and Tampico.

[41]Lind to Bryan, Feb. 24, 1914, in Link, ed., *Papers* 29: 286–87.

[42]Haley, *Revolution and Intervention*, 129–40. Grieb, *The United States and Huerta*, 66, 142–45.

[43]SAE, Apr. 18, 1914.

[44]SAE, Apr. 9, 1914; Apr. 18, 1914.

[45]SAE, Apr. 29, 1914.

[46]SAE, Apr. 21, 1914.

[47]SAE, Apr. 21, 1914.

[48]Congressman Mondell of Wyoming in *Congressional Record*, 63rd Congress, 2nd Session, Apr. 20, 1914, vol. 51, pt. 7, 6941.

[49]See note 29. Secretary of war to secretary of state, Apr. 20, 1914, RDS-IA, 812.00/11577. Bliss to adjutant general, Apr. 20, 1914, RDS-IA, 812.00/11798.

[50]EPMT, Apr. 19, 1914. Colquitt's stormy relations with the Wilson administration over border policy are covered in Chapter 2 and in Don M. Coerver and Linda B. Hall, *Texas and the Mexican Revolution: A Study in State and National Border Policy* (San Antonio: Trinity University Press, 1984).

[51]WP, Apr. 15, 1914.

[52]War Department to Funston, Apr. 26, 1914, RDS-IA, 812.00/11773. General Funston was commander of the Veracruz occupation and had served on the border.

[53]Arthur S. Link, *Woodrow Wilson and the Progressive Era, 1910–1917* (New York: Harper & Row, 1963), 123–26.

Chapter 5

[1]Obregón's uneasy relationship with Carranza and his ultimate rise to the presidency are covered in Linda B. Hall, *Alvaro Obregón: Power and Revolution in Mexico, 1911–1920* (College Station: Texas A & M University Press, 1981). John Womack, Jr., skillfully delineates the limits of the Zapatista revolt in *Zapata and the Mexican Revolution* (New York: Alfred A. Knopf, 1969).

[2]Memorandum for the chief of staff, May 16, 1914, HLS.

[3]Hall, *Alvaro Obregón*, 122–31. Villa himself placed his casualties at six thousand.

[4]See Chapter 2.

[5]See Linda B. Hall, "The Mexican Revolution," 27–35. Frederick Funston to adjutant general, Oct. 22, 1915, AGO/VR, 7645. Funston to James E. Ferguson, July 1, 1915, AGO/VR 7644.

[6]See Chapter 3.

[7]Clendenen, *Blood*, 187–89. The account of the sole survivor of Santa Ysabel, Thomas B. Holmes, is in Cobb to secretary of state, Jan. 12, 1916, *FR, 1916*, 652. Cobb, customs collecter at El Paso, had earlier warned of possible reprisals as a result of recognition of the Carranza regime. See also EPMT, Jan. 14, 1916. SAE, Jan. 14, 1916. WP, Jan. 14 and 16, 1916.

[8]Carothers to secretary of state, Mar. 8, 1916, *FR, 1916*, 480. Also weekly report in RDS-IA, 812.00/17513. Dallas *Morning News*, Mar. 10, 1916. Clendenen, *Blood*, 202–204.

[9]There has been considerable historical debate as to Villa's presence at Columbus and to the motivation behind the attack. Some maintain that Villa actually led the attack, while others claim that he remained outside of town. Motives for the attack include: desire for revenge, an effort to provoke American intervention, German intrigues, need for supplies, and manipulation by

American business interests. See Chapter 2, note 35. An earlier review of the debate may be found in E. Bruce White, "The Muddied Waters of Columbus, New Mexico," *The Americas*, 32 (July 1975):72–98.

[10]Col. Frank Tompkins, *Chasing Villa: The Story Behind the Story of Pershing's Expedition into Mexico* (Harrisburg, Pa.: The Military Service Publishing Company, 1934), 55.

[11]Tompkins, *Chasing Villa*, 56.

[12]Tompkins, *Chasing Villa*, 56–57.

[13]Funston to adjutant general, Mar. 10, 1916, RDS-IA, 812.00/17396. The pursuing force was outnumbered by the raiders it was chasing.

[14]WP, Mar. 10, 1916.

[15]Eliseo Arredondo to Jesús Acuña, Mar. 9, 1916; Andrés García to Venustiano Carranza, Mar. 9, 1916; both in Archivo de la Secretaría de Relaciones Exteriores, Mexico City, 7-9-14. Hereinafter cited as ASRE.

[16]Funston to adjutant general, Mar. 10, 1916, RDS-IA, 812.00/17396.

[17]Adjutant general to Funston, Mar. 10, 1916, RDS-IA, 812.00/17398. Adjutant general to Funston, Mar. 13, 1916, RDS-IA, 812.00/17457. Disagreement over the success of the Pershing Expedition is partially a product of these two different sets of orders. The March 10 communique spoke of "capturing Villa" while the orders of March 13 called for the "pursuit and dispersion" of the raiders. The orders relayed by Funston to Pershing again spoke of Villa's capture. See Frank E. Vandiver, *Black Jack: The Life and Times of John J. Pershing* (College Station: Texas A & M University Press, 1977), 2:605.

[18]Carranza to Arredondo, Mar. 11, 1916, *FR, 1916*, 486. Carranza to Millán, Mar. 11, 1916, *Diplomatic Dealings of the Constitutionalist Revolution of Mexico* (Mexico City: Imprenta Nacional, 1919), 142. Carranza ordered General Millán to go to Veracruz and to resist any landing by U.S. forces.

[19]Acting secretary of state to consular officers in Mexico, Mar. 14, 1916, *FR, 1916*, 490. Link, *Woodrow Wilson*, 137.

[20]Jesús Acuña to John R. Silliman, Mar. 10, 1916, ASRE 7-9-14. The proposal read, "el Gobierno que preside el C. Primer jefe . . . se dirige al gobierno de los Estados Unidos solicitando el permiso necessario para que fuerzas mexicanas puedan pasar a territorio americano en persecución de esos bandidos, concediendo la reciprocidad debida a las fuerzas de Estados Unidos para pasar a Territorio Mexicano, si la irrupción registrada en Columbus se repitiera desgraciadamente en cualquier otro punto de la linea fronteriza."

[21]Carranza envisioned restrictions on crossing similar to those attached to the Porfirian agreements dealing with Indians. See Coerver, *Porfirian Interregnum*, 136–39. Michael L. Tate, "Pershing's Punitive Expedition: Pursuer of Bandits or Presidential Panacea?", *The Americas*, 32 (July 1975): 55–57. Link, *Woodrow Wilson*, 137–38. Arrendondo to secretary of state, Mar. 27, 1916; *FR, 1916*, 501–502.

[22]See for example, Villavicencio to Rafael E. Muzquiz, Mar. 13, 1916; José Delgado to Cándido Aguilar, Apr. 2, 1916, ASRE 7-9-14.

[23]*FR, 1916*, 493–95. Clendenen, *Blood*, 223–24.

[24]Pershing to Scott, undated [late March or early April 1916], HLS.

[25]Luis Cabrera to Charles G. Douglas, Mar. 15, 1916, ASRE 7-9-14.

[26]Gilberto Magaña to Marcelino Dávalos, Mar. 15, 1916; Eliseo Arredondo to Jesús Acuña, Mar. 9, 1916, ASRE 7-9-14.

[27]Funston to Scott, Apr. 5, 1916, HLS.

[28]Funston to Scott, Apr. 5, 1916, HLS.

[29]Carranza to Gen. M. M. Diéguez, Mar. 11, 1916; Carranza to Gen. Agustín Millán, Mar. 11, 1916; ASRE 7-9-16.

[30]Clendenen, *Blood*, 234, 240.

[31]Clendenen, *Blood*, 260–66. Vandiver, *Pershing*, 2:627–36.

[32]Arredondo to secretary of state, Apr. 13, 1916, *FR, 1916*, 515–17.

[33]Clendenen, *Blood*, 216–66. Tate, "Pershing's Punitive Expedition," 60–61. Vandiver, *Pershing*, 2:636. The Expedition was originally organized into a provisional division of three brigades, two of which were cavalry brigades.

[34]Scott to secretary of war, Apr. 22, 1916, HLS. Colonia Dublán was approximately one hundred miles south of Columbus.

[35]Adjutant general to Scott, Apr. 23, 1916, HLS.

[36]Adjutant general to Scott, Apr. 26, 1916, HLS. Also in *FR, 1916*, 530–32.

[37]Obregón to Carranza, Apr. 28, 1916; Luis Cabrera to Obregón, no date, in Archivo de Fernando Torreblanca, AO/I.3/3. Archives hereinafter cited as FTC.

[38]Scott and Funston to secretary of war and secretary of state, Apr. 29, 1916, HLS.

[39]Adjutant general to Scott, Apr. 30, 1916, HLS. Secretary of war to Scott, May 1, 1916, HLS.

[40]Scott and Funston to secretary of war, May 1, 1916, HLS. Scott also spoke of a widespread report of a split between Obregón and Carranza.

[41]Secretary of war to governors of Arizona, New Mexico, and Texas, May 1, 1916, RDS-IA, 812.00/18144 1/2. Texas, adjutant general, *Biennial Report of the Adjutant General of Texas 1915–1916* (Austin: Von-Boekmann-Jones Co., 1917), 118.

[42]Obregón to Cándido Aguilar, Apr. 30, 1916, FTC A.O/I.3/4; Carranza to Obregón, May 1, 1916, ASRE 7-9-14.

[43]Scott and Funston to secretary of war, May 2, 1916; HLS. See also *FR, 1916*, 538–39.

[44]Obregón to Carranza, May 3, 1916, FTC AO/I.3/7; Obregón to Carranza, May 3, 1916, three telegrams, ASRE 7-9-14.

[45]Ronnie C. Tyler, "The Little Punitive Expedition in the Big Bend," *Southwestern Historical Quarterly*, 78 (Jan. 1975): 277–82. Hines, "Mexican Punitive Expedition," 186–95.

[46]Tyler, "Little Punitive Expedition," 283–85. Hines, "Mexican Punitive Expedition," 196–203. Langhorne had led a small force into Boquillas, Mexico, on May 10, but had returned the same day.

[47]Funston to adjutant general, May 17, 1916, RDS-IA, 812.00/18186.

[48]WP, May 9, 1916. Tyler, "Little Punitive Expedition," 285–87. Hines,

"Mexican Punitive Expedition," 211–19. Sibley spent most of his time pursuing Langhorne's force, which was pursuing the raiders.

[49]Carranza to Obregón, May 7, 1916; Carranza to General Ricaut et al., May 8, 1916, *Diplomatic Dealings*, 181–84.

[50]WP, May 10, 11, and 15, 1916.

[51]Silliman to secretary of state, May 20, 1916, *FR, 1916*, 551–52. Carranza to Generals Ricaut and Garza, May 18, 1916, *Diplomatic Dealings*, 207.

[52]Funston to Pershing, May 19, 1916, in Funston to adjutant general, May 19, 1916, RDS-IA 812.00/18270.

[53]Funston to adjutant general, May 22, 1916 in secretary of war to secretary of state, June 3, 1916, RDS-IA, 812.00/18313. In case of hostilities, Funston was also planning a "cross-country dash with a small force" to seize the strategic railroad bridge at Sabinas, ninety miles south of Piedras Negras. See Funston to Scott, May 29, 1916, HLS.

[54]Secretary of foreign relations to secretary of state, May 22, 1916, *FR, 1916*, 552–63. See also Mexico, Ministerio de Relaciones Exteriores, *Nota enviada por el gobierno constitutional al de la casa blanca* (Mexico City: Compañía Editora Mexicana, 1916).

[55]Secretary of state to secretary of foreign relations, June 20, 1916, *FR, 1916*, 581–92. An item-by-item analysis of the Mexican note of May 22 is in Memorandum from the Assistant to the Chief of Staff, June 5, 1916, HLS.

[56]Scott to Charles, May 16, 1916; Scott to Allen, May 31, 1916, HLS.

[57]Funston to Scott, May 29, 1916.

[58]Consul Johnson at Matamoros to secretary of state, June 15, 1916, *FR, 1916*, 575. United States Senate, *Investigation of Mexican Affairs*, Senate Document 285, 66th Congress, 2nd Session, 1:1247–49. Hereafter cited as IMA. WP, June 18, 1916.

[59]Scott to Chief, War College Division, June 16, 1916, HLS.

[60]United States, War Department, *Annual Report*, 1916, 1: 12–13.

[61]WP, June 17 and 19, 1916. Huerta to municipal presidents, June 17, 1916, AGES, Tomo 3072, pt. 1.

[62]Treviño to Pershing and Pershing to Treviño, June 16, 1916, in Funston to secretary of war, June 17, 1916, *FR, 1916*, 577.

[63]Clendenen, *Blood*, 303–11. Vandiver, *Pershing*, 2: 650–52.

[64]Vandiver, *Pershing*, 2: 652.

[65]Adjutant general to Funston, June 22, 1916, RDS-IA, 812.00/18590. Scott to Funston, June 22, 1916, HLS.

[66]Haley, *Revolution and Intervention*, 219–23. Vandiver, *Pershing* 2:654. Funston to adjutant general, June 25, 1916, HLS.

[67]Scott to Carothers, July 21, 1916, HLS.

[68]Scott to Thomas, August 7, 1916, HLS.

[69]Funston to adjutant general, August 17, 1916, RDS-IA, 812.00/18974. Vandiver, *Pershing*, 2: 659.

[70]Scott to Ryan, September 5, 1916, HLS. The Wilson administration was particularly interested in influencing the mining and petroleum policies of Carranza.

[71]Tate, "Pershing's Punitive Expedition," 68–69. Gilderhus, *Diplomacy and Revolution*, 47–51. The joint commission lingered on until January 1917 without producing a final agreement.

[72]Pershing to Scott, Sept. 23, 1916, HLS. Pershing attributed the failure to capture Villa to diplomatic delay following the Parral incident.

[73]SAE, September 9, 1916. The total cost of the Expedition alone was $130 million. See Tate, "Pershing's Punitive Expedition," 70.

[74]Haley, *Revolution and Intervention*, 241. Vandiver, *Pershing*, 2: 667–68. Funston to adjutant general, February 6, 1917, *FR, 1917*, 908. Prophetically, the return of the Expedition was virtually lost in the news concerning rapidly worsening relations with Germany, which had resumed unrestriced submarine warfare on February 1. See WP and SAE, Feb. 6, 1917.

Chapter 6

[1]Lorenzo Meyer, *Mexico and the United States in the Oil Controversy, 1917–1942* (Austin and London: The University of Texas Press, 1977), 7, 10.

[2]Henrietta M. Larson and Kenneth Wiggins Porter, *History of Humble Oil and Refining Company: A Study in Industrial Growth* (New York: Harper and Brothers, Publishers, 1959), 13–14. Harold F. Williamson, et al., *The American Petroleum Industry: The Age of Energy 1899–1959* (Evanston: Northwestern University Press, 1963), 22–23. *Boletín del Petroleo*, 1 (January 1916): 40–41.

[3]Williamson, *The American Petroleum Industry*, 29. Richard Mancke, *Mexican Oil and Natural Gas: Political, Strategic and Economic Implications* (New York: Praeger Publishers, 1979), 47.

[4]Meyer, *Mexico and the United States*, 8–9. See, for example, Statement of Expense and Loss Incidental to the Revolution to December 1, 1919, Penn-Mex Fuel Company, Archivo Histórico de Pemex, Sistema General Sinclair, Roll 44. Cited hereinafter as SGS-Pemex, followed by roll number.

[5]Marjorie McLernon, interview with Linda B. Hall, July 27, 1978, Trinity Border Studies Oral History Project III/1. Project cited hereinafter as TBSOH, followed by number.

[6]Mancke, *Mexican Oil*, 32. San Antonio *Light*, June 23, 1912.

[7]Lon Tinkle, *Mr. De: Biography of Everette Lee DeGolyer* (Boston-Toronto: Little, Brown and Company, 1970), 37–51, 60–61, 101–102. McLernon interview, TBSOH III/1.

[8]*The National Cyclopedia of American Biography* (New York: James T. White and Company, 1961), 43:110. McLernon interview, TBSOH III/1. Sam L. Kone, interview with Linda B. Hall, Sept. 7, 1978, TBSOH III/2-3.

[9]For clandestine activities, see reports of agents in file 112.9, William F. Buckley Papers. For Buckley's expulsion, see William F. Buckley to Edmund L. Buckley, November 24, 1921, file 020.1, in the same collection. Cited hereinafter as BP followed by file number.

[10]Kone interview, Aug. 29, 1978, TBSOH III/2-1, Aug. 31, 1978, TBSOH III/2-2, Sept. 7, 1978, TBSOH III/2-3.

[11]Meyer, *Mexico and the United States*, 22–23. Tinkle, *Mr. De*, 27–29.

[12]University of Texas Catalogue, 1910–11 (Austin: The University of Texas, 1911), 87. University of Texas Catalogue, 1913–14 (Austin: The University of Texas, 1914), 170. University of Texas Catalogue, 1916–17 (Austin: The University of Texas, 1917), 142. University of Texas Catalogue, 1919–20 (Austin: The University of Texas, 1920), 229. Tinkle, *Mr. De*, 63.

[13]Kone Interview, TBSOH III/2-1.

[14]U.S. consul, Tampico, to secretary of state, August 5, 1918, Enclosure, *FR, 1918*, 672–73.

[15]Kone Interview, TBSOH III/2-1.

[16]Penn-Mex Fuel Oil Company, Statement of Expense and Loss Incidental to the Revolution to December 1, 1919, SGS-Pemex, Roll 44.

[17]*Boletín del Petróleo*, 2 (Aug. 1916): 167–68.

[18]Memorandum of Claims, Mexican Petroleum Company, National Archives, Record Group 76, Records of United States and Mexican Claims Commissions: Records of the Agency of the United States. Entry 125, Box 1882. Claims records cited hereinafter as NA RG 76, USMC:125, followed by box number.

[19]Kone interview, TBSOH, III/2-3.

[20]Juan B. Vega to Juan José Ríos, Sept. 11, 1918, ASRE 119, L-E-837. F. J. Huffman to M. C. Schroeder, May 26, 1925, SGS-Pemex, Roll 44.

[21]Kone interview, TBSOH III/2-3. Meyer, *Mexico and the United States*, 50–51. Katz, *The Secret War*, 463.

[22]U.S. consul, Tampico, to U.S. secretary of state, Jan. 27, 1918, 688; Oil Companies' Protest to César López de Lara, Nov. 6, 1918, 684; U.S. consul, Tampico, to U.S. secretary of state, Dec. 7, 1918: all in *FR, 1918*.

[23]Meyer, *Mexico and the United States*, 47–78.

[24]Circular No. 81, Pastor Rouaix for Venustiano Carranza, Aug. 15, 1916, 774–75; Secretary of State Lansing to Special Representative Rodgers, Aug. 16, 1916, 772, in *FR, 1916*.

[25]Meyer, *Mexico and the United States*, 55, 62–63.

[26]U.S. Vice-Consul Bevan to U.S. secretary of state, Jan. 25, 1916, 754; Bevan to U.S. secretary of state, Jan. 26, 1916, 755–56; Decree of Gen. Cándido Aguilar, Jan. 26, 1916, 756–58: all in *FR, 1916*. *Boletín del Petróleo*. 1 (Jan. 1916): 15. Decree of Venustiano Carranza, Aug. 31, 1916, *FR, 1917*, 1063–64.

[27]Meyer, *Mexico and the United States*, 64.

[28]Cándido Aguilar to Venustiano Carranza, July 2, 1919, ASRE-124, L-E-533, Legajo 1 #31. For a further discussion of Aguilar's point of view, see Meyer, *Mexico and the United States*, 72–73.

Chapter 7

[1]*The Mexican Mining Journal*, 10 (Jan. 1910): 57, 60.

[2]*The Mexican Mining Journal*, 10 (Mar. 1910): 15.

[3]For an excellent discussion of this point, see Marvin D. Bernstein, *The Mexican Mining Industry 1890–1950* (Albany: The State University of New York, 1964), 118–23.

[4]Mira Wilkins, *The Making of Multinational Enterprise* (Cambridge: Harvard University Press, 1974), 31.

[5]See Table 6, "Production of the Mexican Mining Industry, 1910–1920," in Bernstein, *Mexican Mining*, 101.

[6]Mexico, Departamento de Minas, *Anuario de estadística minera, Año de 1922* (Mexico City: Talleres Gráficos de la Nación, 1924), overleaf, 139, 145.

[7]Giuseppe Garibaldi, *A Toast to Rebellion* (Indianapolis: The Bobbs-Merrill Company, Publishers, 1935), 219–23.

[8]Bernstein, *Mexican Mining*, 98. Antonio G. Rivera, *La Revolución en Sonora* (Mexico City: Imprenta Araña, 1969), 143. M. Doyle to Consulmex, Naco, Arizona, Jan. 5, 1911, ASRE 119, L-E-625 #127.

[9]S. M. Del Toro to Consulmex, Douglas, Arizona, May 3, 1912, ASRE-119, L-E-867, Leg. 2 #22. M. Doyle to Consulmex, Naco, Arizona, Jan. 5, 1911, ASRE-119, L-E-625 #127. B. G. Hill to Consulmex, Douglas, Arizona, n.d., ASRE-119, L-E-867, Leg. 1 #193.

[10]Memorandum of Claims, Santa Matilde Mining Company, July 24, 1926, Box 786, and Report on Mollie Gibson Oil and Mining Company vs. Mexico, NA RG 76: USMC. Zachary Cobb to secretary of the treasury, Sept. 15, 1916, RDS-IA, 812.63/192.

[11]Memorial of Claim, La Libertad Mining and Milling Co., Apr. 14, 1936, NA RG 76: USMC 125/287. Candelero Mining Co., Basis of Claim, NA RG 76: USMC 125/202. Gunter vs. United Mexican States, June 1, 1929, NA RG 76: USMC 125/636.

[12]Memorial of Dr. Francis C. Nicholas, NA RG 76: USMC 125/282.

[13]Bernstein, *Mexican Mining*, 107–108. L. de la Garza to F. Villa, Oct. 29, 1914, I-I-180; L. de la Garza to F. Villa, Dec. 12, 1914, I-F-141; L. de la Garza to F. Villa, Sept. 14, 1914, I-I-6; L. de la Garza to F. Villa, Dec. 4, 1914, I-I-21; Enrique Salas to L. de la Garza, IX-H-3; Lázaro de la Garza Archive, University of Texas at Austin. Hereinafter cited as DLG, followed by document number.

[14]Enrique Salas to L. de la Garza, Dec. 7, 1916, DLG IX-H-25.

[15]Affidavit to E. F. Knotts, July 15, 1926, NA RG 76: USMC 125/635.

[16]Clendenen, *Blood*, 197–98. Secretary of State Lansing to Consul Edwards, Jan. 3, 1916, 650, and Collector Cobb to Secretary of State Lansing, Jan. 15, 1916, 657, *FR, 1916*.

[17]Clendenen, *Blood*, 197–98. Report of Thomas B. Holmes in Cobb to Lansing, Jan. 12, 1916, and Cobb to Lansing No. 2, Jan. 12, 1916, *FR, 1916*, 652.

[18]Cobb to Lansing, Jan. 13, 1916, 655; Lansing to Cobb, Jan. 13, 1916, 656; Cobb to Lansing, Jan. 14, 1916, 657; Gen. John J. Pershing to Gen. Frederick Funston, Jan. 17, 1916, 662; and Consul Edwards to Lansing, Jan. 27, 1916, 663, *FR, 1916*.

[19]Consul Letcher to Lansing, Apr. 23, 1916, *FR, 1916*, 528.

[20]James Douglas to J. S. Douglas, Oct. 30, 1909, Lewis W. Douglas Papers, University of Arizona. Papers hereinafter cited as LWD.

[21]James Douglas to J. S. Douglas, Jan. 27, 1911; J. S. Douglas to James Douglas, Jan. 31, 1911, LWD.

[22]J. I. Williams to J. S. Douglas, Feb. 28, 1911; J. S. Douglas to James Douglas Feb. 28 or Mar. 1, 1911, LWD. Although the latter entry was dated Feb. 28, internal evidence makes March 1 the more likely date.

[23]Walter Douglas to James Douglas, Apr. 15, 1911, LWD.

[24]J. S. Douglas to James Douglas, June 1, 1911, LWD.

[25]James Douglas to J. S. Douglas, July 5, 1911; James Douglas to Manuel Calero, June 23, 1911; Manuel Calero to James Douglas, June 12, 1911, LWD.

[26]James Douglas to J. S. Douglas, July 26, 1911, LWD.

[27]James Douglas to J. S. Douglas, Mar. 8, 1912; J. S. Douglas to James Douglas, July 8, 1912, LWD.

[28]J. S. Douglas to James Douglas, Apr. 6, 1913; James Douglas to J. S. Douglas, Apr. 22, 1913; J. S. Douglas to James Douglas, Apr. 27, 1913; J. S. Douglas to James Douglas, May 5, 1913; James Douglas to J. S. Douglas, May 14, 1913, LWD.

[29]J. S. Douglas to James Douglas, May 19, 1913; James Douglas to J. S. Douglas, June 2, 1913; J. S. Douglas to Julius Liberman, Oct. 29, 1913; J. Liberman to J. S. Douglas, Nov. 8, 1913; James Douglas to J. S. Douglas Nov. 14, 1913; J. S. Douglas to James Douglas, Nov. 15, 1913; James Douglas to J. S. Douglas, Dec. 19, 1913; J. S. Douglas to J. Liberman, Jan. 30, 1914; James Douglas to J. S. Douglas, Feb. 25, 1914; J. S. Douglas to James Douglas, Aug. 13, 1914; James Douglas to J. S. Douglas, Nov. 6, 1914, LWD.

[30]J. S. Douglas to James Douglas, Feb. 28, 1915, and Mar. 9, 1915; James Douglas to J. S. Douglas, Apr. 17, 1916, LWD.

[31]Robert Glass Cleland, *A History of Phelps Dodge, 1834–1950* (New York: Alfred A. Knopf, 1952), 161–62, 193, 241.

[32]Cleland, *A History*, 136. List of Loans Outstanding, The Bank of Douglas, July 21, 1911, LWD.

[33]F. Simpich to Secretary of State, Sept. 15, 1916, RDS-IA, 812.63/184.

[34]J. A. Ryan, Intelligence Office, to the department engineer, Southern Department, May 3, 1915, MD 165, 8536-7. See, for example, Richfield Copper Company vs. Mexico, May 20, 1932, in NA RG 76: USMC 125/399, and Memorial of Dr. Francis Nicholas, NA RG 76: USMC 125/635.

[35]Quejas, 1912, Caja 5, Expediente 2, Archivo General de la Nación, Departmento de Trabajo. Ernesto Madero to L. de la Garza, July 27, 1915, DLG IX-H-16; De la Garza to Madero, Aug. 9, 1915, DLG IX-H-17.

[36]Martínez, *Border Boom Town*, 32, 35. García, *Desert Immigrants*, 18.

[37]García, *Desert Immigrants*, 18–20, 107–108.

[38]Secretary of the interior to secretary of state, Apr. 24, 1917, RDS-IA, 812.63/538.

[39]Plutarco Elías Calles, Aviso, Cananea, Mar. 7, 1916; Calles to comandante militar de la plaza, Cananea, Mar. 7, 1916, AGES, 3090.

[40]Mark Reisler, *By the Sweat of Their Brow: Mexican Immigrant Labor in the United States, 1900–1940* (London and Westport: Greenwood Press, 1976), 16–17, 97.

[41]James Douglas, "The Production of Copper in Arizona during 1906," *Engineering and Mining Journal*, V.83 (Jan. 26, 1907): 198; hereinafter cited as EMJ. James Douglas, "The Copper Situation in Arizona," EMJ, (Jan. 4, 1908), n.p. James Douglas, "Copper in Arizona," EMJ, n.d., n.p. James Douglas, "Copper in Arizona in 1909," EMJ, n.d., 263. James Douglas, "Copper in Arizona in 1910," EMJ, n.d., n.p. *New York Times*, Feb. 18, 1904. All above are clippings in LWD. W. C. Greene to James Douglas, Jan. 25, 1904; W. C. Greene to James Douglas, Feb. 26, 1904, LWD. David W. Pletcher, *Rails*, 254; Bernstein, *Mexican Mining*, 118–23.

[42]"Presbyterian Copper," *Fortune Magazine*, 6 (July 1932): 41. "Review of Copper Industry for 1919," *Arizona Mining Journal* (Mar. 1920): 16–17.

[43]Douglas *Daily International*, n.d., n.p. Clipping in LWD.

[44]Sheet distributed to mine and smelter employees, June 14, 1918, LWD.

[45]"Review of Copper Industry for 1919," *Arizona Mining Journal*, (Mar. 1930): 16–17. F. Dyer to secretary of state, Nov. 24, 1920, RDS-IA, 812.63/554. F. Dyer to secretary of state, Nov. 30, 1920, RDS-IA, 812.63/556. Harold Playter to secretary of state, RDS-IA, 812.63/560.

Chapter 8

[1]These figures did *not* include those workers who regularly crossed the line in border cities to work in regular jobs on the U.S. side. *Report of the Commissioner General of Immigration, 1919*, in *Reports of the Department of Labor, 1919* (Washington: Government Printing Office, 1920), 706. Hereinafter cited as *CGI*, followed by date.

[2]Manuel Gamio, *The Mexican Immigrant: His Life Story* (Rpt., 1931; New York: Arno Press, 1969) contains a number of interviews with migrants discussing their reasons for coming to the United States between 1910 and 1920.

[3]*CGI*-1911 to *CGI*-1920.

[4]*CGI*-1912, 279–80. *CGI*-1916, 214–15. *CGI*-1920, 408–11.

[5]*CGI*-1912, 224.

[6]*CGI*-1913, 337.

[7]*CGI*-1914, 458.

[8]*CGI*-1911, 314.

[9]*CGI*-1911, 225.

[10]*CGI*-1912, 337.

[11]*CGI*-1914, 458–59. SAE, Apr. 12, 1914. John Martínez, *Mexican Emigration to the U.S. 1910–1930* (San Francisco: R. and E. Research Associates, 1972), 10.

[12]*CGI*-1916, 397.

[13]*CGI*-1917, 419–20; *CGI*-1919, 710; *CGI*-1920, 699–700. SAE, July 8, 1917.

[14]*CGI*-1919, 710.

[15]*CGI*-1911, 317; *CGI*-1919, 718–19. Abraham Hoffman, *Unwanted Mexican Americans in the Great Depression* (Tucson: The University of Arizona Press, 1974), 31.

[16]Martínez, *Mexican Emigration*, 17.

[17]Martínez, *Mexican Emigration*, 17. Julian Samora, *Los Mojados: The Wetback Story* (Notre Dame: University of Notre Dame Press, 1971), 38.

[18]James E. Ferguson to Woodrow Wilson, May 29, 1917, TSA, GP:JEF, Letter Press Books.

[19]*CGI*-1918, 551.

[20]*CGI*-1920, 700.

[21]Lawrence A. Cardoso's fine work, *Mexican Emigration to the United States, 1897–1931* (Tucson: The University of Arizona Press, 1980), 38, 53, estimates that more than a million Mexicans fled across the border during the Revolutionary decade.

[22]Atchison, Topeka and Santa Fe Railway, signature unreadable, to Sen. Henry Z. Osborne, May 24, 1917; Murrell L. Buckner, The Union Terminal Company, to Senator Morris Sheppard, May 30, 1917; W. J. Hotchkiss to Captain J. F. Lucy, Hoover Food Commission, June 7, 1917, in the United States Department of Labor, Bureau of Immigration, #54261/202. Archive hereinafter cited as USDL/BI, followed by file number. See also discussion in Cardoso, *Mexican Emigration*, 50.

[23]A. Caminetti, commissioner general of immigration, to W. B. Wilson, secretary of labor, May 21, 1917, USDL/BI 54261/129.

[24]Edward F. Parker, Southwest Cotton Company to W. B. Wilson, May 28, 1917, USDL/BI 54261/202.

[25]Atchison, Topeka and Santa Fe Railway to Osborne, May 24, 1917; Buckner to Sheppard, May 30, 1917; F. W. Berkshire to commissioner general, July 8, 1918; USDL/BI 54261/202.

[26]*CGI*-1919, 716; *CGI*-1920, 715. SAE, May 10, 1918.

[27]*CGI*-1920, 715.

[28]Los Angeles *Times*, Feb. 4, 1913.

[29]TBSOH II/1, July 21, 1978.

[30]SAE, Jan. 11, 1914.

[31]SAE, Jan. 11, 1914.

[32]SAE, Mar. 8, 1914.

[33]SAE, Jan. 3, 1915.

[34]SAE, Feb. 13, 1915.

[35]Texas Department of Education, Bulletin No. 124. Annie Webb Blanton and Mrs. R. L. Ragsdale, *Texas High Schools: History and the Social Sciences* (n.p.: Texas Department of Education, 1920), 9.

[36]Blanton and Ragsdale, *Texas High Schools*, 8–9.

[37]Texas Department of Education, Bulletin No. 157. Annie Webb Blanton, *A Handbook of Information as to Education in Texas 1918–1922* (n.p.: Texas Department of Education, 1923), 22–23.

[38]Arizona Territorial Papers, National Archives, Record Group 48, M429, 9-2-1 and 9-2-16. Studies such as Malcolm D. Holmes and Howard C.

Daudistel, "Ethnicity and Justice in the Southwest: The Sentencing of Anglo, Black, and Mexican Origin Defendants," *Social Science Quarterly*, 65 (June 1984): 265–77 have pointed out that even in recent years, Mexican American defendants in the Southwest receive harsher sentences from juries than do Anglos. Carlos E. Cortés, *The Mexican American and the Law* (New York: Arno Press, 1974), also contains a number of studies, beginning with the 1920s, that indicate that Mexican Americans have received unequal treatment before the law. It seems reasonable to infer, therefore, that Mexicans were overrepresented in the convict population in 1911.

[39]U.S. Bureau of the Census, *Thirteen Census of the United States*, Vol. 3: Population (Washington: Government Printing Office, 1913), 798–99. U.S. Bureau of the Census, *Fourteenth Census of the United States*, Vol. 3: Population (Washington: Government Printing Office, 1923); 984, 987. Texas, *Annual Report of the Officials of the State Prison System, 1911* (Austin: Von Boeckmann-Jones, Printers, 1912), 27, 31.

[40]Texas, *Annual Report, 1911*, 31, 136, 143–50.

Chapter 9

[1]Enrique Creel to U.S., Mar. 13, 1907; general commanding officer, 1st Military Zone, to secretary of war, Feb. 20, 1907; governor of Arizona to secretary of the interior, Mar. 30, 1907, in U.S. National Archives, Record Group 48, M429, 9-2-3.

[2]D. R. Dowe to collector of customs, Dec. 27, 1910, NA/RG 36, 144-5.

[3]SAE, Nov. 16, 1910.

[4]SAE, Dec. 24, 1910. D. R. Dowe, Del Rio, to collector of customs, Eagle Pass, Jan. 16, 1911, nos. 154–59; Dowe to collector of customs, Eagle Pass, Jan. 30, 1911, no. 163; both in the National Archives, Record Group 36.

[5]Mexican ambassador, Washington, to the secretary of state, Jan. 19, 1911, 392; secretary of state to Mexican ambassador, Washington, Jan. 23, 1911, 393; secretary of state to Mexican ambassador, Washington, Jan. 24, 1911, 397; acting secretary of state to Mexican chargé, Washington, Feb. 11, 1911; all in *FR, 1911*.

[6]General McCain, adjutant general, to General Hoyt, commanding general, Department of Texas, Jan. 24, 1911, *FR, 1911*, 395.

[7]Acting secretary of war to the secretary of state, Feb. 23, 1911, RDS-IA, 812.00/841.

[8]Gov. Oscar B. Colquitt to Pres. William Howard Taft, Feb. 23, 1911, *FR, 1911*, 410.

[9]SAE, Mar. 17, 1911. Henry Lane Wilson to secretary of state, Mar. 23, 1911, *FR, 1911*, 432.

[10]SAE, May 12, 1911.

[11]SAE, May 13, 1911.

[12]EPMT, May 13, 1911.

[13]WP, Nov. 26, 1911.

[14]Secretary of state to attorney general, Jan. 3, 1912, *FR, 1912*, 708–709.

[15]Francisco I. Madero, Decree, Jan. 20, 1912, and Francisco I. Madero, Decree, May 7, 1912, AGES/2908.

[16]*Congressional Record*, 62nd Congress, 2nd Session, Vol. 48, pt. 4, 3257–58, 3365; Clendenen, *The United States and Pancho Villa*, 33.

[17]SAE, Mar. 15, 1912, Mar. 20, 1912, Mar. 21, 1912, Mar. 24, 1912, and Mar. 31, 1912. Acting secretary of state to Mexican ambassador, Mar. 26, 1912, *FR, 1912*, 765–66.

[18]Attorney general to the president, Mar. 25, 1912, *FR, 1912*, 759–61.

[19]WP, Apr. 5, 1912.

[20]Gilderhus, *Diplomacy and Revolution*, 6. Clendenen, *The United States and Pancho Villa*, 59.

[21]EPMT, Apr. 3, 1913; Apr. 22, 1913; May 8, 1913. SAE, May 6, 1913, May 8, 1913.

[22]Gen. Tasker Bliss to adjutant general, Apr. 19, 1913, in secretary of war to secretary of state, Apr. 24, 1913, RDS-IA, 812.00/7256. WP, Dec. 2, 1913.

[23]Colquitt to secretary of state, Apr. 7, 1913, *FR, 1913*, 877.

[24]Colquitt to secretary of state, Apr. 7, 1913 and May 19, 1913, *FR, 1913*, 877, 879–80.

[25]Acting secretary of state to Mexican chargé, Washington, *FR, 1913*, 878–79.

[26]EPMT, Aug. 6, 1913.

[27]Secretary of state to W. H. Page, Jan. 29, 1914, *FR, 1914*, 445–46.

[28]EPMT, Feb. 4, 1914.

[29]EPMT, Apr. 23, 1914. WP, Sept. 10, 1914.

[30]*Congressional Record*, 63rd Congress, 2nd session, May 6, 1914, vol. 51 pt. 8, 8153.

[31]EPMT, July 11, 1914.

[32]SAE, July 20, 1914.

[33]Penney and Robinson to Plutarco Elías Calles, no date (probably April 1916 from internal evidence), AGES/3809.

[34]R. P. Denegri to Calles, Mar. 2, 1916, AGES/3809.

[35]Lázaro de la Garza to Pancho Villa, Feb. 24, 1914, I-B-10; Villa to De la Garza, no date (probably February 25, 1914), I-B-12; Villa to De la Garza, Feb. 26, 1914, I-B-17: all in DLG.

[36]Villa to Dario Horcasitas, Feb. 26, 1914, I-B-28; Garza to Villa, Feb. 27, 1914, I-B-30; Villa to De la Garza, Feb. 28, 1914, I-B-31, Villa to De la Garza, Mar. 12, 1914, I-C-50: all in DLG.

[37]De la Garza to Villa, Feb. 27, 1914, DLG.

[38]De la Garza to Villa, Feb. 28, 1914, DLG.

[39]De la Garza to Villa, Mar. 4, 1914, I-C-4; Villa to De la Garza, Mar. 5, 1914, I-C-8; De la Garza to Villa, Mar. 4, 1914, I-C-9; Villa to De la Garza, Mar. 12, 1914, I-C-49: all in DLG.

[40]De la Garza to W. Cooley, Sept. 28, 1914, III-I-36; De la Garza to Rio Grande Valley Bank and Trust Co., Sept. 23, 1914, III-I-27, DLG.

[41]Tesorero General del Estado de Chihuahua to De la Garza, Mar. 4, 1915; Banco del Estado de Chihuahua to Rio Grande Valley Bank and Trust, Apr. 7, 1915; and R. A. Sepúlveda to De la Garza, June 4, 1915: all in DLG.

[42]Villa to De la Garza, Mar. 27, 1914, DLG.

[43]SAE, Apr. 8, 9, and 18, 1914.

[44]See Friedrich Katz, "Pancho Villa, Peasant Movements and Agrarian Reform in Northern Mexico," in *Caudillo and Peasant in the Mexican Revolution*, ed. David Brading, (Cambridge: Cambridge University Press, 1980), 64–67; and Hall, *Alvaro Obregón*, 131–32.

[45]Dowe to collector of customs, June 23, 1910, NA/RG36-84. Dowe to collector of customs, June 4, 1910; NA/RG36-78; U.S. Commissioners Criminal Records, Brownsville, Texas, 1915, Case Nos. 245, 254, 255, 269, U.S. vs. Miller and Cortez and U.S. vs. Mar Chew, 1919, Case Nos. 241, 242, 243, and 249, FRC-FW. Douglas *Daily International*, Jan. 11, 1915. E. M. Lawton, Report on Conditions in Sonora, Sept. 12, 1917.

[46]García, *Desert Immigrants*, 29. Martínez, *Border Boom Town*, 46–48.

[47]U.S. Department of Commerce, *Handbook of Cyclical Indicators*, (Washington: U.S. Government Printing Office, 1984), 178.

BIBLIOGRAPHY

Archival Sources

Archivo de Fernando Torreblanca. Private Collection in possession of Hortensia Calles de Torreblanca.

Arizona Historical Society. Tucson, Arizona. Manuscript Collection.

La Colección General Porfirio Díaz. University of the Americas. Puebla, Mexico.

Great Britain. Foreign Office. General Archives.

Mexico. Archivo General de la Nación. Departmento de Trabajo.

Mexico. Archivo Histórico de Pemex. Sistema General Sinclair.

Mexico. Museo de Antropología. Archivo de Francisco Madero. Patronato de la Historia de Sonora.

Mexico. Secretaría de Relaciones Exteriores. Archives.

Mexico. Sonora. Archivo de Gobierno del Estado de Sonora.

Texas State Archives. Austin, Texas. Adjutant General, General Correspondence.

Texas State Archives. Austin, Texas. Governors' Papers, James E. Ferguson.

Texas State Archives. Austin, Texas. Governors' Papers, Oscar Branch Colquitt.

United States. Department of Labor. Bureau of Immigration.

United States. Department of State. *Dispatches from United States Ministers to Mexico, 1823–1906.*

United States. Department of State. *Notes from the Mexican Legation in the United States to the Department of State, 1821–1906.*

United States. Department of State. *Records of the Department of State Relating to the Internal Affairs of Mexico, 1910–1929.*
United States. Department of the Treasury. United States Secret Service. Daily Reports of Agents, 1875–1936, Record Group 87.
United States. Federal Records Center. Fort Worth. District Court Records. San Antonio.
United States. Federal Records Center. Forth Worth. District Court Records. San Antonio.
United States. Library of Congress. Hugh Lenox Scott Papers.
United States. National Archives. Federal Bureau of Investigation. Record Group 65, Mexican File.
United States. National Archives. Record Group 165. Military Intelligence Division.
United States. National Archives. Record Group 48. Arizona Territorial Papers.
United States. National Archives. Record Group 76. Records of the United States and Mexican Claims Commissions. Records of the Agency of the United States.
United States. National Archives. Villa's Revolution #2212358.
University of Arizona. Tucson, Arizona. Lewis W. Douglas Papers.
University of Texas. Austin, Texas. William F. Buckley Papers.
University of Texas. Austin, Texas. Colquitt Papers.
University of Texas. Austin, Texas. Lázaro de la Garza Archive.

Government Publications

Mexico. Cámara de Diputados. *Diario de los debates del Congreso Constituyente.* 2 vols. Mexico City: Cámara de Diputados, 1917.
Mexico. Departmento de Minas. *Anuario de estadística minera, Año de 1922.* Mexico City: Talleres Gráficos de la Nación, 1924.
Mexico. Ministerio de Relaciones Exteriores. *Nota enviada por el gobierno constitucional al de la casa blanca.* Mexico City: Compañía Editora Mexicana, 1916.
Mexico. Ministerio de Relaciones Exteriores. *Correspondencia diplomática cambiada entre el gobierno de los Estados Unidos Mexicanos y los de varias potencias extranjeras.* 4 vols. Mexico City: Tip. de Gonzalo de Esteva, 1882–87.
Mexico. Presidente. *Un siglo de relaciones internacionales de México a través de los mensajes presidenciales.* 2d ed. Mexico City: Editorial Porrúa, 1970.
Mexico. Secretaría de Relaciones Exteriores. *Diplomatic Dealings of the Constitutionalist Revolution of Mexico.* Mexico City: Imprenta Nacional, 1919.
Texas. *Annual Report of the Officials of the State Prison System, 1911.* Austin: Von Boeckmann-Jones, Printers, 1912.
Texas. Adjutant General. *Biennial Reports of the Adjutant General of Texas, 1911–1918.* Austin: Von Boeckmann-Jones Co., 1913–19.
———. *Annual Report of the Adjutant General of Texas for the Year Ending December 31, 1918.* Austin: Von Boeckmann-Jones Co., 1919.

———. *Biennial Report of the Adjutant General of Texas from January 1, 1919 to December 31, 1920*. Austin: Knape Printing Co., 1921.

United States. Bureau of the Census. *Thirteenth Census of the United States*. Washington, D.C.: Government Printing Office, 1913.

United States. Bureau of the Census. *Fourteenth Census of the United States*. Washington, D.C.: Government Printing Office, 1923.

United States. Congress. *Congressional Record*, 62nd Congress, First Session, Vol. 47, Pt. 2.

United States. Congress. *Congressional Record*, 62nd Congress, Second Session, Vol. 48, Pt. 4.

United States. Congress. *Congressional Record*, 63rd Congress, Second Session, Vol. 51, Pts. 7 and 8.

United States. Department of Commerce. *Handbook of Cyclical Indicators*. Washington, D.C.: Government Printing Office, 1984.

United States. Department of Labor. *Reports of the Department of Labor, 1910–1920*. Washington, D.C.: Government Printing Office, 1911–21.

United States. Department of State. *Papers Relating to the Foreign Relations of the United States*. Washington, D.C.: Government Printing Office, 1911–1921.

United States. Senate. *Investigation of Mexican Affairs*, Senate Document 285, 66th Congress, Second Session, Vols. 1 and 2.

United States. War Department. *Annual Reports, 1910–1920* Washington, D.C.: Government Printing Office, 1910–21.

Books

Acuña, Rodolfo. *Occupied America: The Chicano's Struggle toward Liberation*. San Francisco: Canfield Press, 1972.

Aguilar Camín, Héctor. *La frontera nómada: Sonora y la Revolución Mexicana*. Mexico City: Siglo Veintiuno Editores, 1977.

Anders, Evan. *Boss Rule in South Texas: The Progressive Era*. Austin: The University of Texas Press, 1982.

Bernstein, Marvin D. *The Mexican Mining Industry, 1890–1950*. Albany: State University of New York, 1964.

Blanton, Annie Webb. *A Handbook of Information as to Education in Texas, 1918–1922*. N.p.: Texas Department of Education, 1923.

Blanton, Annie Webb, and R. L. Ragsdale. *Texas High Schools: History and the Social Sciences*. N.p.: Texas Department of Education, 1920.

Brading, David, ed. *Caudillo and Peasant in the Mexican Revolution*. Cambridge: Cambridge University Press, 1980

Cardoso, Lawrence A. *Mexican Emigration to the United States, 1897–1931*. Tucson: University of Arizona Press, 1980.

Carman, Michael Dennis. *United States Customs and the Madero Revolution*. El Paso: Texas Western Press, 1976.

Carreño, Alberto María. *La diplomacia extraordinaria entre México y Estados Unidos, 1789–1947*. 2 vols. 2d ed. Mexico City: Editorial Jus, 1961.

Carroll, John M., ed. *The Black Military Experience in the American West*. New York: Liveright, 1973.

Cleland, Robert Glass. *A History of Phelps Dodge, 1834–1950*. New York: Alfred A. Knopf, 1952.

Clendenen, Clarence C. *Blood on the Border*. London: Macmillan Company, 1969.

———. *The United States and Pancho Villa*. Ithaca: Cornell University Press, 1961.

Cockroft, James D. *Intellectual Precursors of the Mexican Revolution, 1900–1913*. Austin and London: The University of Texas Press, 1968.

Coerver, Don M. *The Porfirian Interregnum: The Presidency of Manuel González of Mexico, 1880–1884*. Fort Worth: Texas Christian University Press, 1979.

Coerver, Don M., and Linda B. Hall. *Texas and the Mexican Revolution: A Study in State and National Border Policy*. San Antonio: Trinity University Press, 1984.

Cortés, Carlos E. *The Mexican American and the Law*. New York: Arno Press, 1974.

Cosío Villegas, Daniel, ed. *Historia Moderna de México*. 9 vols. Mexico City: Editorial Hermes, 1955–72.

———. *The United States versus Porfirio Díaz*. Translated by Nettie Lee Benson. Lincoln: University of Nebraska Press, 1963.

Cumberland, Charles C. *Mexican Revolution: The Constitutionalist Years*. Austin and London: University of Texas Press, 1972.

———. *Mexican Revolution: Genesis under Madero*. Austin: University of Texas Press, 1974.

Dabdoub, Claudio. *Historia de El Valle del Yaqui*. Mexico City: Librería Manuel Porrúa, S.A., 1964.

Espinosa de los Reyes, Jorge. *Relaciones económicas entre México y Estados Unidos, 1879–1910*. Mexico City: Nacional Financiera, 1951.

Gamio, Manuel. *The Life Story of the Mexican Immigrant*. New York: Dover Publication, 1971.

García, Mario T. *Desert Immigrants: The Mexicans of El Paso*. New Haven and London: Yale University Press, 1981.

Garibaldi, Giuseppe. *A Toast to Rebellion*. Indianapolis: Bobbs-Merrill Company, 1935.

Gilderhus, Mark T. *Diplomacy and Revolution: U.S.-Mexican Relations under Wilson and Carranza*. Tucson: University of Arizona Press, 1977.

Gregg, Robert D. *The Influence of Border Troubles on Relations between the United States and Mexico, 1876–1910*. Baltimore: The Johns Hopkins Press, 1937.

Grieb, Kenneth J. *The United States and Huerta*. Lincoln: University of Nebraska Press, 1969.

Haley, P. Edward. *Revolution and Intervention: The Diplomacy of Taft and Wilson with Mexico, 1910–1917*. Cambridge, Mass.: MIT Press, 1970.

Hall, Linda B. *Alvaro Obregón: Power and Revolution in Mexico, 1911–1920*. College Station: Texas A & M University Press, 1981.

Hansen, Roger D. *The Politics of Mexican Development*. Baltimore: The Johns Hopkins Press, 1971.

Hill, Larry D. *Emissaries to a Revolution: Woodrow Wilson's Executive Agents in Mexico*. Baton Rouge: Louisiana State University, 1973.

Hoffman, Abraham. *Unwanted Mexican Americans in the Great Depression*. Tucson: University of Arizona Press, 1974.

Katz, Friedrich. *The Secret War in Mexico: Europe, the United States, and the Mexican Revolution*. Chicago: University of Chicago Press, 1981.

Kerig, Dorothy Pierson. *Luther T. Ellsworth: U.S. Consul on the Border during the Mexican Revolution*. El Paso: Texas Western Press, 1975.

Larson, Henrietta M., and Kenneth Wiggins Porter. *History of Humble Oil and Refining Company: A Study in Industrial Growth*. New York: Harpers and Brothers, 1959.

León, Arnaldo de. *The Tejano Community, 1836–1900*. Albuquerque: University of New Mexico Press, 1982.

Link, Arthur S., ed. *The Papers of Woodrow Wilson*. 29 vols. Princeton: Princeton University Press, 1966–79.

———. *Woodrow Wilson and the Progressive Era, 1910–1917*. New York: Harper & Row, 1963.

Mancke, Richard. *Mexican Oil and Natural Gas: Political, Strategic and Economic Implications*. New York: Praeger, 1979.

Martin, Roscoe. *The People's Party in Texas: A Study in Third Party Politics*. Austin and London: University of Texas Press, 1970.

Martínez, John. *Mexican Emigration to the U.S., 1910–1930*. San Francisco: R. and E. Research Associates, 1972.

McBride, George McCutchen. *The Land Systems of Mexico*. New York: American Geographical Society, 1923.

Mendieta y Núñez, Lucio. *El problema agrario de México*. 9th ed. Mexico City: Editorial Porrúa, 1966.

Meyer, Lorenzo. *Mexico and the United States in the Oil Controversy, 1917–1942*. Austin and London: University of Texas Press, 1977.

Meyer, Michael E. *Huerta: A Political Portrait*. Lincoln: University of Nebraska Press, 1972.

———. *Mexican Rebel: Pascual Orozco and the Mexican Revolution, 1910–1915*. Lincoln: University of Nebraska Press, 1967.

Obregón, Alvaro. *Ocho mil kilómetros en campaña*. 1917 Reprint. Mexico: Fondo de Cultura Económica, 1970.

The National Cyclopedia of American Biography. Vol. 48. New York: James T. White and Company, 1961.

Pletcher, David. *Rails, Mines and Progress: Seven American Promoters in Mexico, 1867–1911*. Ithaca: Cornell University Press, 1958.

Quirk, Robert E. *An Affair of Honor: Woodrow Wilson and the Occupation of Veracruz*. New York: W. W. Norton & Company, 1962.

Raat, W. Dirk. *Revoltosos: Mexico's Rebels in the United States*. College Station: Texas A & M University Press, 1981.

Reisler, Mark. *By the Sweat of Their Brow: Mexican Immigrant Labor in the United States, 1900–1940*. London and Westport: Greenwood Press, 1976.

Rivera, Antonio. *La Revolución en Sonora*. Mexico City: Imprenta Araña, 1969.

Ruvalcaba, Luis N., ed. *Campaña política del c. Alvaro Obregón*. Vol. 5. Mexico City: N.p., 1923.

Samora, Julian. *Los Mojados: The Wetback Story*. Notre Dame: University of Notre Dame Press, 1971.

Schmitt, Karl M. *Mexico and the United States, 1821–1973*. New York: John Wiley and Sons, 1974.

Scott, Hugh L. *Some Memories of a Soldier*. New York and London: The Century Co., 1928.

Scott, James B., ed. *Diplomatic Correspondence between the United States and Germany, August 1, 1914–April 6, 1917*. New York: Oxford University Press, 1918.

Sepúlveda, César. *La frontera norte de México*. Mexico City: Editorial Porrúa, 1976.

Silva Herzog, Jesús. *El agrarismo mexicano y la reforma agraria*. Mexico City: Fondo de Cultura Económica, 1959.

Tinkle, Lon. *Mr. De: A Biography of Everette Lee DeGolyer*. Boston and Toronto: Little, Brown and Co., 1970.

Tompkins, Frank. *Chasing Villa: The Story Behind the Story of Pershing's Expedition into Mexico*. Harrisburg, Pa.: The Military Service Publishing Company, 1934.

Trimble, Marshall. *Arizona: A Panoramic History of a Frontier State*. Garden City, N.Y.: Doubleday and Company, 1977.

Tuchman, Barbara. *The Zimmermann Telegram*. New York: Viking Press, 1958.

University of Texas Catalogue, 1910–1920. Austin: University of Texas, 1910–20.

Vandiver, Frank E. *Black Jack: The Life and Times of John J. Pershing*. 2 vols. College Station: Texas A & M University Press, 1977.

Vernon, Raymond. *The Dilemma of Mexico's Development*. Cambridge, Mass.: Harvard University Press, 1963.

Wagner, Jay J. *Arizona Territory, 1863–1912: A Political History*. Tucson: University of Arizona Press, 1970.

Webb, Walter Prescott. *The Texas Rangers*. 2d ed. Austin: University of Texas Press, 1965.

Wilkins, Mira. *The Making of Multinational Enterprise*. Cambridge, Mass.: Harvard University Press, 1974.

Williamson, Harold F., et al. *The American Petroleum Industry: The Age of Energy, 1899–1959*. Evanston: Northwestern University Press, 1963.

Wilson, Henry Lane. *Diplomatic Episodes in Mexico, Belgium, and Chile*. Garden City, N.Y.: Doubleday, Page and Company, 1927.

Womack, John, Jr. *Zapata and the Mexican Revolution*. New York: Alfred A. Knopf, 1969.

Zorilla, Luis G. *Historia de las relaciones entre México y los Estados Unidos de América, 1800–1958*. 2 vols. Mexico City: Editorial Porrúa, 1965–66.

Articles

Cumberland, Charles C. "Border Raids in the Lower Rio Grande Valley—1915." *Southwestern Historical Quarterly* 57 (1954): 284–311.

———. "Mexican Revolutionary Movements from Texas, 1906–1912." *Southwestern Historical Quarterly* 52 (1949): 301–24.

Gerlach, Allen. "Conditions along the Border—1915: The Plan de San Diego." *New Mexico Historical Review* 43 (1968): 194–212.

Hackett, Charles W. "The Recognition of the Díaz Government by the United States." *Southwestern Historical Quarterly* 28 (1924): 34–55

Hall, Linda B. "The Mexican Revolution and the Crisis in Naco, 1914–1915." *Journal of the West* 16 (1977): 27–35.

Harris, Charles H., III, and Louis R. Sadler. "The 1911 Reyes Conspiracy: The Texas Side." *Southwestern Historical Quarterly* 83 (1980): 324–48.

———. "The Plan of San Diego and the Mexican-United States War Crisis of 1916: A Reexamination." *Hispanic American Historical Review*, 58 (1978): 381–408.

Hill, Larry D. "The Progressive Politician as Diplomat: The Case of John Lind in Mexico." *The Americas* 27 (1971): 355–72.

Holmes, Malcolm D., and Howard C. Daudistel. "Ethnicity and Justice in the Southwest: The Sentencing of Anglo, Black, and Mexican Origin Defendants." *Social Science Quarterly* 65 (1984): 265–77.

Katz, Friedrich. "Alemania y Francisco Villa." *Historia Mexicana* 12 (1962): 88–103.

———. "Labor Conditions on Haciendas in Porfirian Mexico: Some Trends and Tendencies." *Hispanic American Historical Review* 54 (1974): 1–47.

Machado, Manuel A., Jr., and James T. Judge. "Tempest in a Teapot?: The Mexican-United States Intervention Crisis of 1919." *Southwestern Historical Quarterly* 74 (1970): 1–23.

Mayhall, Pamela. "Bisbee's Response to Civil Disorder." *The American West* 9 (1972): 22–31.

Meyer, Michael C. "Albert Bacon Fall's Mexican Papers: A Preliminary Investigation." *New Mexico Historical Review* 40 (1965): 165–74.

———. "The Mexican-German Conspiracy of 1915." *The Americas* 23 (1966): 76–89.

Munch, Francis J. "Villa's Columbus Raid: Practical Politics or German Design?" *New Mexico Historical Review* 44 (1969): 189–214.

Niemeyer, Vic. "Frustrated Invasion: The Revolutionary Attempt of General Bernardo Reyes from San Antonio in 1911." *Southwestern Historical Quarterly* 67 (1963): 213–25.

Raat, W. Dirk. "The Diplomacy of Suppression: Los Revoltosos, Mexico, and the United States, 1906–1911." *Hispanic American Historical Review* 56 (1976): 529–50.

Rausch, George J., Jr. "The Exile and Death of Victoriano Huerta." *Hispanic American Historical Review* 42 (1962): 133–51.

Richmond, Douglas W. "La guerra de Texas se renova: Mexican Insurrection and Carrancista Ambitions, 1900–1920." *Axtlan* 11 (1980): 1–32.

Sandos, James A. "German Involvement in Northern Mexico, 1915–1916: A New Look at the Columbus Raid." *Hispanic American Historical Review* 50 (1970): 70–88.

———. "The Plan of San Diego: War and Diplomacy on the Texas Border." *Arizona and the West* 14 (1972): 5–24.

Sepúlveda, César. "Historia y problemas de los límites de México, I. La frontera norte." *Historia Mexicana* 8 (1958): 1–34.

Tate, Michael L. "Pershing's Punitive Expedition: Pursuer of Bandits or Presidential Panacea?". *The Americas* 32 (1975): 46–71.

Tyler, Ronnie C. "The Little Punitive Expedition in the Big Bend." *Southwestern Historical Quarterly* 78 (1975): 271–91.

White, E. Bruce. "The Muddied Waters of Columbus, New Mexico." *The Americas* 32 (1975): 72–98.

Newspapers and Periodicals

Arizona Daily Star (Tucson)

Arizona Mining Journal

Boletín del Petroleo

Express (San Antonio)

Morning News (Dallas)

Morning Times (El Paso)

El Universal (Mexico City)

Excelsior (Mexico City)

La Patria (Chihuahua City)

The Mexican Mining Journal

New York Times.

Post (Washington)

Texas. Department of Education. *Bulletin*

Interviews and Unpublished Manuscripts

Sam L. Kone with Linda B. Hall. September 7, 1978. Trinity Border Studies Oral History Project III/2-3.

Luis L. León with Linda B. Hall, July 30, 1974.

Marjorie McLernon with Linda B. Hall. July 27, 1978. Trinity Border Studies Oral History Project III/1.

Bryan, Anthony T. "Mexican Politics in Transition, 1900–1913": Dissertation, University of Nebraska, 1969.

Hines, Calvin W. "The Mexican Punitive Expedition of 1916." Master's thesis, Trinity University, 1961.

Huckaby, George P. "Oscar Branch Colquitt: A Political Biography." Master's thesis, University of Texas at Austin, 1946.

Index